# BIRD BEHAVIOR

# BIRD BEHAVIOR

## ROBERT BURTON

CONSULTING EDITOR
DR BRUCE CAMPBELL

ALFRED A. KNOPF
NEW YORK
1985

THIS IS A BORZOI BOOK
PUBLISHED BY ALFRED A. KNOPF, INC.

This book was created and produced by
Roxby Natural History Limited
Roxby and Lindsey Press
98 Clapham Common Northside
London SW4

Editor: Linda Gamlin
Art Direction: David Pearce
Design: Dorothy Marschall
Assistant Editor: Elspeth Boardley
Typesetting: Tradespools Limited
Reproduction: F. E. Burman Limited

Library of Congress Cataloging in Publication Data

Burton, Robert, 1941–
Bird behavior

Includes index
1. Birds—Behavior. 1. Title.
QL698.3.B87 1985    598.2'51    84-48677
ISBN 0-394-53957-5

Manufactured in Spain by Graficromo S.A., Córdoba
First American Edition

# ACKNOWLEDGMENTS

Roxby and Lindsey Press would like to thank Bruce Coleman Ltd for providing almost all the photographs that appear in this book; Jane Burton and Kim Taylor whose enthusiasm and willingness to experiment have resulted in some very remarkable photographs and the following people and organizations for their help with additional photographs: Doug Allan, Bruce Pearson, Peter Prince, National Geographic and Robert F. Sisson, National Oceanic and Atmospheric Administration.

ARTWORK
Graham Allen, John Woodcock
After the following authors: 23, William Jameson, *The Wandering Albatross* (1958); 41, John K. Terres, *The Audubon Encyclopedia of North American Birds*, Knopf, New York (1980); 130, W.H. Thorpe, *Ibis* 100 (1958); 131, P.C. Mundinger, *Science* 168 (1970); 205, S.C. Lincoln, *Migration of Birds*, U.S. Fish and Wildlife Service, (Washington D.C.) 1950.

PHOTOGRAPHS
T top B bottom C center L left R right
Front cover photograph: Granada edition great white egret (Christian Züber); Knopf edition European robin (Kim Taylor). Back cover photographs, left to right, from top: great grey owl (Pekka Helo), woodpecker finch (Alan Root), gannets (Diana & Rick Sullivan), black-necked storks (Konrad Wothe), black-and-white casqued hornbill (Günter Ziesler), spotted flycatcher (Kim Taylor), carmine bee-eaters (M.P.L. Fogden), snow geese (Charlie Ott), pink-backed pelican (Jane Burton), reddish egrets (M.P. Kahl). Title page photograph: grebes (Charlie Ott).
Doug Allan 29TR , 71BL&C, 97TR, 135, 173TL&R, 195BL, 220–1; Patrick Baker 166R; Jen & Des Bartlett 18BR, 20B, 27T&BL, 34C, 35T, 37, 38BL, 56BL&R, 60L&R, 61L, 69L, 71TL&C, 72BR, 81T&B, 82BL&R, 85, 89T&BL, 116TR, 125B, 126R, 130, 131R, 133TL, 138L, 143T, 144TL&R, 145T, L&R, 147BL, 162TL, 168TL, 169BL, 170C, 171C, 172TR, 176L&R, 177, 178R, 179C, 180C, 188CL, 194TR, 206L&C, 208TL&R, 209T, 214B, 215B, 216CT&CB, 219; Erwin & Peggy Bauer 181; Rod Borland 194L; J.R. Brownlie 119T; Jane Burton 10T, 24L, 25CT&BRC&L, 26T, 31TL, 32, 35L, 43TB&KM 44, 46C, 55T&BR, 56TL&R, 67CR, 69BR, 72T, 76, 77TR, 90L, 95BL&R, 102, 114T, 124C&BL&R, 132L, 147T, 148T, 162RC, 170BR, 179BL, 182, 184, 185TL&R, 190, 192TL, 193BR, 204TR; Robert Burton 97BR; Bob & Clara Calhoun 19B, 64C, 151R, 162BL&TR, 207R, 214B; Guiliano Cappelli 139C; Robert P. Carr 64B, 187BR, 199; Brian Coates 80B, 83R, 88T, 117TR, 123T, 150BR, 164, 169CB, 212TR&BL; Bruce Coleman 24R, 72CT, 79L, 127L, 133BL, 150BL, Alain Compost 89BR, Gerald Cubitt 82T, 142T; Peter Davey 49R, 94, 126L, 167, 212BR; L.R. Dawson 51B, 69TR, 114B, 195TL, 201R; A.J. Deane 18TL, 55TL, 152T, 156LCR, 157L, 187CB, 212B; Jack Dermid 193CB; Martin Dohrn 218R; G. Downey 101BR; Jessica Ehlers 113; Francisco Erize 9R, 54C, 55BL, 80L, 83L, 97TL, 117BR,

143BL, 149BR, 152 3from T&B, 154, 155CL&R, BL&R, 173BR, 188BR; Yossi Eshboli 134R, 189TR; Inigo Everson 97BL, 216R, 218R; M.P.L. Fogden 50R, 133R, 142B, 189CR, 193BL, 214BL; Jeff Foott 18CT, 26BR, 64T, 67CL, 160R, 168TR, 200, 206R; Michael Freeman 153T; C.B. & D.W. Frith 90R, 116BR, 165BL, C, BR, 193CT, 203BR; C.B. Frith 39BR; J.L.G. Grande 173BL, 186R, 203T, 204TL; Dennis Green 40, 201BL, 217; M.P. Harris 23; Pekka Helo 47, 78L&R, 108; Peter Hinchcliffe 9L&R, 11L, 13T, 52; Udo Hirsch 46R, 53, 148 2from T; D. Houston 54B, 109T, 148 3fromT, 153BL; Carol Hughes 51R, 101L; 215C; David Hughes 62T, 63TL; Peter Jackson 166L, 210; M.P. Kahl 72BL, 147BR, 149BL, 168BR; M. Philip Kahl Jr. 101T; Stephen J. Krasemann 9C, 34TL: O. Langrand 141 BR, 179TR, 187TL, C & R; Gordon Lomgsbury 12C, 31TR, 100, 123BR, 205; Wayne Lankinen 91R, 116TL, 180BL, 214TR; Cyril Laubscher 162BR, 179TL, 193TR; Antti Leionen 74R; Norman L. Lightfoot 109TL; Rocco Longo 171BL; Lee Lyon 68R, 175B, 195R; J. Mackinnon 117BL, 176TR, 185TL; J. Markham 74L, 87L, 184TL&C; L.C. Maringo 161BR; A.J. Mobbs 83T, 163, 174; L.M. Myers 11, 96, 109R, 118B; Norman Myers 112; NOAH 211BL; Charlie Ott 34BL, 99T&C, 116BL, 150TL&R, 195CL, 209L&R; Pearson & Prince 49L, 95TL&R; John Pearson 59TL&R&C, 161TR, 194BR; R. Tory Peterson 67T, 175L; Graham Pizzey 171T; Dieter & Mary Plage 106, 107, 137TL&R, B, 139L; G.D. Plage 21BR, 22T&B, 93, 111, 149TL, 188BR; Andy Purcell 103B, 185BL; Mike Price 18BR, 51T, 73, 75BL&R, 88B, 110R, 169C; Masood Qureshi 68BL; Hans Reinhard 41, 188TL; Hector Rivarola 63R, 169TL, 201TL; Alan Root 25TL, 57R, 115T; Donn Renn 192R; Leonard Lee Rue III 50L, 125T, 132BR, 178L, 186R, 187L, 208B; Frieder Sauer 72CB, 189BR; John Shaw 25TR, 173C, 183CB; Jeff Simon 71R, 115B; Robert F. Sisson c 1974 National Geographic Society 58, 59BL&R, M.F. Soper 39TR, 48C, 77BR, 99BR, 168BL, 171C, 175T; Diana & Rick Sullivan 123L; Jan Taylor 84T&B, 165TR; Kim Taylor 12T, 13BL&R, 14, 15, 16C&R, 17, 19, 27B, 30, 31BR, 45T&C, 48R, 62B, 63B, 86L,R&C, 87C&R, 124T, 127R, 132TR, 169T&BR, 170T, 191, 203C; R. Tidman 45B, 92TL, 99BL, 131L, 202; Norman Tomalin 38R, 39L, 117TR; William E. Townsend Jr. 193TL; Simon Trevor 92B, 139L; R.J. Tulloch 180TL; Nicholas de Vore 216L; Peter Ward 35B, 48R, 92TR, 134L, 136T, 157R, 212TR, 215T; Rod Williams 114C; Roger Wilmshurst 10R, 12BL, 20T, 21 T&R, 54T, 80C, 129L, 172BR; Joe Van Wormer 18CB, 38TL, 79R, 84C, 129R, 161L, 186BL, 189BL, 207L; Konrad Wothe 8, 9C, 10L, 26BL, 33B, 34R, 61R, 141TR, 146TL&R, BL, C&R, 148B, 151L, 155T, 160L. 212T; Nathan T. Wright 143BR,T&B; WWF/Eric Oragescoe 119B; WWF/Jörg 75T; WWF/ Tanşu Gürpinar 204B; WWF/Y.J. Rey-Millet 203BL; WWF/H. Jungius 101BL; WWF/J. Watson 46L; Günter Ziesler 21BL, 31BL, 49C, 57L, 65, 67B, 68TL, 70, 77L, 91L, 109BL, 118T, 128, 136B, 138R, 140, 141L, 149TR, 152 2fromT, 153BR, 158, 159, 165TL, 170BL, 172L, 179BR, 180T&BL, 183R, 214T; Christian Züber 33T

# INTRODUCTION

Birds are, perhaps, the most popular group of animals and they give pleasure to thousands of people around the world. For many, the pleasure comes simply from watching birds in the garden, while others will travel hundreds of miles to see a rarity that is, itself, a very long way from home. For all kinds of birder the ease of jet-age travel and the excellence of television wildlife programs are bringing the native haunts of many of these foreign species within reach, and their habits are becoming almost as familiar as those of birds at home.

In the last two decades a growing band of people have been making scientific studies of birds. Not all are professional ornithologists, but the details of their findings are published in specialized journals that are not always readily accessible. In addition they can be difficult to understand, being written in the formal language of science and, increasingly, peppered with mathematical symbols. Yet this research should be of interest to anyone wanting to know more about birds. It is bringing some exciting insights into the ways that birds behave and, by providing explanations for everyday observations of what our familiar birds are doing, it makes watching them that much more stimulating.

While researching this book, I found it particularly exciting to come across a passage of someone's scientific work that helped to explain my own casual observations, or which confirmed my own interpretations of what I had seen. There was also the pleasure of finding some unexpected nuggets of unusual bird behavior, and the more solid satisfaction of learning how the basic rules governing bird life are being pieced together.

The aim of this book is to bring together such information and ideas about bird behavior in an easily accessible form. To avoid interrupting the text, scientific names have not been included, but they are given in the index beside each bird's common name, for more precise identification. The scientific names used for living birds follow *A Checklist of the Birds of the World* by Edward S. Gruson.

One of the difficulties in writing a book such as this lies in deciding exactly what should be included in a discussion of behavior. Should it be just feeding habits, social interactions, rearing the family and so on, or should it include the more mundane questions of how an animal gets about, perceives its environment and digests its food? There is no doubt that it is impossible to get a true idea of an animal's behavior without investigating all these essential requirements. So the chapters in this book discuss the basic necessities of processing food, maintaining the plumage in good condition and keeping warm or cool, as well as the more obvious subjects of social organization, rearing a family and migration. Ultimately, all aspects of behavior are determined by an animal's anatomy and physiology, so it is necessary to introduce the mechanisms of birds' flight and the capacities of their sense organs, both of which set limits on their reactions to the environment around them.

I have a great debt to the many authors whose work has provided the substance of this book. I have been fascinated, and delighted, by their revelations of the richness and complexity of bird behavior or, conversely, its frequent neat simplicity and economy of design, and I hope that I can convey some of this excitement to a wider audience. I would also like to acknowledge the assistance given by my ornithological friends in response to my requests for help, in particular, Brian Bertram, John Croxall, Peter Evans, David Houston and Peter Prince. Bruce Campbell has been especially helpful in putting his immense experience at my disposal, while Linda Gamlin has provided the essential editorial functions of giving an author encouragement and keeping his prose clear and to the point.

Robert Burton

# CONTENTS

# CHAPTER 1
# THE LIVING BIRD

There are over 8,600 species of birds alive today and as a group of animals they are remarkably successful. They have colonized virtually all habitats, except the deep ocean, and have penetrated the remotest corners of the earth, so that only in the most desolate places is it possible for five minutes to pass without either sight or sound of a bird.

The major ingredient in the success of birds is their power of flight, a freedom of movement that man has always envied. It permits birds to move about much faster than other animals so that they can cover

Atlantic puffins, razorbills, black-legged kittiwakes and northern gannets.

Of all the birds on the cliff, the black-legged kittiwake is the best suited for nesting on narrow ledges. Altough its nesting habits are similar to those of gulls which nest on flat ground, there are a number of important differences related to the cliff-nesting habit and the kittiwake's specialization is one of the classic examples of how a species' behavior is suited to its environment and way of life.

The advantage of nesting on cliffs is the immunity it

huge distances, taking advantage of feeding opportunities when and where they arise. Some birds even exploit two distant and contrasting habitats as a regular part of their yearly cycle, migrating thousands of miles between their winter and summer quarters.
LIFE ON THE EDGE
The power of flight also gives birds access to places from which other large animals are excluded, such as the fragmented array of islands forming the North Atlantic coast. Here thousands of birds gather every summer to mate, lay eggs, and rear their young on the heavily indented coasts of Newfoundland, Cape Breton and Nova Scotia. Although exposed to violent storms and bitterly cold winds during the winter months, the cliffs here become the nesting places for immense throngs of seabirds: common murres,

gives from foxes which cannot scale the sheer rocks, and from ravens and gulls which have difficulty in landing on narrow ledges to steal eggs. This immunity has been followed by a relaxation of the defenses, and kittiwakes do not react to predators nearly so fiercely as do ground-nesting gulls. A colony of Bonaparte's gulls responds to the appearance of a predatory herring gull by flying up *en masse*, with a clamor of alarm calls, followed by concerted mobbing, but kittiwakes simply ignore these birds, since they pose little threat to them. Neither do kittiwakes attempt to conceal the nest. Most gulls keep the nest area clear of droppings, and remove empty eggshells after the chicks have hatched, so that the position of the nest is not given away, but kittiwake colonies are splashed with white "flags" beneath each nest, and littered with

*The black-legged kittiwake is a gull which nests on narrow cliff ledges. Its behavior has adapted to exploit this situation, and it has stronger toes and sharper claws than other gulls.*

eggshells.

On the other hand, nesting on a narrow ledge has its own peculiar problems and kittiwake behavior has become adapted to overcome them. The female kittiwake sits when mating, whereas other gulls stand, so the pair will not overbalance and fall off the ledge. The nest is a deep cup, made of mud or seaweed, to hold the eggs safely, compared with the shallow scrape of other gulls, and the chicks are remarkably immobile until fully grown. They do not run from the nest when approached and, if they should come near to the cliff edge, they instinctively turn back.

## ADAPTING TO CHANGE

These and other special adaptations of cliff-nesting birds are the product of evolution through natural selection. The kittiwake probably developed from ground-nesting gulls by a gradual process, in which

inflexible pattern belonging to a species is to miss much of the richness of bird life. Because many pioneering studies stressed the behavior patterns of a species, as for instance in kittiwakes behaving differently from other gulls, the impression is often given that all birds of the same species behave in the same way. But if this was true, there would be nothing for natural selection to work on, because variability is the indispensable raw material of evolution. The kittiwake could never have evolved at all unless there was variability in behavior.

Close observation of birds usually reveals individual differences. The ethologist Niko Tinbergen noted that many of the kittiwakes in the colony he studied showed little peculiarities. One pair built an unusually high nest, year after year, and in another instance, a female returned to the colony each season,

*The kittiwake's winter is spent largely at sea, where flocks feed at the surface on fish and other marine animals (top left). The birds sometimes come inshore to roost communally at traditional sites (top center).*

*Courtship takes place at the colony in spring and, like so much of kittiwake breeding behavior, it is adapted for life on a narrow ledge. Here, a female is squatting during mating which lessens the chance of the pair overbalancing. These are red-legged kittiwakes, a species which is confined to the far north of the Pacific, around the Bering Sea.*

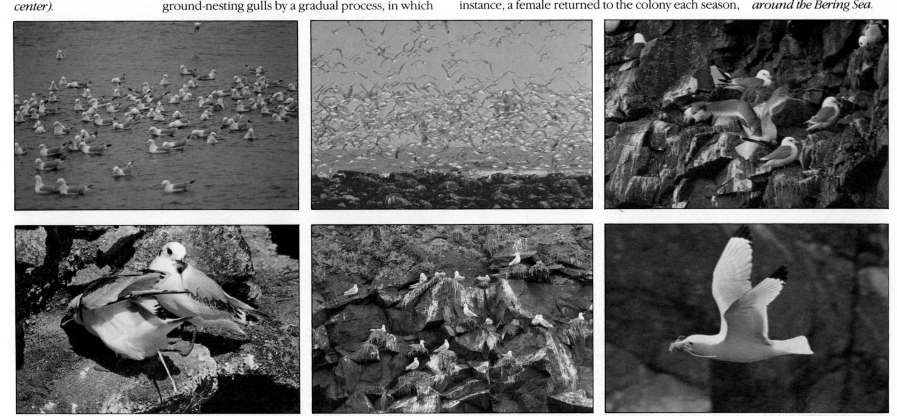

*Unlike ground-nesting gulls, kittiwakes do not attempt to conceal the nest. They defecate over the edge of the nest (bottom left), which keeps it clean, but makes its position very conspicuous (bottom center).*

the nests became situated on progressively more precipitous slopes with narrower ledges. This change in nesting site must have gone hand-in-hand with the development of traits that promoted survival in such situations. A bird that produced chicks which wandered over the cliff edge would not perpetuate its lineage, whereas one that did not bother to mob herring gulls would have more time and energy to devote to its young. In time, the process of natural selection resulted in a cliff-nesting bird showing a remarkable set of interlinked adaptations.

Among the thousands of species of birds living today, there are many, equally beautiful, examples of adaptation, illustrating the very precise way in which a species' behavior is attuned to its environment. However, to think of behavior in terms of an

and approached various males, but was too fearful to settle down and mate with any of them. Such quirks are only the more noticeable aspects of variable behavior, but they confirm that the very small differences in behavior on which natural selection can operate are likely to be there.

The mistaken belief that each species has an invariable behavior pattern is often linked with an idea of birds as simple-minded automatons, rigidly following a routine pattern of behavior. Again, this is far from the truth. In its daily life an individual bird is faced with many choices about where to look for food or what kind of food to select, and the breeding season involves major decisions about the bird's partner and nest-site. The decision-making process has been best studied in relation to feeding (pp. 61–2)

*A kittiwake returns to its cliff ledge with nesting material. The deep nest of mud and vegetation, which holds the eggs and young, requires many collecting trips. This may be a communal activity with a flock of kittiwakes gathering material together.*

*Kittiwakes are superbly adapted to the narrow cliff-ledges on which they normally nest but, like most birds, their behavior shows some flexibility and they can nest in other situations if the need arises.*

*When a kittiwake returns to the nest, it performs a greeting ceremony with its mate (below left). They toss their heads up and down, with mouths wide open, and utter the "kitti-w-a-ak" calls that give them their name.*

*Young kittiwakes do not wander from the nest and they spend much of their time facing the cliff (below right). They have limited opportunities for movement and they do not exercise as vigorously as other gulls.*

and it has been shown that birds and other animals follow simple "rules-of-thumb" when deciding on a course of action.

SECRETS OF SUCCESS

To see the flexibility of bird behavior, it is necessary to go no farther than the garden and watch that familiar and ubiquitous bird, the starling. Originally an inhabitant of Europe and western Asia, the common starling has been introduced to North America, South Africa, Australia and New Zealand and in each area it has multiplied enormously. From a hundred birds released into Central Park in the early 1890's, the population has spread such that the starling's breeding range now extends from east to west coasts and from arctic Canada to Mexico. The success of the species on colonizing new places has come about through its adaptability and opportunism, particularly in its diet.

Starlings are basically insect eaters, but they also prey on other small animals, up to the size of lizards and frogs, and they exploit a range of vegetable foods. Typically, starlings forage on the short grass of pasture and lawns, where they stride rapidly over the ground, probing and peering for hidden animals. The bill and its muscles are adapted for a special feeding technique known as "open-bill probing" in which the tip of the bill is pushed into the soil and then forced open to make a hole, down which the starling peers to seek out worms, cutworms, caterpillars and grubs. This particular form of feeding is believed to be important in the starling's success, for it gives it access to insects overwintering in the soil, and provides it with a highly nutritious source of food during the cold months. Finding food hidden in the ground is not easy, but starlings make use of their ability to learn and adapt. Once one has located a patch riddled with worms or larvae, it will return to the precise spot.

To supplement the basic diet, starlings are quick to exploit new opportunities. When ants begin to swarm on sultry summer days, starlings join the swallows in catching them on the wing, though they are not as adept as the professional hunters of flying insects. Starlings also follow large mammals for the insects they disturb, or land on their backs and pluck ticks from them, oxpecker-style (p. 66).

At certain times of the year, starlings turn to vegetable food. The result is that the bird changes from being the farmer's friend, for destroying insect pests, to being an enemy, through depredations of cherry orchards, vineyards, olive groves, the barley in cattle feeders and fields of newly sown winter wheat. Starlings also learn to scavenge human garbage and they become regular visitors to bird feeders.

## DECISION-MAKING

With such a range of food available it is clear that the starling must have to decide what is the best food to eat at a particular time. It is not just a question of consuming whatever is closest or most readily available, because nutritional value and other factors play a part. In winter, male starlings gather at cattle feeders and gorge themselves on barley, but female starlings concentrate on eating invertebrates, which helps them build up a good reserve of protein in their pectoral muscles, a "deposit account" on which they draw during egg manufacture in the spring. Somehow the individual bird must decide which food to go for.

When feeding nestlings, the decisions become even more critical and the factors to be taken into account are more complex. In one nest colony in Europe, the young were fed on two main types of food, crane fly larvae and antler moth caterpillars. The former were near the nest and fairly easily collected, unlike the caterpillars that were found some distance away and were much more difficult to gather. Even so, the caterpillars were a better food, because chicks fed

*Kittiwakes and pelagic cormorants nesting on a wreck off Alaska. Kittiwakes have also taken to nesting on piers and windowsills, which resemble their natural cliff-ledge sites. They will even, in some places, nest on flat ground, where they exhibit the same behavior that they have evolved for cliff nesting.*

*Kittiwake nestlings take food from the parent's bill (below left) whereas other gulls pick it up after it has been regurgitated onto the ground. In the confined space around the nest it is important to prevent rotten food accumulating.*

*When there is no room for retreat, an effective method of defusing aggression is essential. Unlike other young gulls, kittiwake nestlings have a black band across the neck (below right) which appears to act as an appeasement signal when the chick turns its head away from its nestmate or parent.*

on crane fly larvae produced very wet droppings, that soiled the nest and reduced its insulating properties. It was found that birds with small broods fed their young mainly on caterpillars while those with large broods relied on crane fly larvae to meet the extra-high food demands of their chicks, and brought in only a few caterpillars.

The crucial part of the study involved removing a small brood of healthy, well-fed chicks from a nest and substituting another brood of thin, hungry chicks. The parents, who had previously brought a steady stream of caterpillars for their young, immediately switched to crane fly larvae to satisfy the increased demand, this now being more important than the problem of nest sanitation. Changing tactics in this way must have involved a complex decision-making process, in which prey availability, food quality, and the intensity of the chicks' begging all played a part.

The problem of how a bird makes a difficult decision like this has still to be solved, and there is a great deal of exciting research being carried out. In recent years the whole focus of animal-behavior studies has shifted from describing the basic pattern of a species' behavior to examining how an individual adapts its habits to changing circumstances. The starling, admittedly, is an unusually adaptable species, but the behavior of most birds proves to be flexible enough for an individual to have several courses of action open to it.

## PROFIT AND LOSS

One way of examining how a bird adapts its behavior to a continuously changing environment is to calculate the costs and benefits of its actions and the time spent on them. All behavior uses energy through muscular activity and other body functions, such as digestion, manufacturing the eggs and keeping warm. Energy for these processes comes mainly from food, so all living things are faced with a basic economic equation if they are to survive: they must maintain an income of

*Starlings have a varied diet and need to make decisions as to which food to concentrate on finding. Crane fly larvae and other insects which they extract from the ground are an important food (top) and they occasionally search large animals for parasites (center). In winter, when other food is short, windfall apples are a welcome source of much needed energy (bottom)*

*High-protein food is needed for nestlings (below). When very young they are fed on small insects and spiders, and as they grow, larger insects are brought to them*

*Cold weather and deep snow can be disastrous for birds. They can fluff out their plumage to reduce heat loss and perch quietly to save energy, but food must soon be found. Unless this starling can find a bird feeder, cattle trough or other source of food not covered by snow, it may have to set out across country in search of milder conditions.*

*When the fledglings leave the nest (below left) their demand for food is at a maximum. They follow their parents to the feeding ground and keep up a chorus of cries to show where they are and indicate their hunger.*

*Thousands of starlings flooding into a roost make a marvelous sight on a winter's evening (below right). Their rapid, erratic flight seems to be a maneuver to avoid predation, but the advantage in joining mass roosts is not fully understood.*

energy greater than expenditure. They can exist for a short time on their fat reserves, but in the long run they must have an assured food supply.

Maintaining the energy budget is a particularly critical matter for birds because flying is expensive in terms of energy. A shortage of food can cause a fatal deficit, but there are many ways in which a bird can make savings. At night, when feeding stops, a sheltered roost saves energy, which would otherwise be needed to keep the bird warm. This is the most obvious explanation for the huge communal roosts which starlings join in winter, but a closer study of the profits and losses involved showed that, while heat conservation may account for communal roosting in other birds, it is not the whole story for starlings.

Calculating the energy budget of joining a winter roost involves measuring the temperature inside and outside the roost, and the amount of energy a captive starling uses up when flying in a wind tunnel. Having worked out the amount of energy consumed per miles flown, it is possible to work out how much a starling would use traveling 12.5 miles (20 kilometers) a day to and from the roost. This is an average distance for starlings as a whole, and some cover as much as 50 miles (80 kilometers).

The interesting discovery that has emerged from such calculations is that starlings often use up more energy traveling between the feeding ground and the roost – up to 27% of their daily intake – than they could possibly save as a result of the higher night-time temperatures in the roost. This suggests that there must be some other, non-energetic advantage to communal roosting, such as obtaining information about sources of food (p. 134).

THE BIRD'S YEAR

By looking at a bird's behavior in terms of gains and losses of energy, not only can the way it arranges its everyday activities be appreciated, but the entire annual cycle is put into perspective. Except in parts of

the tropics, the lives of birds are governed by the regular annual cycle of seasons. There is a season of plenty – the summer of temperate and polar regions, or the wet season in warm climates – followed by a season of shortage – the winter or dry season. The birds must gear their essential physiological functions to this cycle, fitting those that make the greatest demands on their resources into the season of plenty, while ensuring that they can survive the subsequent season of shortage.

The most important activity is breeding and it constitutes a substantial drain of energy lasting for several months. The second vital activity is the molt. Regrowth of the feathers is not only expensive in terms of the raw materials and energy required for their manufacture, but flying and keeping warm is more costly while feathers are missing.

flowers attract an abundance of insects, on which the young can be fed. Mockingbirds, thrushes and orioles also produce their broods to coincide with this food peak.

When parental duties have ended, the adults immediately embark on the molt, which takes three months to complete. Then, with flight surfaces in perfect condition, the starlings are ready to prepare for the winter. They put on weight and, according to geographical location, they either remain near the breeding area or migrate, In general starlings from the northern part of the range migrate, while those in the south are resident. Between them, there are populations of partial migrants (p. 198) in which some individuals are migratory and others are resident. Because of the constraints of fitting their long flights into the yearly cycle, migratory starlings

*The natural nesting places for starlings are in hollow trees or under boulders, but they adapt to a variety of sites, such as disused nests of larger birds, nest-boxes and buildings. This male has found an entrance into an old metal ventilator cowl, and is singing to proclaim his ownership.*

Migration is a third energy-draining activity, and although there are exceptions, these three vital activities do not generally overlap. However, the manner in which breeding, molt and migration are fitted into the annual cycle varies from species to species. Breeding requires the greatest expenditure of energy and it therefore takes place at the time when food is most plentiful. In most birds, the molt starts after breeding has ceased, but it may take place either side of the autumn migration.

The European starling provides an example of a "basic" annual cycle. It starts courtship and breeding activities in early March, as the days begin to lengthen, in Alabama (progressively later farther north) and the eggs are laid from late March to early May. There may be two clutches and the nestlings are reared when food is plentiful. For the first clutch, this coincides with the blooming of oak trees, when the emerging

rarely raise a second brood.

The starling's year can be visualized as a series of peaks of energy requirement – breeding, a molt, sometimes two migratory journeys and winter survival. Whenever energy expenditure is greater than intake, as during migration, the starlings have to draw on reserves of fat laid down in less strenuous times.

The time when the young are becoming independent is the point around which breeding, and the rest of the annual cycle, is centered. The parents need to maintain themselves, as well as meet the demands of their offspring. After the young have fledged, food needs to be in good supply because the population is at its maximum, the fledglings need easy meals while they learn to fend for themselves, and their parents must make good the weight losses sustained during the breeding season.

*The resident starling has to fight off other males that covet his nest-site, but he has time to start building the nest.*

## CONTROLLING THE CYCLE

The peak food supply is the ultimate factor in deciding when birds breed but eggs must be laid before the peak, and courtship takes place earlier still. Some migrants even start pairing, and prepare physiologically for breeding, while on the wintering grounds, thousands of miles away. So the food supply itself is not the trigger that starts breeding.

Internal timing mechanisms tell birds when to start preparations for breeding, and the most important of these mechanisms responds to daylength, the only quality of the environment which has a regular, unchanging annual cycle. Both molt and migration seem to be under the control of daylength changes, which are, surprisingly, perceived by light penetrating the skull to the brain, rather than acting through the eyes.

daylength changes very little.

Although timing of breeding is inborn, it can be modified from year to year by local conditions. A warm spring starts birds nesting earlier, but a drought prevents barn and cliff swallows gathering mud for their nests. Food supply may be an important modifier at the start of the breeding season, since the female cannot lay until there is sufficient food for her to manufacture the eggs, and many other environmental factors may play a part in deciding exactly when birds breed.

## THE LIVING BIRD

To understand a bird's behavior, it is necessary to look at the whole bird's life, not only in such striking features as its nesting habits, but also the details of where it roosts at night or how it picks up food for its young. Everything is geared to helping the bird in its

*When the nestlings hatch out, both parents become very busy bringing food into the nest (center). The effort involved in feeding nestlings is two to three times the energy expenditure of everyday activity outside of the breeding season.*

*A female is attracted by the half-built nest, which the male often decorates with flowers, apparently as an enticement. She will finish off the nest and add the lining of feathers and grass.*

Some species, however, have a timing mechanism which is not based on daylength or any other external cue. This is a fixed internal rhythm of approximately one year's duration. How such a rhythm is produced is a mystery, but it seems that changing daylength is used to reset the bird's "internal clock" each year and keep it in step with the seasons. Several species of birds, including starlings and some European warblers, have a fixed internal rhythm and if they are kept in a laboratory under a constant twelve hours light – twelve hours dark regime, they continue to show seasonal changes. Warblers put on weight and become restless when it is about the time to migrate, they molt roughly at the correct time and their reproductive organs develop as the breeding season approaches. This fixed rhythm may be important in giving the signal for the spring migration by birds which spend the winter near the equator, where

struggle for survival and it includes such diverse things as the color of its plumage, or the structure of its digestive system for dealing with a particular diet. The bird must keep itself in good condition by preening and bathing, or its flight will be impaired and its life put at risk. It needs to defend itself against predators, communicate with its fellows and navigate long distances on its migrations. Its behavior also includes the way it perceives the world through its senses, and the way it moves. Ultimately, however, behavior concerns the survival of the bird so that it can rear healthy offspring to carry its genes into the next generation.

Birds have been changing and adapting for millions of years and what we see in every species is a solution to the problem of life. Each species has a different solution and the study of birds reveals the extraordinary complexity and subtlety of their ways.

*Removing the young birds' droppings is another vital activity. Observation of nesting starlings has shown that if a parent bird has to spend more than three hours per day flying to and fro it will start to lose weight because it has insufficient time to feed properly.*

# CHAPTER 2
# FLIGHT

Flight is the main characteristic of the birds. Almost every aspect of bird biology has been modified for an aerial existence, and bird behavior cannot be considered without reference to the benefits and problems of flight. Flight has conferred great advantages on the birds in terms of fast and sustained locomotion. Not only can they cover a large area in a day's foraging, but they can also migrate thousands of miles to exploit two different habitats in the course of a year. On the other hand, the changes to the body needed for flight have caused constraints on other activities. The transformation of the forelimbs into wings is so complete that they can have few other functions. Some birds use their wings for signaling in courtship displays, a few herons employ them as sunshades when fishing, and young hoatzins and rails use them for clambering through branches. But,

surfaces are unequal; air flowing over the upper surface travels farther and hence faster, so that pressure is reduced, while the air traveling under the wings increases in pressure. The result is the upward force of lift (see diagram) which increases with the angle presented to the airstream – the angle of attack. Most of the wing's lift comes from the reduced pressure on the upper surface, and it reaches a maximum when the angle of attack is around 15°. Above this, lift disappears suddenly, and the wing stalls, because the airstream over the top of the wing breaks up and becomes turbulent, while pressure increases under the wing to push it backwards.

The key to bird flight is the flight feathers' ability to change shape automatically through the wingbeat cycle. The trailing edge of the vane of each primary feather is broader and more flexible than the leading

*A great tit's wingbeats photographed at 8-millisecond intervals to show two complete cycles.*

*Center: on the upstroke, the tawny owl's flight feathers separate and, as the wings are flicked straight, they act as individual propellers to push the bird forwards.*

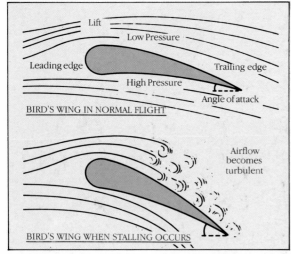

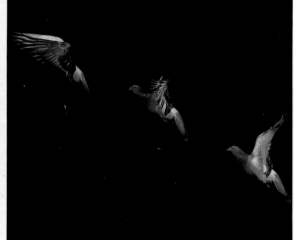

*A bird's wing is shaped to generate lift when it moves forward through the air. Its convex upper surface causes the airstream to travel farther and faster over the wing, which creates low pressure above it. Below the wing, pressure increases to push the bird up. If the angle of attack is too large, the wing stalls, as the airflow becomes turbulent.*

whereas mammals use their forelimbs for holding, manipulating and carrying, birds must manage with the horny bill, assisted occasionally by the feet.

The mechanics of bird flight are extremely complicated – more so than for an airplane with fixed wings – and some aspects are still not fully understood. When gliding, a bird wing is behaving like an airplane wing and lift is generated by its forward movement through the air, but in flapping flight the wing is acting both as lifting surface and propeller. In fast, level flight, the wing performs a fairly simple up and down motion, starting at an angle of 60° above the horizontal and ending just below the horizontal. Forward movement comes from the outer part of the wing beating up and down rather than rotating like an airplane propeller.

In section, a bird's wings are similar to an airplane's wings: convex above, concave below, with the leading edge blunt and rounded, and the trailing edge narrowing to a point. The upper and lower

edge so, when forced down, the vane twists, the trailing edge goes up, and air is forced backwards to produce a forward thrust. To fly faster, the bird either flaps its wings faster or more powerfully, to make the primaries twist more and increase the thrust.

On the upstroke the wrist is flexed so that the outer part of the wing partly folds and the primaries separate, like a Venetian blind opening, to let the air stream through and avoid pushing the bird down again. A small backward sweep of the wing as it comes up forces the primaries against the air, and they act like a paddle to give the bird an extra push forward.

When taking off or hovering, the bird loses the lift created by forward movement through the air. The extra lift has to be created by sweeping movements of the wings, like the rotating blades of a helicopter, and wingbeats become very much exaggerated, almost meeting over the back on the upstroke and ending well below the body on the downstroke. The wings are swept forwards and backwards more or less

*A pigeon photographed at intervals of 275 milli-seconds – slightly shorter than one wingbeat cycle, so the picture shows three stages in the upstroke. On the far right the wings are about to flick fully open at the end of the upstroke. In the center, an earlier stage, the primaries have turned over and are directing the airstream downwards. At the left, near the beginning of the upstroke, the primaries are separating and beginning to twist.*

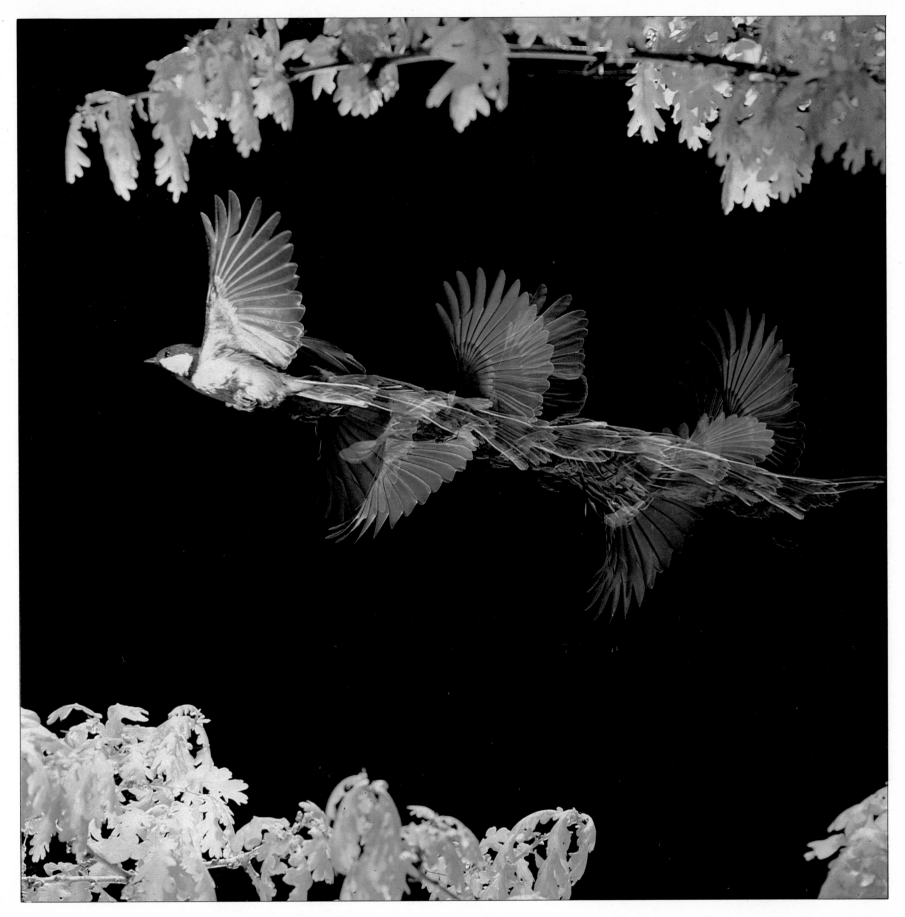

horizontally, so that they create their own movement through the air to generate lift. At the end of the downstroke, the wrist rotates and the elbow bends so that the primaries are turned upwards and the wing partly folds. The wing is then pushed sharply back and the primaries separate to let the air flow through. At the end of the upstroke, the wing is given a backward flick as it straightens out and the primaries give the bird a boost forwards and upwards.

When flying slowly, a bird faces the same problem of stalling as a slow-moving airplane. If the angle of attack becomes so large that the flow of air is turbulent, lift disappears and the wing is said to stall. Both birds and airplanes have the same solution to this problem. The alula, or bastard wing, a bunch of three or four feathers attached to the thumb, performs the same function as the slot on the leading edge of an

airborne without the help ot airtlow over the wings to give it lift. Most birds spring into the air to give the wings room to beat fully. The tail is fanned to deflect the airstream downwards, and it may beat shallowly up and down to increase the lifting effect. The loud "claps" made by a pigeon or dove taking off in a hurry are due to the outstretched wings hitting each other above the body, in an action which is thought to give extra lift at the start of the downstroke.

Some birds cannot take off by jumping, either because their legs are too short, as in swifts, or because they are set well back on the body, like those of many seabirds. Their easiest way of taking off is to drop from a perch or ledge, spread the wings and let gravity provide the momentum for attaining flying speed. Swifts have difficulty in taking off in any other way (although they are not so helpless on the ground

*A flock of African spoonbills climb heavily into the air with their long legs trailing until they are fully airborne.*

*Center: trumpeter swans taking off by running across the snow until they achieve flying speed.*

*After a meal of carrion, scavengers like this Rüppell's griffon vulture have difficulty getting airborne.*

*As it lands, a painted stork is almost hovering. It sweeps its wings forwards to get maximum lift with low forward speed.*

airplane wing. When there is a danger of stalling, the alula or slot is raised and a stream of rapidly moving air is directed over the wing surface to cut out turbulence. Herons and storks have a very large alula to give maximum lift on landing, when they almost hover and gently touch down on their long, spindly legs. The alula can increase lift by 10–20% at low speeds, and some birds cannot take off if the alula feathers are clipped.

## TAKE-OFF AND LANDING

Taking off is a strenuous, energy-demanding action, and the ability to lift straight off depends on the bird being able to generate enough power to get it

as is often believed), and seabirds take off from clifftops in a flat calm by leaping over the edge.

When leaping or dropping is not possible, takeoff has to be achieved by running, like an airplane accelerating down the runway. This is especially true for waterbirds. Some ducks and geese can leap straight into the air but swans, loons, cormorants, alcids and petrels patter over the surface, wings beating rapidly but shallowly, until flying speed is reached. A wind can help by increasing the airflow over the wings and so generating extra lift, and these birds, again like an airplane, take off into the wind. A wandering albatross will not attempt to take off in a

*A blue crane lowers its legs to absorb the impact of landing.*

*Center: an American wigeon about to touch down on a lake. It has swung its feet forwards so that they can break its impact with the water.*

flat calm and, if chased, fails to get airborne, but a strong wind will lift it off after a few steps.

Many birds can hover for a short time while picking an insect off a leaf or choosing a landing place; but few can sustain it for long since it is an energy-draining exercise. The American black-shouldered kite spends only two and a half hours hunting by hovering each day, but this accounts for half its energy budget. Prolonged hovering is mainly limited to specialists such as the kestrels of the Old and New Worlds, but even these birds do no more than fly steadily into a light wind as they lack the muscle power to hover properly in still air. The hummingbirds are the most specialized of hovering birds; the structure of their wings is different from all other birds, except the closely related swifts. The bones of upper arm and forearm are reduced in size so that the wing is almost all 'hand''. The elbow and wrist joints are practically immobile, and the wing acts as a rigid paddle rotating at a very flexible shoulder joint. When hovering, the body is held at an angle of 45° and the wings sweep through a narrow figure-of-eight in a horizontal plane. On the "downstroke", the wings are angled to provide lift, and at the end of the beat the wing turns over, so presenting the same angle of attack and obtaining the same lift. The thrust on up strokes and down strokes is equal and opposite, so the hummingbird stays in the same place, while a slight change in the angle of attack on either stroke will send the hummingbird forwards or backwards.

To touch down gently, a bird must lose height and slow down, yet maintain enough lift to keep control and prevent a crash. Fanning the tail and changing to deep wingbeats, as in take-off, help to slow the bird and also provide extra lift. If landing on a perch, further braking can be achieved by approaching from below and flying up so that gravity is helping to check the forward momentum. Ducks and geese rock when they drop sharply to land: they tumble and slide from side to side so air spills between the widely spread primaries, with a clear tearing sound, shedding enough lift to lose height quickly and then turning the wings into airbrakes before hitting the ground. Sometimes they twist onto their backs and so lose lift completely.

FLIGHT CONTROL

Control of flight, whether to maintain a straight-and-level course, or to turn, dive and climb, requires the greatest skill. When watching a bird in flight, it is almost impossible to see how it is controlling its flight, and photographs that freeze movements only reveal the many small means of control and fail to show how they are integrated into the overall flight mechanism.

An airplane has a tail unit which acts as a stabilizer to counteract any deviations from straight-and-level flight. *Archaeopteryx*, the earliest-known bird in the fossil record, had a long, lizard-like tail, fringed with feathers, which also acted as a stabilizer but would have hampered maneuverability. This forerunner of modern birds probably did little more than glide from tree to tree. In becoming more skillful

Lift (Backward Stroke)

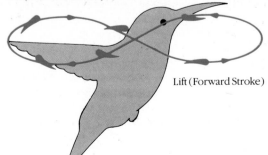

Lift (Forward Stroke)

*Hummingbirds' wings are almost rigid and swivel at the shoulder. When hovering the wing sculls to and fro. At the end of the forward stroke, the wing flips over so that it generates lift equally on the back as well as the forward strokes.*

fliers, birds have reduced the tail to a stump with a fan of feathers, and stability is achieved by correcting movements of the wings and tail. In effect, a modern bird is essentially an unstable flying machine and cannot remain airborne without continuous control.

To maintain its course, a gliding bird trims its wings: to dive and increase speed, the wings are swept back and partly folded; to rise nose-up, they are pushed forward and straightened. Stability can be increased by raising the wings in a shallow V, as is often noticeable in soaring birds of prey and gliding pigeons. In this posture, if the bird rolls slightly to the right, lift increases on the right wing but decreases on the left wing, so any tendency to roll is immediately checked and the bird tilts back to an even keel. Frigatebirds have turned-down wings which make them less stable than other birds but more maneuverable. From a slow, soaring flight, a frigatebird spots its prey and can instantly tilt over to one side and plunge headlong after it.

Steering is also achieved by movements of the wings. By altering the angle of attack, or flexing or extending one wing, the lift on that wing is increased or decreased and the bird slews round. The tail reinforces the effect of the wings by twisting one way or the other. The most maneuverable birds have wings and tail that can vary considerably in area. This is seen at its best when a bird, a fulmar or chough for instance, hangs in the air currents swirling and eddying up a cliff face and maintains perfect control by fanning its tail and extending or half folding its wings. The forked tails of swallows, terns and frigatebirds provide very sensitive rudders for maneuvering at low speed because they can be spread widely for greater effect.

POWER FOR FLIGHT

Mastery of the air has required more than the provision of wings to provide lift, thrust and control. During their evolution birds had to face two further problems. They needed to shed excess weight and to generate a high and continuous output of power. To lose weight, the bones are hollow, tail bones are reduced to a single plate, and jaws and teeth, which are the heaviest structures in other animals' bodies, have been abandoned for the horny bill.

The power of flight is generated in the breast muscles, which, in pigeons, make up one third of the body weight. To supply the flight muscles with the necessary fuel, and the oxygen for burning it, birds are equipped with highly efficient circulation and breathing systems. The heart is much larger than in comparably sized mammals, and the breathing system is unique. The lungs are connected to a series of thin-walled airsacs which spread through the body, penetrating the muscles and even entering the hollow bones. The air passages in the lungs do not end blindly in tiny sacs, or alveoli, as in mammalian lungs, but consist of about a thousand tubes, called parabronchi, each of which gives off thousands of microscopic, branching air capillaries where gases are exchanged with the blood. The function of the airsac

A black-and-white casqued hornbill shows the primary flight feathers widely separated, like fingers, a feature of large, slow-flying birds.

A display of aerobatics as a lammergeier attacks a griffon vulture in the Himalayas. The griffon vulture is turning away from its assailant by beating strongly with one wing – outstretched and primaries bending – and the other wing partly folded to reduce its lift.

*A lammergeier and several alpine choughs soar in the breeze blowing up a rock face in the Himalayas.*

system has been debated for years, but it now seems certain that it creates a one-way flow through the lungs by the air shuttling between the airsacs, as distinct from the tidal to-and-fro system in mammals.

Flapping flight requires a huge expenditure of energy. Fuel consumption for steady flight is usually in the order of ten to fifteen times greater than for a bird at rest, so economy is a virtue. It can be neglected only when there is a certainty that fuel is cheap, or when there is another overwhelming advantage, such as the advertisement of its territory by the skylark in its song-flight. Hummingbirds and kestrels use energy-expensive hovering flights only because it enables them to exploit a rich food supply.

The simplest way of saving energy is to stop flapping and glide: a gliding gull uses only twice its resting energy expenditure. So birds take the opportunity to "free-wheel" whenever possible. Gamebirds take off explosively when disturbed, but once airborne they use their momentum to carry them to safety in a fast, shallow glide. Many species typically have a flap-and-glide style of flight, especially when traveling a long distance, either in search of food or on migration. The bout of flapping is used to regain the height lost during the glide. Small birds of woodpecker size or smaller often have a bouncing flight in which they close their wings completely between bouts of flapping. It pays to fold the outstretched wings because the amount of drag on them outweighs any advantage they would get from lift generated by gliding.

*Snow pigeons, or Tibetan doves, live at heights of 6,500 feet (2,000 meters) or more in the Himalayas. Slope soaring is a useful aid in their daily migrations between their roosts on snow-covered crags and feeding grounds in cultivated valleys below.*

### SOARING

Soaring is a good energy-saving device because movements of the air are used to buoy up the bird. There are three main ways in which the atmosphere contributes a source of energy for soaring. The first depends on the flow of the wind being deflected upwards by an obstacle. A cliff or hill provides an opportunity for "slope soaring" in the breeze blowing up its face. Gulls and fulmars use this phenomenon to soar and hover along cliff faces while searching for food or prospecting for mates. It is also used by eagles as they patrol their hunting grounds. Ocean swell provides a similar updraft for seabirds, and petrels and albatrosses can soar along, traveling with the swell even in calm weather. When a strong wind is blowing, even a gently rounded hill will throw up a series of air waves in its lee, so that birds can "wave soar" beyond and above it. Gannets and other seabirds use the air waves thrown up by sea stacks. These tall rocks, as well as ships and large buildings, also provide an opportunity for "gust soaring", as when gulls and albatrosses hover over the stern of a ship and make use of the eddies of air swirling around it.

Updrafts are also created by weather fronts, and these can be used for soaring. Weather systems consist of moving masses of air, hundreds of miles across, and the boundary between two masses is called a front. Because it is denser, the air in a cold mass slides under neighboring warm air to create a cold front. Birds soar up the sloping face of the approaching front

to heights of over 20,000 feet (6,000 meters) as a means of escaping the storms associated with the mixing of the air masses. Swifts also soar in the lesser fronts formed by sea breezes along coasts.

A second source of energy for soaring is provided by air rising as it is warmed. When the ground warms in the sun, the air close to it heats up, becomes lighter and rises through the atmosphere as a thermal. Thermals are normally invisible, but one type consists of a whirling column of air which sucks in dust at its base and becomes visible as a "dust devil". A more widespread form is a spinning vortex ring, like a smoke-ring, which commonly forms over an outcrop of rocks that is warming more rapidly than the surrounding ground. A series of vortex rings rises, then drifts downwind, their positions being shown by a line of small cumulus clouds. In all types of thermal

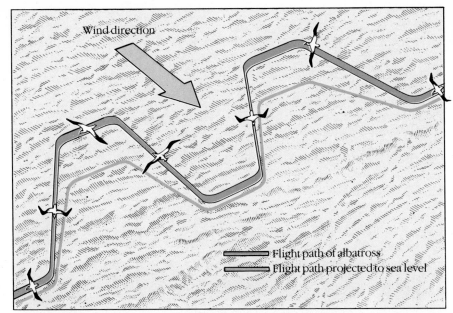

Wind direction

Flight path of albatross
Flight path projected to sea level

provide a vantage point from which they can scan the ground for carrion and then use a line of thermals to reach it before other animals get there. It has been calculated that when soaring and gliding white-backed vultures use one thirtieth of the energy of flapping flight.

Indeed, flapping flight for the heaviest vultures and condors requires so much power that they are barely able to remain airborne without the assistance of an updraft, and it is essential when the birds have a crop full of food. As thermals begin to form under the early morning sun, the smallest vultures take off first and only when the thermals become stronger are they followed by larger species, unless slope soaring can give them enough lift for an early start.

Thermals do not form over the sea, or only weakly so, because water is slow to warm, but the oceans are the home of a second group of great soaring birds: the albatrosses. Constructed on a very different pattern from the vultures, albatrosses are fast gliders with streamlined bodies and long slender wings to reduce drag. They, and other members of the tubenose order of seabirds, save energy by slope soaring above the waves, but they also employ dynamic soaring, the third method of extracting energy from the air.

Dynamic soaring is possible because friction slows the layer of air in contact with the sea surface, and full wind speed is only reached at about 165 feet (50 meters) above the sea. Albatrosses use this wind gradient to gain energy for soaring. The albatross glides downwind, picking up speed, then turns into the wind and begins to rise. Its speed relative to the water surface drops as its impetus is used up, but as it climbs it meets a stronger wind. Its speed relative to the air will either actually increase, or at least decrease more slowly than the groundspeed, depending on windspeed and the rate of climb. When the wind gradient has dropped and the bird cannot continue its climb, it turns downwind again and glides downward, gathering momentum ready to repeat the cycle.

A wandering albatross, the largest species, frequently soars to 50 feet (15 meters) or more, although calculations suggest that dynamic soaring on the wind gradient alone is unlikely to lift it more than 15 feet (3 meters). The extra impetus probably comes from energy gathered from slope soaring along a wave, which is used to lift the albatross so that it can then glide away to another wave and repeat its slope soaring. The dynamic soaring acts only as a boost to the ascending albatross.

Whichever way the albatross gains its energy, its soaring is very efficient. It can travel long distances without flapping if there is a good wind, and a 20 pound (9 kilogram) wandering albatross uses only 1% of its body weight to fuel a 60-mile (100-kilometer) flight. This form of travel is used by smaller petrels, gannets and gulls and is even employed by swallows migrating across the rock plains of the Sahara, but, as they are not such good gliders, some flapping is needed to maintain height.

*Albatrosses use the wind gradient above the sea to provide energy for soaring. On the downward flight the bird partially folds its wings to increase speed. Leveling out above the sea, it slope soars on the wave, for a short distance, then turns into the wind, relying on the wind gradient to carry it to heights of up to 50 feet (15 meters).*

*After the long glide downwind, a black-browed albatross turns across the wave tops and climbs again.*

there is a rising draft of air in the center which birds use for soaring. Tall buildings generate thermals just as rocks do, and other man-made thermals include parking lots, concrete highways, and in the Sahara oilfield flares used by migrating storks.

Small birds are probably assisted by thermals while migrating, but the specialists are such birds as eagles, hawks, storks, cranes, pelicans and especially the New and Old World vultures. They are all heavily built birds, some having long legs for wading, others being equipped with strong legs and talons. These birds have broad wings, and the primaries separate like spread fingers, which will give them good lift at low speeds and the ability to turn in tight circles. They soar to the top of one thermal, perhaps 6,500 feet (2,000 meters) high, then glide to the next, several miles distant, and soar again. Vultures use thermals to

The ancestors of modern birds are thought to have been animals which clambered through the trees and used their wings to glide or flap from one tree to the next. *Archaeopteryx* is almost certain to have lived this sort of life. Its big toe, or hallux, was turned back, as in modern birds, for grasping branches. The three hooked fingers on the wrist of each wing were probably used for scrambling through dense foliage, in the same way that nowadays young hoatzins in the swampy forests of South America use the two claws on their wings, or young moorhens and other rails use their single claw. Hoatzins and rails nest among aquatic vegetation and, if disturbed, the unfledged

ankles flex, tendons running down the back of the leg automatically pull tight and the toes clamp down. As long as the bird is squatting, its toes remain tightly curled around the perch, even while it is asleep.

Many birds use trees as roosts, nest sites, song posts and feeding grounds, but specific adaptations for life in trees occur in only a few families. The birds that feed on buds, seeds and fruit rely on the sense of balance and perching mechanism of the legs described above. No more than a heightened agility is required by the titmice and others that glean insects from leaves and can hang upside down from the flimsiest of perches. The parrots, mousebirds and

*Although strong fliers, vulturine guineafowl spend most of their time on the ground, scratching for food with their feet and running for cover when alarmed.*

nestlings scatter through the undergrowth and even leap into the water. When danger is past, they scramble and flap back into the nest, with their claws giving an extra purchase.

By the time hoatzins and rails have become adult, the wing claws have been lost, but some other adult birds use the wings to assist scrambling through dense foliage. Most tree-dwellers, however, rely on the sense of balance to control hopping and clambering through branches, and the passerines, or true perching birds, are aided by a locking mechanism in the legs. As the bird settles after each hop and its

crossbills use their bills to give extra support when clambering from perch to perch – a trait which leads to fatalities when parrots climb on power transmission lines, since they short-circuit cables as they stretch from one wire to hook the bill onto the next.

The most highly adapted climbers are the birds which feed on tree trunks, the woodpeckers, the creepers and the South American woodhewers, or woodcreepers. All these birds cling vertically and use their long tails as a prop. Other birds may do this from time to time – house sparrows inspecting nestboxes and roosting swifts cling vertically in this way – but

*The roadrunner is a North American desert bird that feeds on small animals. It has the speed and agility to capture fast-moving lizards and snakes.*

*Center top: silhouetted against a frozen lake, an amphibious Eurasian coot shows its strong legs designed for running and the toes bearing lobes for swimming.*

*Long hind-claws anchor a white-breasted nuthatch as it hops down a tree trunk.*

only the birds which forage regularly on tree trunks have stiffened tail feathers, sometimes with the tip of the vane missing to make a "spike". The spine-tailed swifts, such as the chimney swift, have a similar adaptation. Woodpeckers which rely on the two central tail feathers for support delay shedding them at the molt until the replacement set has grown. These birds' grip is enhanced by sharp curved claws and powerful thigh muscles; a strong grip is particularly needed when chiseling into timber.

Progress up tree trunks and along branches is by hopping with the tail pressed down firmly. The usual pattern of food searching is to hop up one tree and then to fly down and start at the base of the next. Creepers and most woodpeckers can shuffle down a

as do many passerines, while those that feed and nest on the ground have changed to walking. The larks, crows, starlings and the American troupial families are examples of walking passerines. Exceptions to the rule are the ground-dwelling pittas of tropical forest and scrub, and the West African rockfowls which feed on ground-living insects: both of these proceed by hopping.

Birds which spend most of their time on the ground have, like the hoofed mammals, evolved strong legs with smaller or fewer toes. Pheasants and shorebirds have small hind toes, and the ostrich – the ultimate running bird which reaches speeds of 45 mph (70 kph) – has only two toes. Extreme agility is seen in the roadrunner, a member of the cuckoo

*Center bottom: the enormously long toes spread the weight of the African jaçana so that it does not sink as it walks over waterlily leaves.*

*Young hoatzins leave the nest at an early age and scramble among the vegetation, using the bill and two movable claws on each wing for support.*

trunk only with difficulty. The nuthatches and the piculets of the woodpecker family display more agility and hop up and down trunks with equal facility, always proceeding head first, without use of the tail, and getting extra grip on the way down from a very long claw on the hind toe.

## BIRDS ON THE GROUND

As a general rule, those birds that spend much of their time in trees progress along the ground by hopping,

family, which hunts lizards and rodents, and runs rather than flies to safety. It can out-maneuver dogs, no doubt using its long tail to help steer and balance. The opposite trend is seen in marsh-dwelling birds, such as the rails, which have long toes to give support and spread the weight over a large area, like snowshoes. This reaches its culmination in the enormous toes of the jaçanas, or lily trotters, which tread delicately over floating vegetation.

For many birds, contact with water is limited to drinking and bathing, and a fall into deep water is likely to be fatal. Unless they can struggle clear, the plumage will become waterlogged and the bird will drown. To exploit the water medium, a degree of adaptation is needed. For some waterbirds this is slight. Herons keep clear of the water on their long legs, although they occasionally swim. Shorebirds, also, usually keep clear of the water, although phalaropes are swimmers and the common sandpiper dives underwater if chased. Exploitation of water may involve minimal contact, as with the frigatebirds which are ocean-goers yet avoid getting wet, plucking their food from the water without settling on it, even for a moment. At the other extreme, penguins and alcids are almost wholly aquatic and spend their entire lives at sea, except when breeding.

The first considerations for birds entering the water is that, like boats, they should be waterproof and buoyant. Waterproofing is provided by the structure of the feathers and the fact that they overlap closely; dead waterbirds soon become wet and bedraggled as the feathers go limp. Air trapped under the feathers provides buoyancy, and the airsacs of the respiratory system further reduce the density of the body, so most birds are extremely buoyant. However, the heavy, flightless cassowaries sink if they stop swimming.

For birds wishing to submerge, reducing buoyancy is more of a problem, and diving birds have heavier bones and smaller airsacs than landbirds. The grebes, the loons and the stiff-tailed ducks can adjust their buoyancy further by compressing their feathers and respiratory airsacs to force out air. When they are disturbed, they can sink so that only the head and neck are showing. The cormorants, and the closely related darters, or anhingas, are a puzzle because there is a comparatively greater gap between each barb on their feathers, so that they easily become waterlogged. This might seem to be a disadvantage for a waterbird, but the cormorants feed in deep water and waterlogging makes diving to depths considerably easier. When a

*Below left: an American darter or anhinga comes up from a dive with a fish impaled on its bill. To reduce its buoyancy before the dive it squeezed the air out of its plumage and is consequently swimming with the body submerged. Darters, grebes and loons also swim in this way when alarmed.*

*Below right: the waterlogged plumage of these Indian darters has to be dried after diving.*

*A common goldeneye "duck-diving". First it lifts its body out of the water, then plunges head-first and disappears.*

cormorant is about to start fishing, it raises its feathers to let water in and displace the trapped air, so reducing its buoyancy. On its return to the surface, the waterlogged cormorant finds take-off difficult until it can dry its feathers. To dry them, it perches with wings outstretched. Waterlogging of the feathers also destroys insulation, so cormorants and darters may also be warming themselves in the sun when they spread their wings.

Buoyancy makes it difficult for some diving birds to get below the surface, and an impetus is needed in the form of a "duck dive" – a sharp leap up and plunge from the surface – or by diving from the air. Gannets, brown pelicans, terns, gulls and kingfishers plunge from a height directly onto their prey and stay submerged only long enough to seize it.

The legs of some waterbirds have moved to the rear of the body where they act as more efficient paddles, or as rudders, while swimming or flying. This makes walking difficult. Petrels, loons and some ducks can only shuffle awkwardly on their breasts to their nests, but the alcids and penguins have solved the problem by standing upright and waddling on their short legs. Penguins can not only run at a fair speed but pick their way over boulders and scramble up almost sheer cliffs.

Cormorants, ducks, loons and grebes swim underwater by paddling, but the most specialized diving birds – the alcids, shearwaters, diving petrels and penguins – use their wings to "fly" underwater, the feet being used, with the tail, as rudders. With the increased resistance of water, large wings are a hindrance, and these diving birds have evolved narrow, almost paddle-like wings, linked to powerful flight muscles. Another need for specialization is in fast flowing water. Dippers search for invertebrate prey among the stones in mountain streams. They swim with their wings but also have the ability to walk on the bottom, holding on with stout legs and claws. Their only other significant adaptation to underwater activity is a very dense plumage. A similar but more perilous way of life has been adopted by the torrent duck, which lives in the headwaters of the Amazon where they pour down the side of the Andes. It searches for food in seemingly impossible conditions by making use of eddies, hanging on with its sharp-clawed toes and bracing itself with a stiff tail and spurs on its wings.

For most waterbirds, these adaptations amount to

*Like gannets, the brown pelican dives headlong into the sea to catch fish. It folds its wings right back as it hits the water to prevent them being broken.*

*Having the feet set well back on the body is an adaptation for swimming, but it makes many waterbirds, like this red-throated loon (below left), very clumsy on land. Loons only come on land to shuffle to their nests at the water's edge. Common murres (below right) have the same problem but they solve it by standing upright when on land. The black-legged kittiwakes, which often share their nesting cliffs, are more normal in shape, as they do not dive or swim underwater.*

*Torrent ducks in a mountain stream: the female is using her sharp claws and stiff tail to keep a footing while the male swims in the foaming water.*

a compromise between swimming and flying. As a result, flight is often labored, maneuverability is poor, and take-off and landing are difficult. The alcids and their southern hemisphere counterparts, the diving petrels, fly with rapidly whirring wings, like giant bumble-bees. When a puffin or guillemot, or a waterlogged cormorant, is chased by a boat, it is more likely to escape by diving than by trying to struggle into the air. The diving petrels, however, seem to have reached a good compromise: they surprise visitors to

This is not an effective way of alighting on firm ground, and those waterbirds that can do so adopt the same techniques as landbirds, whereas others try to avoid coming down on land. Loons almost always land on water, and petrels and albatrosses land with a thump at their nests unless there is sufficient wind to let them float down gently. Alcids land gently on the nesting ledge by coming in low and flying steeply up to lose speed, but there is not enough airspace for this maneuver when guillemots nest near sea level, so they

*Center: the dipper can swim with its wings or walk along the riverbed.*

*A tufted puffin displays its narrow, paddle-like wings which are well suited to propelling the bird underwater.*

*Like other alcids, these razorbills and common murres have a problem in taking off. Their glide down from the cliff-top may continue until they are just above the sea.*

the Southern Ocean by flying through steep waves, entering one side and coming out of the other without a pause.

Small wings and backwardly placed legs makes take-off difficult, and alcids launching from low cliffs are sometimes hard pressed to get airborne without crashing into the sea. Landing presents similar difficulties. Instead of slowing down until almost hovering, waterbirds brake as much as possible with the wings, then put their feet out and slide to a halt.

land on the water and walk up the rocks.

The penguins, along with the extinct great auk, have made the greatest adaptation to swimming. They have abandoned flight totally in favour of a marine way of life. The wings have become rigid, sabre-thin paddles for propelling the penguins underwater, and the wingbeat is different from that of flying birds. The whole flipper twists, in much the same way as a single flight feather on a flying bird, with the trailing edge forced up on the downstroke so that water is deflected

*Alcids also find it difficult to land at their nest sites. Here a puffin brakes by throwing its wings back and its legs forward.*

downwards and backwards. This is reversed on the upstroke, so that thrust is produced throughout the cycle. The upstroke is powered, unlike that in a fast-flying bird in which it is largely a "recovery" stroke generating little lift. The result is a net balance of forces pushing the penguin up and down, and it is propelled in a straight line, the speed being controlled by the wingbeat frequency.

Emperor penguins have been recorded as swimming at 6 mph (10 kph), although the average

penguin is swimming just below the surface, it encounters resistance caused by the surface wave that its own movement is creating. The faster it swims, the greater the resistance, until a point when resistance exceeds the energy needed to leap clear of the water and porpoising becomes the economical way to travel. The penguin could avoid the surface drag by swimming at a greater depth, but it has to come up to breathe, so porpoising is more efficient.

From the few investigations made, it seems that

*Penguins can swim fast enough to propel themselves out of the water and leap 6 or 7 feet onto rocks and ice floes.*

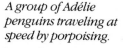

*A gentoo penguin swimming underwater shows its superbly streamlined shape.*

*A group of Adélie penguins traveling at speed by porpoising.*

speed is 4.5 mph (7.5 kph). These figures are less than one would have expected from seeing a penguin zip through the water, and wildly exaggerated estimates used to be given for penguin speeds. The figures for emperor penguins were calculated by timing a penguin swimming under the ice from one breathing hole to the next, but for sustained journeys penguins usually travel by "porpoising", that is, repeatedly leaping out of the water and plunging back. Porpoising is an energy-saving device. When a

penguins and other diving birds are not as well adapted as whales and seals for diving to great depths, or remaining submerged. Most dives are shallow and short, but emperor penguins have been recorded, with an instrument package strapped to the back, as descending to 850 feet (265 meters) and staying down for 18 minutes. Other seabirds have been recovered from great depths by fishing nets: common loon and common murre at 250 feet (80 meters) and oldsquaw at 180 feet (54 meters).

*The feather of a domestic pigeon, with the barbs partially separated to show the barbules. The feathery distal barbules are equipped with hooks as shown in the diagram below. These link up with the concave surface of the proximal barbules, to hold the feather vane together.*

A bird must keep its feathers in perfect condition. If the plumage is in disarray, insulation and waterproofing will be spoiled and flight will be less efficient. It will cost the bird more in terms of energy to keep warm and fly, and labored flight may even cost the bird its life. Flight maintenance is a two-tier process comprising the everyday regime of cleaning, oiling and preening the feathers, and the renewal of the suit of feathers at the molt.

A feather is a complex structure, delicately pieced together, so that it must be treated with care. From the central shaft, or quill, there run two rows of barbs which are linked together by overlapping barbules. Maintenance consists of ensuring that the thousands of barbules stay hooked up, because the integrity of the feather is responsible for its unique flexibility and strength, as well as for its waterproofing properties. Air trapped between the barbs increases the surface tension of the feather vane and causes water to pearl into droplets and run off (like the air held between the fibers in tent canvas). In waterbirds, the air trapped in the plumage also increases buoyancy.

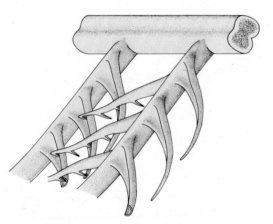

### BATHING

Most birds bathe, even in cold weather, and starlings have been seen to break thin ice so they could immerse themselves. The typical bathing action gives the bird more of a shower bath than a soaking. Standing in shallow water, it bends down to immerse the belly and vigorously flicks its bill from side to side in the water. At the same time the wingtips are vigorously beaten so that sprays of water are thrown over the body. In heavy rain, drops of water run off the plumage leaving the bird dry, so, to make bathing effective, the bird ruffles its plumage to allow wetting. But it must not get soaked or it will be unable to escape if danger threatens.

Some birds bathe in the rain. Larks, for instance, squat on the ground with wings outstretched when it rains, and parrots stand with feathers ruffled and

Far left: a yellow-fronted Amazon parrot rain-bathing. It fluffs out its feathers and carries out all the normal actions of bathing, without leaving the safety of its perch.

Left: even waterbirds like this mute swan need to bathe. Without such treatment the condition of the feathers will deteriorate and they will lose their waterproof qualities.

Far left: a little cormorant speeds the drying of its feathers by giving them a good shake.

Left: a song thrush soaking its plumage thoroughly in a birdbath. The nictitating membrane has been drawn across the eye to keep water out.

wings and tail spread. Hornbills, and some other birds bathe by flapping among rain- or dew-soaked foliage. The plunge bath is a feature of the most aerial of birds, such as swifts, swallows, owls, nightjars, kingfishers and hummingbirds, which dip into the water for an instant before continuing their flight.

## PREENING

After bathing, the bird retires to a safe place to preen. Wetting the feathers before preening helps the spread of preen oil. Most birds have a preen gland at the base of the tail whose contents are smeared over the plumage. The function of the oil is not known for certain. It was once believed to act as a lacquer that helped to increase the surface tension, and hence the waterproofing of the feathers, but ducks treated with a solvent to remove the oil remained waterproof. Neither is there any support for the notion that preen oil contains a substance which is converted into Vitamin D under the influence of sunlight. The oil does seem to keep the feathers from becoming brittle, and it has antibacterial and fungicidal properties.

Several actions, involving sensitive movements of the bill are used in preening. The most thorough movements are gentle nibblings of each feather as it is drawn between the tips of the beak. This cleans and rearranges the barbs and barbules. Sometimes the bird digs vigorously at one spot to clear away dirt or remove a parasite; at other times it draws the feather rapidly through the bill. Stroking movements help to smooth the feathers and to dry them. Finally, the bird shivers its body feathers and beats its wings to settle everything comfortably into place.

## DUSTING, SUNNING AND ANTING

As well as being a frequent visitor to the bird-bath, the house sparrow also indulges in dustbathing, particularly in fine weather. Sandgrouse, bustards and the gallinaceous order – chickens, grouse, guineafowl and others – dustbathe but never bathe in water. These are birds of open, often dry, country where there is plenty of dust but little water. The bird scrapes with its feet and shuffles its wings so that its ruffled plumage becomes filled with dust.

The value of dusting is not clear, and neither is that of sunbathing. At its simplest, the bird sits with its feathers ruffled and wings drooping. At higher intensities, it leans away from the sun with the nearer wing drooping and half-spread, or it lies flat with both wings spread. Pigeons raise the wing nearest the sun over the back, and bateleur eagles perch with their wings spread to catch the sun, like heraldic eagles.

Some birds probably sunbathe to warm their bodies in the morning, but it is noticeable that others sunbathe when the sun comes out even though the air is very warm. They pant at the same time so they are presumably already too hot. Furthermore, a sunbathing bird looks "stupid": it appears to be in a trance and often loses its natural wariness. A possible function for sunbathing in large birds is to assist in feather maintenance. When birds such as vultures, storks and pelicans soar for extended periods, their long flight feathers become bent. These birds

*Far left: a juvenile barn owl pays attention to its tail feathers during a bout of preening. Feather maintenance is an important activity and birds spend a considerable time preening. The preen gland at the base of the tail has been exposed by the raising of the covering feathers.*

*Left: a great white egret preens its long plumes. The feather is gently nibbled as it is drawn through the bill.*

*Even birds with large, awkward bills like these white pelicans, show great delicacy when preening their feathers.*

sunbathe, whereas large birds that flap – herons, swans and cranes – and those that have short wing feathers, such as albatrosses, do not. It has been found that a twisted vulture feather straightens out in four to five minutes when exposed to the sun, but takes two to three hours in the shade.

Perhaps sunbathing for some birds, as for human beings, is more than a functional pursuit and is positively enjoyable through the sensation of physical well-being. The same may be said for anting. This is an odd performance in which a bird picks up ants, one at a time, and applies them to the underside of the wings, as if oiling the feathers. Then the ants are dropped, or eaten, and the performance is repeated. Some species, notably members of the crow family, squat over the ants, often with wings spread as if

*In the Sonoran desert of North America, a Gambel's quail uses dust as a substitute for water. It scrapes at the ground to loosen the soil, then ruffles its plumage so that the dust can penetrate the feathers.*

## MOLTING

Despite the daily servicing of the plumage, feathers eventually wear out. As well as abrasion against the ground or foliage, and continuous rubbing in the nest, the feathers eventually become worn through flying. The primary flight feathers of the swift, which spends almost the entire year in the air, are reduced to little more than quills.

The old set of feathers must be replaced before it becomes unserviceable and almost all birds molt their entire plumage once each year. Some molt twice and a very few three times. Second and third molts typically involve only the body feathers and are usually concerned with color changes, either into the breeding dress or for camouflage, like the ptarmigan turning white to match the winter snow.

*Center: turkey vultures roosting on cacti in northern Mexico. One has its wings spread to catch the weak rays of the rising sun. Sunbathing in the early morning helps such birds to warm up after a cold night.*

*A Steller's jay spreads its wings and tail and raises its feathers to let the sun penetrate.*

sunbathing, and let them swarm over the plumage.

The usual explanation is that the formic acid from the ants may kill or dislodge lice from the feathers, or that other secretions may act like preen oil in preserving the feather structure. There is no evidence that fluid from the ant's body has any beneficial effect on the feathers, however, and anting appears to be something of an addiction. Some birds ant avidly while others seem never to ant. Such is the passion for anting that "addicts" twist their wing and tail feathers against the ground in a way which is hardly calculated to improve the condition of the plumage. Captive birds have anted with such odd things as mothballs, matches and cigarette ends, while starlings and crows occasionally display the same type of behavior over smoke and flames. Taking "beakfuls" of the smoke, they place it under the wing, as with a beakful of ants.

Where possible the rule is for a bird to molt when not undergoing the hardships and strains of breeding or migrating, and to avoid the winter or other periods when food is short. The molt is a time of increased energy expenditure for birds. They have to manufacture the new feathers, which are equivalent to over a quarter of the total body protein in a small bird. They will need to eat more food to replace the energy lost as heat through the patchy feather covering, and flying is more strenuous because of the gaps in the wings. If a molting bird is held in the hand, the new flight feathers are distinguished by their fresh appearance, as compared with the worn, faded feathers which they are replacing. The gap between the two is partly filled by the growing feathers, the newest being a "pin" still in its waxy sheath. When about one-third grown, the feather breaks out of the

*Painted storks strike statuesque postures when they sunbathe. Sunbathing may help large soaring birds keep their flight feathers in good condition.*

sheath and attains its full length and shape. A little while later, the blood supply to the new feather ceases and it becomes a dead structure. The sequence continues down the line of feathers. As each new feather is half grown, its old neighbor drops out.

Most birds molt after the breeding season but the female European sparrowhawk which, like some other birds of prey, incubates continuously on the nest while being fed by her mate, starts to molt after laying the eggs and loses her feathers very rapidly. The nest rim becomes thickly covered with molted feathers and, if flushed from the nest, she appears to fly heavily. This arrangement allows her to pass the difficult period of the molt at a time when she would be inactive anyway. Her mate, who is hunting for himself and his family, does not molt until later, when

covering intact. A penguin cannot afford the loss of heat through an incomplete plumage, and the old feathers do not drop before their replacements appear, as in other birds. The new feathers grow into the old feathers so that the plumage has a thick, unkempt appearance. The old feathers are torn away by the penguin's preening, leaving patches of sleek, new plumage.

The birds described so far lead seasonal lives. Other species, especially those living in the tropics and subtropics or at sea, occupy a more equable environment and there is not the same constraint to fit molting into a limited timespan. Consequently their molts are often a slow process. Parrots, for instance, may take eight or nine months to renew their plumage, and large birds of prey are in a state of

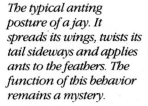

*The typical anting posture of a jay. It spreads its wings, twists its tail sideways and applies ants to the feathers. The function of this behavior remains a mystery.*

*Penguins lose all their feathers in a sudden molt, but insulation is not impaired since the new feathers are already well grown.*

*Molt of the flight feathers can often be seen as a bird flies overhead. This black kite also shows "fault bars" on the outer primaries. These are lines of weakness caused by the bird going hungry while the feathers were growing.*

there are plenty of young birds, fresh out of the nest and easily caught. Where males take no part in rearing the family they may molt immediately after mating. In the cotinga family there is a link between feeding, nesting and molting. Among insect-eating species both sexes care for the brood and they molt after breeding is complete. The fruit eaters have brightly plumaged males which take no part in family life, and they molt as the females begin egg laying.

Some hornbill females imprison themselves in their nesting holes behind a wall of dried droppings and are fed through a slit by their mates. They take advantage of this period of enforced immobility to change their feathers in a very fast molt that leaves them naked and completely flightless.

Penguins have a unique molting system which is extremely rapid but which leaves the plumage

continuous molt. The golden eagle takes two years to replace its feathers completely but, by the time one sequence of molt has been completed, another will have begun. The advantage of a slow molt, especially for birds such as albatrosses and vultures which spend most of their time airborne, is that by dropping only one feather in a sequence at a time, flying efficiency is not lost.

An alternative solution is to molt all the flight feathers at once. This is only feasible for birds which can continue to feed and avoid danger while flightless. It is the solution adopted by a number of water and marsh birds that include the waterfowl, grebes, loons, many alcids, cranes and rails. Molting geese, for instance, retire to lakes: they come out to feed along the shores, but are very wary and rush back into the water at the slightest hint of danger.

*Ostriches running at full speed on the Etosha Pan in Namibia. Their long legs enable them to escape from danger quickly, and to cover a wide area when searching for food in barren country.*

Despite the advantages of flight, a few birds have given up an aerial existence for life on the ground or in the sea. There are about forty species of flightless birds living today, and many others have become extinct only in recent times. The largest groups of flightless birds are the penguins, which have abandoned flight in favour of swimming, and the ratites – the ostrich, emu, cassowaries, kiwis and rheas – which specialize in running. Other flightless birds, living and extinct, belong to a variety of bird families, and include ducks, grebes, a cormorant, an alcid, a parrot and a wren. One family which is particularly well represented is the rails, with over thirty flightless species, a dozen of which have become extinct within the last 300 years.

All flightless birds are descended from flying ancestors but the ratite birds have lost so many of the adaptations for flight that they were once believed never to have flown. The name is derived from the Latin *ratis*, a raft, and it describes the flat breastbone or sternum, which lacks the keel that acts as an extra anchorage for the large flight muscles of flying birds. The ratites also have very small wings; the kiwis' wings are so small that they are hidden under the plumage and their flight muscles have atrophied giving the birds a pear-shaped outline. The ostrich retains some use of its wings: they are spread for balance when running and in display, and for shading the brood from the sun. The tail of ratites is small or absent, the preen gland is missing and the feathers have lost their barbules so that the vanes are loose and fluffy like the down of a chick.

Linked with the loss of flight is the development of the running habit. Paralleling the evolution of the hoofed mammals, the ratites have long legs and short toes. The ostrich has reached the peak of this development and has only two toes; one takes most of the bird's weight and is provided with a flat nail while the other is smaller and without a nail. Ostriches can run at over 38 mph (60 kph), and their speed, combined with wariness and a powerful kick, enables them to survive among lions, cheetahs, hyenas and hunting dogs. The South American rheas are also speedy and spread one wing as a brake to help make a swift, sharp turn. In Australia there are two groups of running ratites, the emu which is found over most of the continent, and the cassowaries which replace it in the forests of northern Australia and New Guinea. The cassowaries' wing feathers have lost their vanes, and the stout quills that remain form a palisade on each side of the body which, with the bony casque, or helmet, on the head, are thought to protect the birds as they race through the dense forest vegetation. As well as being fast runners, these ratites can defend themselves with powerful kicks and cassowaries have, on rare occasions, killed human beings.

The remaining living ratites, the three species of kiwis, have not attained the size of the others. About chicken-sized, they are short-legged and lead a secretive life in forests. The kiwis have been described as honorary mammals because, in the isolation of New Zealand where there are no native mammals except a few bats, they have developed several mammalian characteristics: they are nocturnal, they rely more on the sense of smell and less on eyesight than other birds, and their unbarbed feathers resemble fur.

Two groups of huge ratites became extinct in recent times. The aptly named elephant birds which stood over 10 feet (3 meters) high and weighed half a ton (500 kilograms) lived on Madagascar. Well-preserved skeletons of these giants and their 18-pint (10-liter) eggs are still found in swamps. Their memory lingers in the legend of Sinbad the Sailor's *roc*, an enormous white bird that was believed to prey on elephants, carrying them in its talons to its nest among the mountains. The moas, of which there were about nineteen species, were confined to New Zealand. There are a few accounts of strange birds, unlike any known today, that suggest that some of the smaller species survived to be seen by Europeans, but most moas were probably extinct by the end of the seventeenth century.

Apart from the ratites and the penguins (p.29), flightlessness has occurred throughout the bird world where the power of flight has become unnecessary or where its advantages no longer compensate for the anatomical and physiological constraints it imposes. Trends towards flightlessness appear in many families and there are several birds which fly reluctantly. The tinamous, a South American family of quail-like birds which may be related to the ratites, have strong wings but fly only when flushed and then in such an uncontrolled fashion that they are likely to crash into tree trunks or branches. The New Zealand wattlebirds climb up trees and then glide back to the ground. The mesites, which are distant relatives of the rails living in the forests of Madagascar, walk like pigeons with a nodding head. Their habits are poorly known, but despite well formed wings it seems that they rarely fly. Many other ground-dwelling birds are reluctant to fly and prefer to run for cover if threatened.

Complete flightlessness among landbirds is more likely in species which live on islands where the absence of mammal predators removes one reason for flying and the danger of being blown out to sea may become a good reason for not flying. The rail family has been a frequent colonizer of islands. Although rails are typically retiring birds which run or hide in vegetation when disturbed, several species are long distance migrants. Island rails undoubtedly evolved from migrants which were blown off course, and many have either become flightless or fly only feebly.

An island species has a precarious existence because its population is necessarily small. Four species of rails are known only from bones found in

caves on Bermuda; they had become extinct before the earliest human colonizers arrived. Many extinctions of flightless island birds can, however, be attributed to man. These birds were adapted to life without mammalian predators and succumbed after the arrival of men and the cats, rats, dogs and other animals they brought with them. The most famous extinction is that of the dodo of Mauritius, which disappeared in the 1680s, but many flightless birds have been exterminated more recently. The Laysan rail was destroyed by rats from a ship in World War II at about the same time as the last of the Wake Island rails were devoured by the beleaguered Japanese garrison. The Stephen Island wren of New Zealand,

*Two male ostriches displaying at each other. The spread wings and raised tails show how these are useless for flight but make excellent signals. The flight feathers form fluffy plumes rather than stiff airfoil surfaces.*

*A lesser rhea "kneels" to drink. Birds look as if their knees bend the wrong way, but in fact the joint is not a knee at all. The rhea is resting on an elongated ankle bone and its knee is hidden under its plumage, as in other birds. The bird's elongated legs are an adaptation for fast running.*

believed to be the only flightless passerine, was reputedly wiped out in 1894 by a single lighthouse keeper's cat. Other flightless birds which survive under threat of extinction include the kagu of New Caledonia and the kakapo, a New Zealand parrot. The takahe, also of New Zealand, was thought to be extinct until rediscovered in 1948, living in a remote, isolated valley. Only one bird has managed to turn the tables on introduced mammals: the weka, a chicken-sized New Zealand rail, thrives on a diet that includes mice and rats.

In the case of waterbirds, flightlessness is linked with the development of swimming (p. 26) but their habit of nesting in safe places where they cannot be reached by ground predators has also been essential for them to survive without flight. When a team of

sledge dogs gets loose among a penguin colony in the Antarctic, they quickly demonstrate how vulnerable flightless birds can be, but even those penguins breeding on the coasts of warmer lands are normally safe from predation because they nest in inaccessible places. This must have been a significant factor in the evolution of three groups of flightless or near-flightless waterbirds in South America. The short-winged, Atitlan and Junin grebes live on isolated, mountain lakes, the two flightless steamer ducks live in coastal waters of South America, and the flightless cormorant lives on the Galapagos Islands.

At one time it was thought that penguins represented a primitive stage of bird evolution or

*The bony helmet or, casque, and the spiny, vaneless wing feathers of this double-wattled cassowary are thought to help protect the bird as it runs through the dense undergrowth of the forest.*

even that they had evolved independently from the reptiles, but they are now known to be descended from flying birds, and seem to be related to the petrels. In the course of their evolution they probably went through a stage like the modern alcids and diving petrels. These birds have achieved a compromise between flying and swimming with their wings. Their flight is not very efficient but they continue to fly long distances between feeding grounds and nesting colonies, which are usually sited on or above cliffs. On the coast of Labrador there is a colony of murres breeding near the bottom of the cliff and the birds walk up the rocks to their nests. They would have no need of flight at all if they could feed within swimming distance of the colony, and this could show how the flightless alcids and penguins came into being.

For smaller birds the best size of wing for flying is also the best for swimming. As body weight increases, relatively larger wings are needed for flying whereas smaller wings are better for working in the denser medium of water. At about 2.2 pounds (1 kilogram), large enough wings for flying in air become ineffective for "flying" through water: the largest living alcids, the murres, are just within this limit.

The penguins' course of evolution took them away from the air and, once they were flightless, the wing could be reduced to an oar-blade, and their weight could increase. Unlike ratites, penguins have a keel on the breastbone and very large "flight" muscles for working the flippers. The largest living penguin is

One advantage of being flightless is that a bird can afford to put on weight. The great auk and the dodo (related to the pigeons) were both the largest members of their type, and the ratites and penguins attain body weights in excess of any flying bird. There is a theoretical limit on the weight of a flying bird because of the physical limitations of the power of its muscles, the strength of its bones and the relationship of wing area to weight. The Kori bustard of Africa is near this limit and it only flies when hard-pressed.

The benefits of extra weight are varied. For penguins, a thick layer of fat, to keep out the cold and act as a large reserve of energy, is one advantage. The male emperor penguin spends the long winter

*Like all cormorants, the flightless cormorant of the Galapagos Islands holds out its wings to dry after fishing. The picture shows how degenerate the wings have become, but they are still used for steering while swimming underwater and for shading the chicks from the sun.*

*The kokako, one of the wattlebirds that inhabit the forests of New Zealand, is almost flightless. It feeds on leaves and fruit and climbs trees by leaping from branch to branch, using its wings to help balance.*

*A flightless rail showing the tameness that delights visitors to its island home of Aldabra in the Indian Ocean. This is a common trait in island birds, whether they can fly or not, and has contributed to the extinction of many species.*

the emperor, which stands 3¼ feet (1 meter) high and weighs 66 pounds (30 kilograms), but an extinct penguin which lived in the Miocene period (from 11 to 25 million years ago) is estimated on the basis of fossilized bones to have been 5 feet (150 centimeters) high and weighed 220 pounds (100 kilograms).

The increase in weight is associated with an improved diving ability and a greater foraging range. The only other birds to have made this transformation into heavy underwater "fliers" are now extinct. Several species of flightless alcids once lived in shallow seas around California and another, the great auk, or garefowl, survived in the North Atlantic until 1844, when the last birds were killed on Eldey, near Iceland. These goose-sized alcids had once nested on islands from St Kilda, off Scotland, to the Gulf of St Lawrence.

months incubating an egg without any opportunity of feeding and prepares for this by putting on a fat layer equal to 50% of its basic body weight, which would be an encumbrance for a large flying bird. In the case of the ratites, the loss of weight limitations has enabled them to develop robust leg bones for running, and their height and bulk is probably also a defense against predators. Some extinct flightless birds took this one step further and were predators themselves. *Phororhachos*, a South American bird of some ten million years ago, stood 10 feet (3 meters) high and had a head as large as that of a horse. Its massive beak was sharply hooked, like an eagle's, enabling it to prey on fairly large mammals. With the evolution of larger, fiercer mammalian predators, birds such as this disappeared.

# CHAPTER 3
# SENSES AND INTELLIGENCE

Birds are equipped with the same set of sense organs as other land-dwelling vertebrates, but they have been altered and adapted during their evolution to suit the requirements of flying animals. Traveling rapidly through the air is only possible if an animal can make an accurate and rapid assessment of its environment. It must also have a very fine appreciation of the forces acting on its body, and have precise muscular control for the complex movements of flight. To see a bird sweeping in to make a precision landing on a perch or chasing a rival through the trees gives an idea of the finesse needed for flight. It is no wonder that earthbound humans have always envied birds and sought to emulate their freedom of movement.

To understand the behavior of birds, it is essential to appreciate the birds' view of the world and to imagine the world as recorded by bird senses and processed by a bird's brain. The basic physiological mechanisms of the senses supply only part of this understanding: we also need to know how the senses are used in various departments of bird behavior and how the different senses are integrated. For instance, flying requires the sense of balance, centered in the inner ears, vision to help balance by watching the horizon, and the sense of touch which, through forces acting on the feathers, tells the bird about the airflow over the body. There is also the sense of proprioception, in which tiny sense organs buried in the muscles record their state of contraction. (Proprioception is the sense which enables us to clap our hands while our eyes are shut.) So four senses are used to control flight, but exactly how the information they supply is integrated to keep the bird in the air has yet to be explained.

At present it is only possible to examine each sense separately, describe the information it collects, investigate the role it plays in bird life and perhaps show how any one species of bird is using its senses for particular purposes. Sense-organ physiology has largely been investigated in a small number of birds commonly used for experimental studies, notably chickens and pigeons. Generalizations have many exceptions, and it is not often known whether the results of experiments on one bird can be applied to birds in general. Nor is it always obvious how they relate to a wild bird's behavior in its natural environment away from the confines of the laboratory.

*A merlin in flight with all its senses alert as it hurtles toward its quarry. The head is held horizontal to help with its aim.*

## VISION

It is to be expected that animals which travel swiftly should have good eyesight to perceive instantaneously the position of objects around them. The size of the eyes is an indication of the importance of vision in the lives of birds: hawks and owls have eyes as large as the human eye and, in some, the eyeballs almost meet in the middle of the skull, dwarfing the brain. They cannot rotate much in their sockets, hence the fixed stare of hawks and owls, although the eyes are not so immovable as is sometimes stated. In compensation, such birds have very flexible necks and can turn their heads to look around them. The owls are famous for turning their heads almost completely round to follow someone circling them. When they get to 270° from the front, they rapidly swivel round in the opposite direction and continue the scan.

In basic structure and function, there is little difference between bird and mammal eyes. Most birds' eyeballs are rather flattened, but raptors and others with increased visual acuity have globular or tubular eyes, which increase the distance between lens and retina. The focusing power of the vertebrate

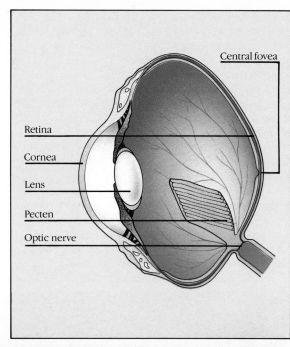

Central fovea

Retina

Cornea

Lens

Pecten

Optic nerve

*A cross-section through the eyeball of a bird, to show the main structures. Many birds have a more flattened eyeball than this, while some owls have a tubular eyeball. The pecten, a structure found only in the eyes of birds, is filled with blood vessels and is believed to help nourish the retina.*

*A Bonelli's eagle surprised with its prey. It has turned its head through 180° to look over its back.*

eye comes from the refraction (bending) of the light as it enters the cornea and passes through the lens. In both birds and mammals, accommodation, or the fine adjustment of focusing to different distances, is carried out by changing the shape, and hence the strength, of the lens. Birds obtain additional focusing power by changing the curvature of the cornea through contraction of a surrounding muscle, and most species have twice the focusing power of human eyes. This allows them to focus on food at very close range, but also gives them the accurate distance vision necessary for flight.

The focusing power of the cornea depends on light rays being bent, or refracted, when they travel from air into the corneal tissue. This can be expressed in terms of "refractive index" by saying that there is a large difference between the refractive index of air and that of the cornea. But corneal tissue has a refractive index very similar to that of water, so there

the penguin dives, but the lens is very strong to compensate for the lack of focusing by the flat cornea.

The retina of a bird's eye is composed of cone and rod cells as in human eyes. Rod cells are sensitive to low light levels and predominate in owls; cones are sensitive to colors and are used for resolving fine detail in good light. Birds of prey have a concentration of visual cells in the upper half of the retina, which is the area on which images of the ground will fall when they are in flight. When perching, they often turn their heads upside down to look at other birds overhead.

The acuity of birds' vision has often been said to be far superior to our own. This assertion was supported by anecdotes of birds catching sight of tiny or distant objects out of range of the human observer. Physiologists have now refuted these claims with experiments showing that birds of prey have an acuity no more than two and a half times better than that of man. Other birds actually have less acute vision than

A red-backed hawk scans the ground below with head cocked to one side.

is very little refraction when the eye is underwater. As soon as a bird puts its head underwater, its eyes lose most of their focusing power and it becomes long-sighted. To compensate, diving birds need some extra focusing power, and the solution of the hooded merganser, a diving duck, is for part of the lens to bulge through the rigid iris on submergence, thereby increasing its strength. Other diving ducks, alcids and loons increase the refractive power of the eye by covering it with the transparent nictitating membrane (the third "eyelid" which is responsible for keeping a bird's eye clean by blinking).

It used to be thought that penguins were highly adapted for underwater vision and therefore short-sighted on land. They do indeed look as if they are peering about myopically, but in fact their eyes are adapted for vision in both air and water. The cornea is flat, so there is little change in its refractive power as

ours. Birds appear so keen eyed because they are continually surveying their surroundings, and their eyes can pick out details at a glance while humans make a slow scan.

The ability of nocturnal birds to see in dim light is also much exaggerated. The light-collecting power of the eye depends on the aperture of the iris, that is, the size of the pupil. It is expressed in the photographer's f-number, which is an indication of the brightness of the image falling on the retina. Human eyes have an f-value of 2.1. Owls' eyes have a value of 1.3, which means that the image is two and a half times brighter, but this is not a significant difference in practice and the conclusion is that owl and human eyes have similar light-collecting powers.

Birds' eyes, like those of humans, have a pit in the retina, called the fovea, which is packed with cone cells. This is the center for the most acute vision and nearly all birds have a central fovea which receives light on the plane of the eye. Many birds have a second, "temporal", fovea set in the rear part of the retina to enable them to look forward. Temporal foveas are found in high-speed hunting birds such as raptors, kingfishers, terns and swallows, which need good forward vision for catching their prey. The fovea is important for sensitive daytime vision, and owls usually have no central fovea. The temporal fovea is not well developed either, except in daytime hunters such as the short-eared owl.

All birds have both monocular vision – seeing independently with each eye – and binocular vision – seeing with both eyes together. It is difficult for us to appreciate what monocular vision entails, but it can be seen when a robin or thrush turns its head to peer closely at the ground with one eye searching for food, or a sparrow cocks its head to look out for a hawk overhead. They are directing their view onto the

*A European woodcock on its nest merges perfectly with the background and its bulging eyes, set high on the head, give it all-round vision to warn it of danger.*

*Parrots have difficulty seeing to the front so they turn their heads and scrutinize the scene with one eye, focusing objects of interest on the sensitive fovea in the retina.*

central fovea of that eye to get the sharpest image. Most birds have their eyes on the side of the head, which gives them good all-round vision to spot danger. Pigeons, for instance, have a 340° field of view (the human one is 200°), and can see all round except immediately behind them, but the fields of left and right eyes overlap by only 24° to give a small binocular field to the front. The woodcock, which feeds by thrusting its long bill deep into the soil, has eyes set high on the head, and their fields overlap both fore and aft. As a result, there is binocular vision to the rear as well as to the front, and the woodcock can spot danger when it is feeding. Some birds raise the head and peer under the bill to get a better view ahead. When bitterns "freeze", with their bills pointing skyward and the streaked neck plumage blending with the surrounding reeds, they can fix an approaching predator with both eyes.

*The grey heron's eyes are set far enough forward on the head to give it good binocular vision when it stabs at fish.*

Birds which hunt have eyes placed to the front of the head to give increased binocular vision. Hawks have overlapping fields of 30–50°, and the owls with their very forward-looking eyes have binocular vision covering 60–70°. So far as is known, owls are the only birds with true stereoscopic, or three-dimensional, vision. The sensation of depth through stereoscopic vision is a very useful attribute to a hunting animal, because a solid image will stand out from a matching background and its position will be easier to compute for an accurate strike. Humans and other mammals experience stereoscopic vision because the slight differences between the position of the image on each retina can be compared. To do this, nerve fibers from both eyes must link up on each side of the brain, instead of all fibers from on eye going only to one side of the brain. Among birds, only owls have this overlapping arrangement of the nerve fibers.

Birds other than owls have to judge distances by a number of tricks, such as using perspective and the relative size of images. Bobbing the head gives views from different angles and makes objects move in relation to the horizon so their position can be judged. Even owls bob or nod their heads from side to side to assist range-finding.

When pigeons and peacocks walk, they nod their heads to and fro, but this has a different function from head bobbing. They are stabilizing the head, throwing it forward then keeping it steady while the body moves up. With the head steady, the eyes are better able to pick out tiny objects and slight movements. Anyone who has tried spotting birds through binoculars on a heaving ship will appreciate the need for a steady platform!

Head stabilizing can often be demonstrated by holding a bird by its body and gently tilting or rolling it: the head remains fixed in space. When a goose makes a rocking descent, turning onto its back, its neck twists so that the head remains the right way up. Hovering birds also need to keep their heads steady while aloft. A surveyor once lined up the cross-wires of his theodolite on a kestrel's head as it hovered in a strong wind. The head was held rock-steady while the body pitched and yawed around it.

Birds have well-developed color vision that is broadly similar to our own and plays an equally important role in their lives, but there are some basic differences. Like amphibians and reptiles, but unlike any mammals, birds have colored droplets of oil in the cone cells of the retina. The function of the droplets has long been disputed, but there is now evidence that they significantly affect the bird's perception of its environment.

The droplets are mostly red, orange-red or yellow. These are colors with long wavelengths, and the droplets act as selective filters removing shorter wavelengths at the blue end of the spectrum, but transmitting the longer wavelength light. In combination with the sensitivity of different types of cone cells, this gives pigeons, and other plant-eating species which have been tested, a peak discrimination

of shades in the red, yellow and green range. The part of the pigeon retina on which images fall when the bird is aiming its pecking is particularly rich in red droplets, which will heighten this sensitivity. Green is the color of chlorophyll, and the subsidiary leaf pigments are red and yellow (causing autumn colors when the chlorophyll has broken down), so the sensitivity of the pigeon retina matches the colors of the pigeon's food. This enables it to distinguish different leaves and, presumably, choose which to eat.

It is probably also significant that flowers which are pollinated by hummingbirds and other birds are mainly red, and will, to a bird, stand out against the background foliage. A world-wide survey of bird-pollinated plants showed that 80% had mainly red flowers. Similarly, plants whose seeds are dispersed

by attracting birds to their succulent fruits are mostly red, while caterpillars, frogs and wasps, which advertise their distasteful or venomous properties, are brightly colored with red or yellow. Once birds established a significant sensitivity to reds, oranges and yellows for their feeding habits, it is probably no coincidence that plants and animals developed warning or advertising colors in the same range. Similarly, the birds themselves have evolved display plumages which are frequently of the same colors.

A second property of red, orange and yellow filters is to cut through haze, as photographers know. This is probably the function of droplets in the eyes of birds which hunt above the sea. Cutting out blues makes the sky darker, so white-bodied gulls, gannets, albatrosses and terns are able to see each other at greater distances because they contrast strongly with the background of sky or sea.

There are occasions when this filtering effect is disadvantageous. Cormorants, alcids and shearwaters, which pursue their prey underwater, have few red and orange droplets and so can see better in an environment bathed in blue and green light. As droplets reduce the total amount of light stimulating the retina, they are also a disadvantage in dim light, and nocturnal owls and nightjars, which need great sensitivity to low light levels, also have few droplets. Filters that darken the sky would likewise be a disadvantage to birds that have to catch dark insects on the wing, and there is far less colored oil in the eyes of swifts, swallows and martins.

There are two further attributes of the bird's eye which makes their world different. The human eye is insensitive to short-wave ultra-violet light, but the bird eye has two peaks of sensitivity: one in the green and a second in the ultra-violet. This sensitivity must affect what birds see, but it is a subject which has not been studied. Ultra-violet light penetrates clouds and may enable migrating birds to detect the position of the sun on overcast days. They may also see the ultra-violet "nectar guides" on flowers that orient visiting insects. The many palatable fruits and noxious animals that are black to the human eye may reflect ultra-violet and so be a bright signal to birds.

Birds can also detect polarized light, which for us is as hard to imagine as seeing ultra-violet light. Dust and other particles in the sky scatter sunlight and set up a pattern of polarization which changes through the day. Bees are known to navigate by polarized light, and some migrant birds use the pattern of polarization in the sky to locate the position of the sun when it is obscured by cloud or just below the horizon.

## HEARING

The ears of birds, like their eyes, are similar in structure and sensitivity to our own, although birds do not have a cartilaginous external ear, or pinna. A single bone, the columella, replaces the three small bones of the mammalian middle ear. Birds have a peak of sensitivity, similar to humans, to sounds between 1.5 and 4 kiloHertz. However, the range of hearing varies considerably between species. Hearing

*Ivy berries photographed by daylight flash (above) and in ultra-violet light (below). Birds' eyes are sensitive to ultra-violet light, so that berries which look black to the human eye look bluish to birds and may be more visible to them.*

*While hovering, a European kestrel stabilizes its head position so that it can scan the ground below for prey. The black streak under the eyes of some falcons is thought to help reduce glare.*

is generally very acute, as illustrated by the use of parrots and waterfowl as "watchdogs" throughout history, the geese that alerted the citizens of Rome being the most famous example.

Birds use their sense of hearing for four, or possibly five, purposes. The most obvious and important is the role of hearing in communication. Birds sing and call to advertise territories and attract mates, keep contact in flocks and give warning of danger. Unless they wish to avoid attracting a predator, their sounds may be structured to make it easy for other birds to pinpoint their positions, and some birds, at least, are known to have peaks of hearing sensitivity that are tuned to the songs and calls of their species. The subject of communication is discussed more fully in Chapter 6. Birds also use hearing to find their prey. This may be through incidental association, like the ravens which find carrion by homing on the howling of wolves, or by listening to the sounds generated by the potential victims: woodpeckers are said to listen for the

centimeters) in diameter. This is because resolution is related to frequency: the higher the frequency, the shorter the wavelength and the smaller the object which can be detected. Lower frequency sounds have long wavelengths that fail to reflect from small objects. However, they do travel farther, which may be useful in navigating through large caves. The swiftlets have made one behavioral adaptation to allow them to exploit this use of sound. Unlike other swifts, they carry nest materials with their feet to leave their mouths free for clicking. Only the glossy swiftlet, which nests in the mouths of caves and lacks the power of echolocation, has been observed carrying nesting material in its bill.

Finally, there have been suggestions that sounds could assist migrating birds to fix their positions. High-flying birds could hear choruses of croaking frogs which emanate from the same ponds every year and use them as landmarks. The recent discovery that birds can hear infra-sounds (frequencies too low for the human ear) has opened up another possible use

*Facial disks are seen in most owls, except diurnal species, and are especially well developed in the great grey owl. The disks are edged with a ruff of short feathers and serve to funnel sounds to the ears, which are located on the side of the head just below the level of the eyes.*

*A nesting colony of cave swiftlets. Those species that nest deep in caves use echolocation to guide them to their nests.*

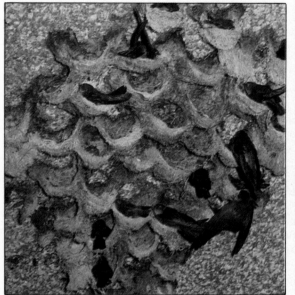

*Center: the capercaillie's song is described as sounding like sticks being knocked together, followed by a cork being pulled and a knife being ground. Although fairly loud at close quarters, the sound does not carry far. The very loud infra-sound component is completely missed by human ears, but may be heard over long distances by rival males and susceptible females.*

chewing sounds of insect grubs working in timber, and the Australian black-backed magpie finds beetle larvae in the soil by listening for the sounds of their burrowing. By the same token, birds must be aware of sounds made by approaching predators, especially at night or in dense cover.

A few birds are known to use sound for finding their way in the dark. These are the oilbird of Venezuela and some cave swiftlets of southern India and South-east Asia which possess the power of echolocation, although it is less sensitive than that used by bats to find their insect prey. The birds emit streams of clicks audible to human ears, at frequencies of 1.5 to 2.5 kiloHertz, compared with the largely inaudible 20–115 kiloHertz of bat pulses. These birds' echolocation systems are useful only for finding nests and roosting places in the pitch-dark of caves. When plastic discs were suspended in a cave, oilbirds avoided only those larger than 14 inches (35

of sound in migration. Pigeons are sensitive to infra-sounds with frequencies between 0.05 and 10 Hertz. Such sounds are generated by storms, the passage of wind over mountains and the sea breaking on the shore, and travel through the atmosphere for hundreds of miles. These noises could be particularly helpful when birds migrate at night or in heavy clouds, but as yet there is no proof that any use is made of them.

For all uses of the ear, localization of sound sources is vitally important. In humans, pinpointing a sound is achieved by comparing tiny differences in pitch and timing of the sounds entering two ears. Depending on the position of the source, a sound takes longer to reach one ear than the other, and is louder on one side than the other. These minute differences are increased by the head forming an obstacle around which sound has to travel. Birds use a similar system but, because their heads are so much

*Above: a pair of bald ibises, their naked heads revealing the position of the ear opening, which is covered by feathers in most birds. One ibis is cleaning the surface of its eye by drawing the transparent nictitating membrane across it.*

smaller, the time differences in the arriving sound waves are too small to measure. However, like amphibians and reptiles, but unlike mammals, birds have a passage through the skull which links the two eardrums. As sound waves travel down the passage, each eardrum receives the sound on both its faces. The result is to enhance the difference in response between the two eardrums and, given the birds' greater ability (compared with mammals) to discriminate time differences in sounds, this enables them to pinpoint the source.

Sound location has reached a peak in the owls, some of which can pounce on prey accurately in pitch darkness and are four times better than any other animal tested. The owl's hearing system has several features not found in other birds. There is a circular ruff of very fine feathers around each eye that funnels sound to the ear opening, which is hidden under a flap of skin. The ear openings are asymmetrically placed on the head as a further aid to

veracity of the missionary's story has been proved by burning wax candles set out in trees.

The bird first proved by experiment to use a sense of smell was the kiwi, whose abilities in this direction were suspected because the olfactory bulb of its forebrain is much larger than in most other birds. Kiwis feed by probing for earthworms, and experiments have demonstrated that they are guided by smell, the nostrils being conveniently placed at the tip of the bill rather than at the base, as in most long-billed birds. Large olfactory bulbs are found in some other birds, especially albatrosses, petrels and some New World vultures, suggesting that they too are using a sense of smell.

Robert Cushman Murphy, the doyen of American seabird studies, suggested in 1936 that smell was important to tubenosed seabirds – storm-petrels, fulmars, shearwaters and albatrosses – after he had attracted them to slicks of warm bacon fat and whale oil. Serious experiments, which were not carried out

*Honeyguides attack bees' nests and eat the wax of the comb. Wax is an important part of their diet and they are attracted by its smell. On this juvenile honeyguide the nostrils can be seen at the base of the upper mandible.*

*Center: kiwis are the only birds known to use the sense of smell for finding food in the ground. The nostrils open at the tip of the bill and experiments show that they can locate earthworms by smell. Whether they use scent for other purposes is not known.*

location, the left ear being placed higher and its opening tilted downwards, so it is more sensitive to sounds from below. Comparison between the ears gives a very good measurement of the angle of elevation of a sound source, so the owl can judge the position of a mouse on the ground below. Extreme accuracy is needed because the angle is usually shallow, so a slight change results in a large shift in range of the target.

SMELL AND OTHER SENSES
It used to be thought that a bird's sense of smell was so poor that it could be conveniently ignored when considering the way it perceived its environment. Vision and hearing were held to be the essential senses, although the suggestion that a bird might have a sense of smell came as long ago as 1569, when a Portuguese missionary in Africa reported that honeyguides flew into his church when he burnt beeswax candles. Honeyguides attack bees' nests and are uniquely capable of digesting wax. Recently, the

until many years later, involved attaching sponges or wicks soaked in cod-liver oil to floating buoys. After a series of observations it was clear that the tubenosed birds were attracted from downwind, but gannets, gulls and alcids took no notice. A good sense of smell might be especially useful for tubenosed birds because they often forage at night.

Shearwaters and petrels also visit their nests nocturnally, shearwaters preferring very dark nights when visual navigation must be difficult. Leach's storm-petrels approach the nesting colony upwind, and there is experimental evidence that they identify their own nest by its particular smell. They can certainly do this once they have landed nearby, and it may be possible when flying overhead. The use of smell for homing from a distance has been suggested from several experiments with pigeons. In one experiment, pigeons were kept in either an open-sided loft or a loft with baffles that deflected the wind to enter from one or other side. This gave a false

*Shearwaters, like other tubenosed birds, have a good sense of smell and often feed at night. They get their name from the fact that the nostrils extend in a tube along the top of the bill. This probably helps them to locate food by smell.*

impression of the wind direction and the location of odors carried on it. Three groups of pigeons were then released at a short distance: those from the open cage orientated in the right direction and arrived home quickly, but those accustomed to a deflected wind set off to right or left as predicted by the angle of the loft baffles.

A group of birds that might be expected to use a sense of smell for finding food are the vultures, since they feed on dead and often decaying flesh. Odors seem to be important to turkey vultures, and other New World vultures, which have been found to gather over dead animals hidden from view, but Old World vultures appear to forage entirely by sight.

The remaining senses of birds are not well known either in terms of their physiology or their use in the birds' behavior. The discovery that smell plays a more important role in bird life than was realized, shows that touch, taste and the temperature sense should not be overlooked either. Another sense, that

different foods, and the fact that many insects rely on an unpleasant taste for protection from predatory birds confirms this.

The sense of touch is well developed and birds are quick to react to a touch on the plumage. They do this by means of specialized, bristle-like feathers, known as vibrissae, which lack vanes and are sensitive to the slightest deflection. These vibrissae may allow a bird to detect the pattern of airflow over the body in flight, giving it an advantage over a human pilot who is ill-equipped to monitor stresses on his aircraft. Within the skin there are other specialized organs of touch, called Herbst's corpuscles. These occur mainly on the legs and bare skin, but also around the base of each feather and in particular on the bill and tongue. The degree of sensitivity in the tongue is very much related to the feeding habits of the bird. A heightened sense of touch is found in the tongues of woodpeckers, for probing into insect borings, the bills of shorebirds for exploring sand and mud, and those of ducks for

*Dove prions fly to their burrows on Antarctic islands at night to avoid the attentions of predatory skuas. This is a common habit for the smaller members of the tubenose order and it is believed that they use the sense of smell to find their own nests.*

*Above center: a turkey vulture on a dead killer whale. Such a large corpse would have been spotted from afar, but turkey vultures can also smell carrion hidden from sight when they are flying over the forest canopy.*

of the Earth's magnetism, has only recently been discovered through experiments with migrant birds.

The temperature sense is used in a general way to monitor the bird's environment and inform it whether steps need to be taken to keep warm or cool. The mallee fowl is one bird which has a specialized use for its temperature sense. While the male tends its compost-heap nest, it continually monitors the temperature by probing the heap with its bill.

Taste – the sensitivity to acid, bitter, sweet and salty substances – is apparently the same as in humans, although birds have far fewer taste buds. There are only from thirty to sixty taste buds in a pigeon's mouth and 400 in a parrot's, compared with 9,000 in a human mouth. What we call flavor is the combination of the true taste sense with an appreciation of the smell of food in the mouth. It is often said that birds of prey eat foul-tasting shrews, which are rejected by mammals, because of an insensitivity to flavor. However, tests have shown that birds are aware of the palatability of

sifting edible and inedible particles. A sensitive tongue and bill are also found in wood-storks, spoonbills and avocets, which feed by sweeping the parted bill through the water and snapping it over any small creature that they touch.

The Herbst's corpuscles are very versatile sense organs for, as well as being sensitive to touch, those on a bird's legs respond to vibrations of the ground or perch, alerting the bird to approaching danger when it is roosting. In at least one group of birds, the finches, these corpuscles can also detect infra-sound, so that the bird can "hear" certain noises with its legs.

In some way, perhaps by the sense of touch, birds are also sensitive to atmospheric pressures. Pigeons can detect slight changes which would enable them to determine their height to within 35 feet (10 meters), and it would explain birds' sensitivity to changes in weather. In the eastern United States, migration in the fall often occurs when pressure is rising as this brings the most favorable weather for the journey.

*A delicate sense of touch tells spoonbills when something edible touches their parted mandibles.*

# BIRDS AT NIGHT

*The potoos are relatives of the nightjars which hunt flying insects at night, locating them with their large eyes and capturing them in their huge, gaping mouths.*

The traditional view of birds is that, with certain notable exceptions, they are as much creatures of the day as humans: in the evening, most song ceases and birds fly to their roosts. But it is now becoming clear that many of the familiar daytime birds are also active at night. In Europe, robins can be heard singing until it is almost dark, kestrels have been reported as hunting bats in twilight and flocks of swifts make noisy ascents as darkness falls. Indeed, there is good evidence that swifts may spend the night soaring at considerable heights, up to 6,500 feet (2,000 meters). The nightingale and the mockingbird are famous for singing through the night.

Some of the more unexpected discoveries about nocturnal activity have come about because birds can now be observed in the dark with night-viewing equipment. Black-crowned night-herons, which were long thought to feed mainly at dusk and dawn, were viewed with a light intensifier on the Camargue marshes in France. This revealed that they obtained most of their food not in the twilight hours but in the depths of night, thereby avoiding harassment by little egrets and purple herons.

Three explanations can be given for nocturnal activity, whether by true birds of night, such as the owls, nightjars and kiwis, or by birds that are normally out during the day. Dividing the twenty-four hours into shifts reduces competition, as with the night herons described above, and with the owls which take over from the day-flying raptors: in North America, the great horned owl, short-eared owl, barred owl and screech owl replace, respectively, the red-tailed hawk, northern harrier, red-shouldered hawk and American kestrel. The nightjars, or nighthawks, the potoos and the frogmouths are the counterparts of swallows and flycatchers, which catch flying insects, and the shrikes, which pounce on small ground animals.

A second reason for nocturnal activity is to take advantage of food which is not available during the

*A screech owl caught by the camera as it is about to land in dim light. Its eyes are focused on the perch to judge its approach, and it is about to throw its feet forward for landing.*

day. Kiwis and woodcock probe for worms at night, when they come to the surface, and tubenosed birds similarly feed at night when marine organisms migrate to the surface of the sea. Shorebirds that feed on the shore are governed partly by the cycle of tides and sometimes feed at low tide during the night, particularly in winter when the days are short. Some are feeding by touch, but even those that feed by sight manage to continue at night. Prey may be harder to find, but some small animals are more active at night and thus easier to spot.

Thirdly, darkness brings safety from predators. Colonies of burrow-nesting petrels and shearwaters appear empty by day but the night scene is full of activity as birds approach and leave their nests. These birds can only shuffle clumsily to their burrows, and they nest on islands where there are no native land predators. They are still vulnerable to hawks, gulls, frigatebirds and skuas, and the cover of darkness gives them some protection from these aerial predators. Flamingos fly from lake to lake by night for similar reasons: although strong fliers, they cannot take evasive action and are easily caught by large birds of prey. The night is a good time for many waterfowl to feed; urban mallards especially avoid disturbance by feeding after dark when people are indoors.

Whatever the reason for being active at night, birds must have the sensory equipment to cope with low light levels. It is never pitch dark in nature, so that large-eyed owls, nightjars and oilbirds are not hampered except perhaps on the darkest and stormiest nights. Too little is known about the night vision of different species to explain how it affects their nocturnal activity. The letter-winged kite of Australia hunts mice by moonlight, and it would be interesting to compare its eyes with an owl's. Pigeons, on the other hand, have very poor night vision; they go to roost early and are never active at night.

In many instances, nocturnal activity may involve a switch to another sense, like the petrels finding their nests by smell and shorebirds no longer using vision to find food. This is not so efficient, and oystercatchers find fewer snails at night as they probe blindly into the sand or mud instead of looking for the tell-tale signs of buried animals.

*A painted stork leaves its nest in the light of the setting sun. When there is a family to look after birds have to use as much of the daylight as possible, and they are often more active at night than is generally realized.*

*Far left: the oilbird uses echolocation to find its nest in a pitch-dark cave but its large eyes are used for finding fruit when it is feeding at night. The sense of smell and the long, touch-sensitive rictal bristles around the mouth may also be used for feeding. The only other birds to echolocate are the cave swiftlets.*

*Left: the grey heron often fishes around dusk and sometimes far into the night, especially if the moon is full.*

The study of animal behavior, and especially the comparison of the mental capacities of different species, is surrounded by pitfalls. It is all too easy to slip into anthropomorphism and to ascribe human motives to an animal's actions. As has already been made clear, a bird's senses give it a different view of its surroundings, so that it may be reacting to stimuli that we are not conscious of and ignoring others which are obvious to us. Understanding a bird's motivation, or working out what is "going on in its head", is even more difficult.

The European robin which attacks a bunch of red feathers is responding automatically to a stimulus. To human eyes it is stupid, but to judge that birds are

changes in environment, but not with rapid ones.

One example will serve to show the rigidity of instinctive behavior through what happens when something "goes wrong". Occasionally a pigeon develops a misshapen bill with a long, downcurved upper mandible. This appears to be a congenital deformity, and the pigeon is handicapped because it aims unsuccessfully and pecks at food as if the bill were normal. If the pigeon is caught and its bill trimmed, it can pick up food normally. So its pecking behavior is stereotyped and instinctive. There is no ability to adapt and, not surprisingly, these deformities remain rare in the pigeon population.

In contrast, learning is the process whereby an

*A European robin will attack a stuffed bird as if it is a rival. The attack is automatic and is triggered by the sight of red feathers. If these are covered by dye, the attacks cease.*

simple-minded automatons on the basis of such observations is to miss the point. In normal circumstances, its behavior enables a bird to cope with its natural environment, to keep itself alive and produce offspring.

Behavior is broadly speaking of two types: instinctive and learned. Instinctive, or innate, behavior follows a general pattern within each species, so that it is possible to state that gannets dive for fish or that puffins lay their eggs in burrows. It is fixed and inherited from one generation to the next. Instinct evolves slowly through natural selection and adapts a species to a particular way of life, in the same way as the shape of its bill or wings. It can cope with gradual

individual changes its behavior. It is rapid, and the animal can adapt to a sudden change in its circumstances. There was the instance of the European robin with the whole of its bill missing, which ate at a bird feeder by putting its head on one side and scooping up food with its tongue. It had been able to change its behavior when faced with a catastrophic situation. This does not imply that robins are cleverer than pigeons, only that, in respect to picking up food, an individual robin proved more adaptable.

Deciding whether an action is governed by instinct or learning is not necessarily straightforward. For example, it is easy to believe that young birds learn to fly rather than being born with this ability: while still in the nest they flap their wings as if practicing and, after leaving the nest, the first landings are often heavy. Yet birds reared in constricted circumstances and unable to open their wings go on to make maiden flights as successfully as those with an unconstrained upbringing. Taking to the air is instinctive, and there would be an enormous mortality of young birds if this were not so. The control of maneuvering and landing, however, needs practice.

It used to be believed that much of bird life was under the control of instinct and that birds were mere automata, compared with the quick-thinking mammals. As bird behavior has been studied in more detail and in more natural circumstances, so that the bird's whole way of life is considered, the rigid distinction between instinctive and learned behavior is dissolving. It is now realized that the two are

bill and draw it along the perch in a random fashion. If the food happens to catch on a thorn or a wedge, the shrike immediately concentrates on dragging it repeatedly over the obstacle and very quickly learns to direct the dragging action in the right places. Thus, the instinct to drag prey along the perch is refined into an accurate action for impaling or wedging.

Modification of the basic instinct can take a variety of forms, as is shown in the feeding behavior of farmyard chicks. They emerge from the egg with the instinct to peck at small objects that contrast with the background, so they automatically peck at objects which could be edible grains. They might also be small pebbles, or even marks on the ground, so by a process of trial-and-error the chicks learn what is edible and what is to be avoided. Learning is enhanced by assistance from the mother chicken. When the chicks are newly hatched, she will pick up a

*Young birds sometimes look as if they are learning to fly, like this Sandwich tern with its parent. In fact, birds can fly instinctively, although they need practice at maneuvering.*

complementary in the control of the bird's actions.

Instinct – the fixed response to a situation – is vital when there is no time to learn. Young kiskadees and motmots avoid wooden rods painted with yellow and red rings: this is the pattern of the predatory coral snake. There would be no time for discovering by trial-and-error what pattern spelled danger, any more than for learning the correct way to flap the wings when jumping out of the nest. However, once the instinctive pattern of behavior has started, learning can refine the bird's behavior to make it more efficient. Shrikes impale food on thorns or wedge morsels in the forks of twigs. A young loggerhead shrike of twenty-two days' age starts to hold food in its

morsel and hold it in her bill for the chicks to take. Later she lets it drop for the chicks to pick up themselves. As they grow older and wander farther, she calls them back with a loud "food-call" and indicates the food by pointing with her bill. Learning by observation continues into adult life among birds that feed in flocks. When one finds a new kind of food, others take note and start to search for it themselves.

Imprinting is a special form of learning which takes place when a bird is young and happens only during a short "sensitive" period. Ducklings or other young birds which leave the nest soon after hatching very quickly learn to recognize their parents by sight and sound. Normally the parent bird is the first suitable object the chick sees, but it can be fooled by a substitute. So Konrad Lorenz, the Austrian naturalist who pioneered the study of animal behavior, found when he crept around the garden quacking to a brood of orphaned ducklings: they soon looked on him as "mother" and followed him everywhere.

This "following" response wanes as the young birds become independent, but the effects of imprinting persist in other circumstances. Early impressions are important for later life, and preferences for a particular habitat or food may be learned at a critical period when the bird is young. Young birds recognize others of their own species by identifying them with their parents, and birds reared under a foster parent are likely to make the mistake of mating with one of the foster species when they mature. Among those ducks where the family is reared by the mother alone, this form of imprinting only occurs in males, which learn to recognize a mate of the correct species. Since female ducks never see their brightly colored fathers, instinct guides them to choose their own species, and they make the right choice even when fostered under another species. The exceptions are the few species of ducks in which male and female adults have the same plumage and both care for the chicks. Here, both sexes learn the identity of future mates by imprinting on their parents.

These and many other examples of learning are automatic, and they are not a sign of great intelligence. Moreover, birds and other animals are usually

*An animal's instinctive behavior is sufficient to deal with routine situations but it cannot cope with change. Learning is the process which allows a rapid change in behavior as circumstances alter. Mockingbirds on the Galapagos Islands have been adaptable in their feeding behavior and have learned to open and eat the eggs of waved albatross (far right). The albatrosses' breeding behavior is governed largely by instinct and is adapted to remote islands where there is little threat to their eggs: they have not learned to drive the mockingbirds away. Similarly, fairy terns (right) lay their eggs on branches where they are normally safe, and they have no defense against skinks and toc-toc birds which feed on their eggs.*

*When milk was first delivered to British doorsteps in bottles with foil caps, blue and great tits soon learned to open them. The action is similar to that used in finding insects, but the context is new. The speed with which the habit spread suggests that tits were learning from each other. In some places, they now open paper cartons of milk by pecking at the corners.*

*When a broody bantam hen is given a clutch of ducks' eggs, she accepts the ducklings and cares for them as if they were her own offspring. This can create problems if they do not recognize her calls to come to food or hide from danger. The foster mother is also clearly agitated when her charges instinctively take to the water (below right).*

regarded as being able only to alter their behavior in the light of past experiences and not capable of anticipation. But experiments and observations of animals in the wild are leading to a change of attitude among biologists: the divide between humans and animals may not be the gulf that it once seemed, and birds' mental powers are not so inferior to those of mammals as was once thought. Some birds show signs of reasoning power or insight, and they can appreciate the relations between separate events or even abstracts such as numbers. If this is so, birds can be said to have real intelligence, and their behavior to be more than merely mechanical.

The problem with analysis of animal intelligence is that reports of behavior showing a high mental capacity are often anecdotal. Instances of apparently clever behavior may not be repeatable, and they often involve a pet so that there is the possibility that the owner is too deeply involved to view its behavior objectively. Yet it is mainly through an intimate knowledge of an individual, and the continuous, close observation that is often possible only with a pet, that instances of intelligent behavior come to light. The constraints of laboratory experiments are not always conducive to this sort of study. In his book *The Naked Ape*, Desmond Morris commented that parrots and other "talking" birds merely copy and repeat sequences of sounds without any reference to outside events. People who have kept parrots may well disagree, having noticed that their parrots will match

*The way that a bird handles its food is often stereotyped and not capable of changing. The European purple gallinule (right) is one of many birds which holds food with the foot to make it easier to tear up with the bill. Skuas and jaegers are seabirds whose usual diet of fish does not require the use of the feet. Great skuas (below) often eat flesh, and although they could use their feet for feeding they never do so. This means that tearing pieces off a carcass is very difficult unless a pair of skuas cooperate to pull it apart.*

their utterances with the appropriate event: barking when the dog comes in, for instance. Parrot owners have now received support from the scientific study of an African grey parrot called "Alex". Alex has a vocabulary of forty words and can relate these to objects. He says "shower" when sprayed with water and picks up a colored rather than a plain plaque when given the order "color".

Another remarkable bird was the jackdaw, whose ability to count was tested. It was trained to lift the lids from a row of boxes in turn until it had picked out five morsels of food, and then to return to its cage. On one occasion, the jackdaw retired after taking only four morsels: one from the first box, two from the second, one from the third and none from the fourth. The experimenter was about to record a failure when the jackdaw returned to the boxes. It bowed once in front of the first box, twice in front of the second, once at the third and, ignoring the fourth, it picked up the fifth lid, took the fifth morsel and went back to its cage.

The jackdaw could perceive numbers and had the insight to realize its mistake, but are counting and other intelligent actions of use to birds in their natural world? A frequent question is whether birds count their eggs or chicks and recognize whether there is one more or less. This is not the case, and birds will even continue to sit on an empty nest. Eventually they desert when the lack of physical stimulus of the eggs against the brood patch allows the urge to incubate to wane. The degree of intelligence in a bird's life must be related to its needs. The majority of birds lead short lives, and only a fraction reach adulthood, so there is little time to learn; it is better to rely on instinctive behavior, and follow the habits which contributed to the survival of their parents and have been passed on in their genes. Short-lived birds can use the rapid turnover of generations for adaptation by natural selection to environmental changes. For longer-lived species, individuals need to adapt to changes which happen within their lifetimes, so the rapid response of learning is needed. Higher mental faculties are most valuable to those birds, such as members of the crow family, who are opportunists that survive by taking advantage of every new opening.

*Sometimes a bird's actions are difficult to interpret. This secretary bird was seen throwing a clump of grass into the air, and leaping after it. Presumably it was playing, although play is usually a feature of young birds and is a means of practicing skills.*

*The myth that ostriches hide their heads in the sand probably arose from their habit of lying with their necks on the ground when disturbed on the nest. This instinctive behavior can conceal the ostrich if it nests among vegetation but it is ineffective in an open landscape of pale sand.*

*One instinct can be so strong that it can overpower more appropriate behavior. The male northern phalarope must keep the eggs and chicks warm on its Arctic breeding grounds, and it will return to them even when it would be safer to flee from possible danger.*

## TOOL USE

Tool use by birds was first put on record by John Gould in 1848. Australian aborigines had told him of black-breasted buzzards that frightened emus off their nests and then smashed the eggs by dropping stones on them. Since that time, a small but significant number of animals, including some thirty species of birds, have become known as tool users and even tool makers. It is usually clear that tool using is not evidence of great intelligence, and may be no more than instinctive behavior or involve only simple learning by association. Furthermore, an animal tool maker is working to fulfill an immediate and observable need, unlike human tool makers who have the ability to think ahead and make a tool for a future eventuality. Nevertheless, the superficial similarity to human behavior has made animal tool use of great interest – perhaps more than its importance in the life of the animal really warrants.

Even those who have studied tool use by animals have been unable to agree on a definition, but it clearly involves the manipulation of inanimate objects to enable an animal to perform a task more efficiently. In a sense, nest building could be described as tool use, for the bird manipulates twigs, grasses or mud to make a cup for holding the eggs. But the bird's nest does not conform with most people's idea of a tool, although there is clearly an element of tool use in the nest building of the tailorbirds of southern Asia. They make their nests from living leaves, by fastening them together to form a pouch. The tailorbird punches a hole with its bill through two overlapping leaves, then draws them together by threading strands of vegetable fibres or spiders' web through the hole. It secures these strands by teasing out their ends to form knots: it is usually said that the leaves are sewn or stitched together, but the process is in fact more like riveting and the fiber "rivets" can be thought of as tools.

A classic example of tool use is found in the Galapagos Islands where woodpeckers are absent and a finch fills the vacant niche, feeding on insects which hide in crevices. Unlike woodpeckers, the woodpecker finch does not possess a long tongue for dislodging its prey and instead it uses a cactus

*It is not always easy to decide what is a tool. The tailorbird 'rivets' leaves together to make a container for its nest. The rivets are pieces of fibre or spiders' web which are teased out to make the heads. They can be considered as a form of tool.*

*The woodpecker finch uses cactus spines to pry insects out of wood and will even manufacture or improve its tool. When a woodpecker finch finds an insect in a crack it picks up a broken spine, or snaps one off a cactus. If necessary, it then twists off side branches or trims its length, to make the spine more manageable.*

spine. No one has watched young woodpecker finches to see how they start the habit, but tests with captive birds in the Galapagos show that not all woodpecker finches use cactus spines. On the other hand, some closely related species have proved capable of using spines. One cactus finch learned to pick up spines and push them into cracks by watching woodpecker finches in an adjacent cage. The latter even passed spines through the bars for the cactus finch to use. It seems, then, that this behavior is largely learned.

The problem remains as to how the tool-using habit arose in the first place. It could perhaps have come about as a result of displacement activity, a well-known phenomenon in which an animal that is thwarted in its attempt to carry out an action reacts with some irrelevant behavior. So a woodpecker finch may have fiddled with a cactus spine in frustration at being unable to reach an insect sheltering deep in a crevice. Then, on trying to reach the insect again, it was lucky enough to be holding the spine so that it was thrust down the crevice. The reward of catching the dislodged insect would then be associated with the trick of holding the cactus spine, without the need for special insight or reasoning.

A more widespread form of tool use is seen in the egg-breaking behavior of birds of prey. Only a few years after John Gould had observed that black-breasted buzzards smashed emu eggs with stones, there was a report from Africa that Egyptian vultures used the same technique on ostrich eggs. In recent years this behavior has been studied in some detail, and has been reported from several different parts of Africa. This suggests that the trick has been "invented" several times in different places and that local populations of Egyptian vultures have learned it from each other.

It is fairly easy to see how such behavior could have first arisen. Part of the Egyptian vulture's regular feeding habit is to pick up small eggs and throw them down to smash them. Ostrich eggs are far too large for this to be attempted, and the suggestion is that the vultures were so thwarted by the sight of such a huge but unobtainable meal that they turned to picking up and throwing down nearby stones. This is called redirected behavior – the human equivalent of kicking the cat when everything has gone wrong. If the vulture accidentally broke an ostrich egg, it would associate its prize with its frustrated stone throwing and repeat the action with other ostrich eggs.

Well-documented examples of tool use such as this are all too rare. The problem with trying to understand tool use in animals is that the reports are generally anecdotal and involve just one individual, so that it is impossible to draw much in the way of conclusions. Individuals of several different species have been seen to manipulate sticks or spines in the same manner as the woodpecker finch, although this is not a regular trait in any of them, and brown-headed nuthatches sometimes lever bark from trees using another piece of bark as a tool. Then there was the green-backed heron which had the habit of using

bait to catch fish. For fifteen years this heron was thought to be unique among its kind. Then a second green-backed heron at the Miami Seaquarium was found to be using the same means of fishing. Two more green-backed herons at the Seaquarium learned from the first to fish with bait. Since then another green-backed heron has been seen to use a feather as a lure, and fishing with a bait has now been widely recorded, not only by green-backed herons but in other waterbirds, such as the sunbittern and pied kingfisher.

The crow family is generally reckoned to be among the most intelligent of birds. Its members have a well-developed sense of curiosity, and investigate, probe and pick up any object they find. They sometimes turn such exploratory behavior to good use. A captive blue jay was seen to rip a piece of the newspaper that lined the floor of its cage and poke it through the wires to scoop up food pellets which were out of range of its bill. It did so repeatedly and, as tool using has never been seen in wild blue jays, it was assumed that this bird had learned the trick by accident. Moreover, five other jays in the captive colony then learned to imitate it.

Now that many more birds are being studied, both in the wild and in captivity, it is becoming clear that the occasional use of tools is fairly commonplace. Birds seem to pick objects up occasionally and manipulate them in a random way, but sometimes, by chance, to good effect. If such behavior results in a learning process, then tool use may become a habit, that can be imitated by other birds.

*A green-backed heron using a fish-food pellet to catch fish. Tool-use need not involve high intelligence, but in this instance the heron seemed to understand what it was doing, for it retrieved the bait when it floated away and carried it to another spot to try again if no fish appeared.*

A juvenile Egyptian vulture uses a stone to break open an ostrich egg and then eats the contents. Holding a stone in its bill, the vulture raises its head high and then flings the stone downwards. Its aim is erratic and several throws are usually needed. Sometimes the sequence starts at a considerable distance from the egg and repeated throws bring the stone in range.

# CHAPTER 4
# FINDING FOOD

The shape of the bill gives a good idea of what a bird eats: carnivorous birds have hooked bills to tear at the flesh of their prey, eaters of hard seeds or nuts have stout, powerful bills to crack them open, while hummingbirds have very long, slender bills to sip nectar from trumpet-like flowers. Although these anatomical adaptations are clearly important, they are not the whole story, because behavior is just as crucial in determining what a bird eats. A duck's broad,

tits hanging upside-down from twigs of deciduous trees while coal tits probe into nooks and crannies on conifers. Instinct can even control the complex hunting and killing behavior of predators. Hand-reared European kestrels carry out perfect pounces on the first live mice that they see, and kill them with an accurate peck at the back of the neck. Indeed, they have to learn that it is not necessary to kill a dead mouse. Nevertheless, practice is needed to find prey

*The marabou stork is usually a scavenger on large carcasses and frequently haunts refuse dumps. But it is also a predator, especially when nesting, since it needs to feed its young on smaller prey containing bones, to supply them with the calcium they need for growth. This marabou shows its hunting skills by catching a dove at a watering hole.*

sensitive bill is useless for chipping grubs from a log, woodpecker-style, but a duck is also incapable of recognizing that wood contains food, although it would unhesitatingly eat the same grubs if it found them floating in water. This is an extreme example, but the inflexibility of feeding behavior is shown by the need to hand-feed oiled seabirds which do not recognize dead fish dangled in front of them.

The extent to which feeding behavior is innate or learned has been studied in only a few species and, even then, it is not easy to explain the process by which the characteristic feeding habits are acquired. European blue and coal tits, hand-reared and totally ignorant of their natural food and feeding habits, show an instinctive awareness of where to find food by exhibiting the same preferences as wild tits: the blue

and launch a successful strike. In flocks of brown pelicans off Costa Rica, adults were seen to swallow prey after seven in ten dives, whereas immatures, identified by their distinctive plumage, were successful in only five out of ten dives. During the post-fledging period, the young of many birds continue to receive extra food from their parents as a supplement to their own efforts. Young frigatebirds, which have highly skilled techniques of gathering food in flight, continue to receive supplementary feeding for six months after they have left the nest.

The problem of acquiring full skills at feeding is probably the reason why many birds defer their first attempt at nesting for several years after they are physiologically capable of breeding. Herring gulls do not breed until they are at least four years old, apparently because they need these years to become completely adept at foraging. A study of flocks of gulls feeding at refuse dumps, revealed that their rate of finding food increased with each year of life until full adulthood, and that the older birds got more food for less effort.

In some circumstances, survival is only possible if the bird concentrates on feeding to the exclusion of all other activities. Pigeons and titmice, for instance, are feeding throughout the daylight hours in winter, the titmice needing to find an item of food every two or three seconds to build up sufficient reserves to survive the long, cold night. After the winter, efficient feeding has to be continued when food becomes plentiful, to give the bird time to devote to breeding.

bulk of mice or voles, because it will have to spend much more time and energy finding and catching them. But the eagle will ignore a deer fawn which, although a very good meal, is too strong to be easily overcome. So the cost of handling as well as seeking prey has to be taken into account. The basic need, then, is to get greatest gain for the least expenditure, and those birds which have been studied are clearly using simple rules which allow them to feed with the optimum efficiency.

When flocks of lesser golden plovers and lapwings gather on pastures to feed on earthworms, they crouch with the bill pointing downwards as they pinpoint the position of the worm in the soil, presumably by the sound of its movements. Then they

## OPTIMAL FORAGING

There is plenty of evidence that birds are continually assessing their food supply and deciding on a profitable foraging technique to exploit it. The decisions made by the birds frequently agree with what human observers calculate should be the best for them, but this does not imply that the birds are using high mental processes. A decision can be made instinctively by following basic rules. These instinctive rules have been shaped by natural selection in just the same way as the size of the bird's bill or the length of its legs.

An obvious procedure is to choose the largest possible "packets" of food which will give the most energy. For example, an eagle will profit more from catching a rabbit than from catching the equivalent

plunge the bill into the ground and pull out the worm. Observations show that the plovers are not taking the largest worms as might be expected but are taking those of medium size. (The length of a worm can be gauged by comparing it with the length of the plover's bill). The plovers cannot judge the size of the worm before pulling it out, so they probe for worms using a simple rule-of-thumb that gives a good chance that the correct-sized worms will be obtained. This is based on the fact that larger worms live deeper in the soil, so the plovers probe as deeply as possible (about 1 inch or 2.5 centimeters). This effectively stops them from pulling out the small unprofitable worms that live near the surface. It does not stop them from occasionally pulling out large worms and these are often cast aside because the much longer handling

*A pygmy cormorant feeds a fully grown youngster. Many birds continue to feed their young after they have left the nest, to supplement the food that they gather for themselves.*

*Birds' bills are usually well adapted to their diet, but small vultures do not have very large bills and are often ill-equipped to attack the hides of carcasses. These black vultures cannot tear open the skin of a dead turtle (right) and they have to attack it through the mouth and openings made by other scavengers, or wait for it to decompose. Turtle eggs are easier to deal with and the nests are often plundered (far right).*

time makes them unprofitable.

"Probe deep" is therefore a good rule for efficient feeding, but the plovers face another problem in the form of black-headed gulls, which steal their worms. To combat this threat, the plovers switch to catching the smaller worms which, since they live near the surface, are easier to locate. This means less time in the attention-attracting crouching posture and less time pulling out and swallowing the worms, so it is harder for the gulls to steal them.

Some birds have to cope with great variations in the food available, and they have a wide repertoire of feeding tactics. Flying insects, for example, are a very changeable food supply and birds that feed on them must be adaptable. The European spotted flycatcher gets its name from the characteristic habit of "hawking" in sallies from a conspicuous perch, snapping up passing flies and returning. This way of feeding is most profitable when there are plenty of good-sized flies, such as bluebottles, dungflies and hoverflies, and the flycatcher does not have to fly more than a few yards. Bees, butterflies and the largest flies are usually not profitable because they are difficult to catch and handle, but butterflies are caught in the early morning when their flight is sluggish. Longer flights are avoided by the flycatcher because they use more energy and they are also less successful, as the insects have a better chance of escape. If medium-sized, profitable flies become scarce, the flycatcher has to supplement its diet with small species

The flickers are woodpeckers but they feed mainly on insects found on the ground or plucked from the bark of trees, and on berries and seeds. Although they rarely excavate wood for their food they retain the woodpeckers' chiselling bill, which is used for making nest holes in trees.

of flies which are nutritionally ten times poorer, and when the preferred size of fly becomes too scarce for hawking to be profitable, the flycatcher changes to a new tactic. In the early morning and late evening, or on cold days, when flies are inactive, it searches the foliage for aphids and other small insects.

Foraging birds often give the impression that they are specifically searching for a particular preferred food. The basis of this preference has been investigated using tame carrion crows which were given morsels of food hidden under mussel shells that had been painted in a variety of colors. If a crow first found food under a red shell, it would continue to look under other red shells and ignore shells of different colors. In this situation, a bird is said to have a "search image" for red shells. A search image explains why the food a bird eats does not always reflect what is available. The birds are selecting some items and ignoring others because they have a mental image of what they are looking for, so that they fail to recognize other kinds of food. The same sort of mental image is formed in the human mind when searching for a lost object: finding it is much easier if you have a picture of what you are looking for.

Foraging titmice may ignore a favorite caterpillar when it first appears. Later, they eat the same species of caterpillar avidly and almost to the exclusion of all other food. It seems that, after first overlooking the caterpillars, the titmice start to find them by accident as they become more abundant, because they are

A spotted flycatcher catches a small tortoiseshell butterfly (far left) for its nestlings. Smaller insects are usually preferred, but butterflies are sometimes an easy prey when they are sluggish with cold, or are feeding on flowers. It is also more economical to carry one large prey to the nest (left) than several smaller ones.

*The acorn woodpecker (right) stores dried acorns in holes that it makes in tree trunks (below right), but it also feeds on insects and collects sap from holes in live trees.*

naturally curious and investigate anything likely to be edible. After finding a few caterpillars, a search image for them is formed and the birds then begin specifically to search for them. As the caterpillars' numbers wane, searching for these caterpillars is no longer rewarded, the titmice lose interest and form search images for other prey.

STORING FOOD

When food is temporarily abundant or easily gathered, it pays a bird to store what it cannot eat. Hoarding or cacheing can help the bird to survive the night, when it cannot feed, or see it through the winter, when food is scarce. European kestrels make caches of prey during the day and return to eat them in the evening; so they keep their weight down to save energy while hunting, but retire to roost well fed. Shrikes impale their prey on thorns and barbed wire, or wedge them in the forks of twigs, partly to assist in dismembering them when eating, but also for storage. Impaling and wedging are most frequent during the breeding season when extra food is required, but the habit persists throughout the year. Shrikes "larders" are often abandoned for unknown reasons; perhaps because they have dried out or rotted, or because the shrikes have stored more than they require.

The most common function of hoarding is to build up a food supply for the winter. Nutcrackers rely on burying pine seeds not only for their winter diet but for feeding the young. Seeds are buried in late summer and fall, then recovered in winter and spring. Like the many jays, which bury acorns, nutcrackers remember the position of their caches and can even locate them under several inches of snow, but since one bird buries up to 32,000 seeds – over three times as many as it needs to survive – many are left buried. So the European nutcracker helps to disperse the trees on which it feeds and was responsible for re-establishing Arolla pines in parts of the Alps after they had been destroyed by felling and grazing.

The pinyon jay of southwestern states stores seeds of the pinyon pine but it first tests the soundness of each seed by appearance, weight and tapping it with its bill. Several American woodpeckers cache seeds or insects and the most specialized is the acorn woodpecker. This species drills shallow holes in the bark of tree trunks and jams an acorn in each hole. One large pine contained 50,000 acorns.

A problem with hoarding is that other birds may find the stores. As birds of the same species tend to store and search in similar places, they are in effect switching each other's stores and they gain as much as they lose, but theft by other species which do not make stores for themselves represents a net loss. Thus great tits do not hoard but follow other titmice as they hide food and immediately steal it. The larders of shrikes can be found even more easily, and one was regularly robbed by a mockingbird. To combat theft, Lewis' woodpeckers defend their winter hoards of nuts against other woodpeckers, while nuthatches cover the nuts they have wedged in crevices with shreds of lichen and bark.

## FEEDING TOGETHER

So far, tactics for finding food have been considered in terms of the individual bird, but birds do not live alone and their foraging is affected by interactions with other animals. Interference by other birds can reduce the efficiency of feeding and in any gathering individuals compete for food. Jostling, warning jabs of the bill and brief squabbles, all reduce the time that can be spent feeding. Sometimes one bird is able to defend a limited food supply and keep its fellows away; a starling carefully guards a crust on the lawn, but it may be so busy chasing away other birds that it barely has time to feed. Aggression is most severe in short-lived gatherings of birds which have come together solely to exploit food. In a stable flock a regular rule of precedence, known as the peck-order, is established, so the birds take turns to feed in a more or less orderly way (see Chapter 7).

One advantage of feeding in flocks is that a group of birds can keep a more efficient watch for danger. Each bird in the flock needs to spend less time looking out for an approaching predator, because it will receive warning from its companions. It can also benefit from seeing what food the others have found. Terns and gulls watch for the flashing white plumage of other seabirds diving to show where shoals of fish are swimming just beneath the surface.

Social feeding is a fairly casual business in some species but well organized in others. A technique of some cormorants, the blue-eyed cormorant in the Antarctic waters for instance, is to hunt in "rafts". A flock of cormorants swims slowly forward in close formation and individuals put their heads underwater at intervals to look for fish. If one cormorant spots a fish, it dives and is followed by the rest of the raft. The cormorants benefit from charging together at a shoal of fish because a fish avoiding one cormorant will be snapped up by another. White pelicans "herd" shoals of fish into a tight concentration by swimming in a semicircle, so that they are trapped more easily and caught by their "dip-net" technique.

Some insect-eating birds benefit from feeding together because insects escaping from one bird will be caught by another. Cattle egrets feed mainly on land and specialize in catching grassland insects, their flocks rolling forwards as the birds at the rear leapfrog to the front. When a bird in the front of the flock pursues an insect, it disturbs more which are seized by the egrets following behind. The leapfrogging insures that all the birds in the flock get a fair share. The cattle egret also feeds in association with cattle and benefits from the insects disturbed by their hooves. It has enjoyed a phenomenal increase in its range partly because of this habit. From its original home in the Old World, it crossed the Atlantic to South America, has spread through the continent and now breeds as far north as Canada. In the other direction, it has spread through Asia and into Australia.

The opening up of the country for cattle ranching, by cutting down forests and draining swamps, has increased the amount of suitable country for cattle egrets. They habitually follow a particular herd of cattle, leaving to feed on their own only when the cattle rest. When following cattle, the egrets have been found to expend one third less energy in walking, and catch many more insects than when feeding on their own.

A feeding association with another species is known as commensalism which means, literally, "eating at the same table" and is characterized by one species profiting from another without harming it. Wagtails and the North American cowbirds (once called buffalo birds before the herds of buffalo disappeared from the prairies) run among the legs of grazing mammals to catch the insects they flush, and swallows fly around moving cattle and tractors. In the Arctic, ptarmigan save themselves the task of digging through snow by feeding where caribou and hares have already exposed the vegetation.

Where wild pigs still survive in the forests of Europe, robins follow them for the insects they expose as they root and scratch in the leaf litter. This is most useful when winter frosts send the insects beneath a frozen top layer. David Lack, who is famous for his study of European robins, imitated a large mammal by scraping frosted woodland litter with his feet, and was rewarded by robins dropping down from the trees to feed in the cleared patches. Today, in Britain (though not on the continent of Europe) robins have become garden birds and wait for the gardener's fork to turn up food for them.

Many feeding associations appear to be casual, and the birds are doing no more than switching to a new source of food which makes feeding easier. This is the case for the thirty-five species of birds which have been recorded as sipping at the sap oozing from the holes bored in tree trunks by sapsuckers. The same is true for the several species of gulls, alcids, shearwaters and phalaropes which gather in the shallow parts of the Bering Sea to feed where gray whales have stirred the mud on the seabed, bringing marine organisms to the surface.

By contrast, the oxpeckers or tickbirds have a very definite and regular association with large mammals and two species rely on their hosts for most of their needs. Oxpeckers can be seen on most large herbivorous mammals in Africa, except elephants. They have sharp claws and stiff tails for running, woodpecker-like, over the host's body, and all their food is obtained from their hosts. The bill is flattened from side to side and is used for scissoring parasites from the host's hide, as well as trimming open wounds and scars, and sipping blood. The 2,500 ticks and lice found on the body of one waterbuck show that mammals can supply sufficient food for their entourage of oxpeckers.

The hosts also form a platform for courtship displays and even provide hair for lining the oxpeckers' nests. It is often stated that the association between oxpeckers and large mammals is of mutual benefit. However, there is no evidence that they significantly affect the numbers of ticks on their hosts

*Feeding with large animals, ankole cattle in this case, saves cattle egrets time and energy because they can easily seize insects disturbed by the cattle's movements.*

*Cooperation is a good policy when prey live in a mass, such as a shoal of fish. Cormorants (right) dive together to make a concerted attack on a shoal – the gulls nearby are probably waiting to steal fish as the cormorants surface. White pelicans (far right) form a horseshoe to contain a shoal, all dipping their heads underwater together.*

*These cranes are probing for insects in a stubble field. When one has found a profitable place to search others join it, but do not come so close that they interfere with each other.*

and, rather than cleaning wounds, the oxpeckers may enlarge them by pecking away healthy flesh. Their alarm calls may benefit the mammals by warning of approaching human beings, but the oxpeckers do not react to other predators, such as lions and leopards.

Since Herodotus wrote on the subject 2,500 years ago, there have been scattered reports of birds feeding in the mouths of crocodiles. Five species have been implicated: the Egyptian plover (a courser), the blacksmith plover, the spur-winged plover, the common sandpiper and the water dikkop or thick-knee. All these birds feed near crocodiles and often pluck parasites from their backs as they bask on the river bank, but they also enter the reptiles' mouths to

observers, and even the existence of the association has been disputed, but with the disappearance of crocodiles from wide areas of their former range, it is not surprising that it is now rarely seen.

In most of these examples, the relationship is one-sided and the larger animal does not benefit. It creates feeding opportunities for the smaller animal quite unwittingly and without any modification of its behavior. At other times there is mutual benefit, as in the association between honeyguides and honey badgers, or ratels. The twelve species of honeyguides are insect eaters, related to barbets and woodpeckers, and they show a particular liking for bees and their larvae, and also for beeswax. They have tough skins

*Oxpeckers may not always benefit their hosts but they search for parasites with impunity. The red-billed oxpecker has not disturbed the sleep of a black rhinoceros (below) and a buffalo (right) tolerates yellow-billed oxpeckers, even on the sensitive tip of its muzzle.*

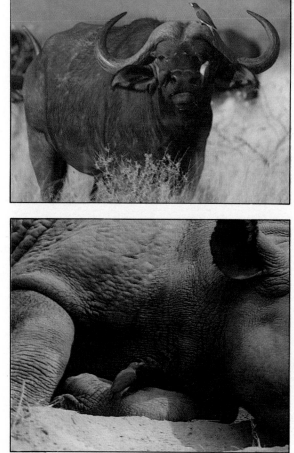

pick remnants of food from between their teeth or leeches from the lining of the mouth. It is said that the crocodiles benefit from having decaying food and parasites removed and that they are also warned of danger, the birds' shrill alarm calls sending the reptiles sliding into the water. It was also said that a crocodile would shake its head to warn the bird that it was about to close its mouth, and while this is not proven, it is noteworthy that the crocodiles do not molest them although they regularly prey on other birds. Whether the association is really two-sided has never been satisfactorily resolved. Crocodile-bird associations have not often been recorded by reliable

which give some immunity to bees' stings, carry bacteria in the gut to digest beeswax and can smell wax from a distance. Preying on bees' nests is a strange enough habit but two species, the black-throated and scaly-throated honeyguides, entice another animal to open the tough fabric of the nest. Having found a nest, the honeyguide seeks a honey badger and attracts its attention by calling insistently and, flying a few yards ahead, leads it to the nest. The honey badger tears open the nest with its strong claws and feeds on the honey and grubs. When it has finished, the bird descends to feed on the remaining bee grubs and the wax of the comb. Like the European

*The Arabian bustard not only helps to provide food for a carmine bee eater by disturbing insects, but also makes a convenient perch.*

robin, the honeyguides transferred the association to human beings, who at one time regularly followed them in search of honey. Although once widespread over Africa below the Sahara, this strange association between honeyguides and men has disappeared, except in remote places where people still search for wild honey rather than buying manufactured sugar at the local store.

The closest relationship between a bird and a mammal for their mutual benefit is that recently discovered between dwarf mongooses and yellow-billed and von der Decken's hornbills. The hornbills, like several other birds, follow packs of mongooses and snap up any small animals that try to escape from

insects and other small animals that they put to flight. These ants are nomads which occupy temporary nests for a period of time, sending out foraging parties each day, then abandoning the nest and wandering across the countryside in huge columns, several inches broad and 330 feet (100 meters) or more long, to a new site. The movements of the driver ants of Africa are not very regular and birds do not make a special habit of following them, but the army ants of America attract a specialized group of followers. Regular followers include antbirds, antpittas, tanagers and woodcreepers. Occasionally small falcons, anis, motmots and toucans join in. The regulars will leave their territories to follow the ant columns and then

*As an African helmeted guineafowl scratches for insects and seeds, a rufous sparrow waits to glean anything left over.*

*A European starling on a sika deer (left) and two wattled starlings on a zebra (far left). Large mammals make a good vantage point on which to perch in open country, and they may either stir up insects or attract flies which the starlings can snap up.*

them. In return, the hornbills give warning of danger. The value of this arrangement is shown by the way that the members of a dwarf mongoose pack spend less time on guard when hornbills are present, and can therefore spend more time feeding. They are even unwilling to leave the safety of their burrows until the hornbills arrive. For their part, the hornbills entice the mongooses to join them. If the mongooses are asleep, the hornbills poke their long bills down the burrows and call "wok" to bring the mongooses scrambling out, yawning and stretching.

In tropical America and Africa, a number of birds follow columns of army or driver ants to prey on the

return to roost. They find the ants by seeking their temporary nests, by returning to where they last saw a column, or by following other birds in the expectation that they will be led to a column.

Army ant columns may have up to fifty birds of ten species following at one time and they spread out over the path of the column according to their perching habits, thereby increasing their own chances of capturing prey. The ground-dwelling antpittas and ground-cuckoos run and hop along the edge of the column, antbirds perch on slender twigs and stems above it, while woodcreepers and flickers cling to the tree trunks.

There is more to a bird's dietary needs than the amount of energy it requires, because raw materials – proteins, vitamins and minerals – are needed to construct and maintain the body. A "balanced diet" is most important when the young bird is growing and building up its tissues, and extra nutrients are needed at the molt or when the female is manufacturing eggs. Non-breeding birds that are merely maintaining their bodies can survive on a poor diet for some time. Feral pigeons (the "town pigeons") can exist for over a month on barley alone. Such a diet is deficient in

*Scarlet macaws and red and green macaws gather at a river bank to eat the soil, which supplies them with the minerals their diet lacks.*

red grouse (willow ptarmigan) pick shoots of *Calluna* heather rather than *Erica* heaths and analysis shows that *Calluna* is richer in nitrogen and phosphorus; it is not known how the grouse distinguish them.

Calcium, which is needed for bones and eggshells, is one dietary component which has been studied in some detail. Female queleas supplement their diet of seeds and insects with snail shells and calcium-rich grit while the shells are being formed on their developing eggs. On the Arctic tundra, the insect diet of sandpipers is deficient in calcium yet the clutch

calcium, vitamin A and other nutrients, but a pigeon can store such substances in the body when a more varied diet is available.

The need for a balanced diet has often been overlooked because it is difficult to study, although it is sometimes clear that birds are not merely choosing the diet that gives them the most energy. Great tits feed their nestlings mainly on caterpillars, but for the first few days of life the nestlings are fed on large numbers of spiders, despite the abundance of caterpillars. The surmise is that spiders contain something that newly hatched chicks need. Scottish

of four eggs contains more calcium than the female's body. To supply the amount needed, she searches for the scattered bones of long-dead lemmings or picks them from regurgitated pellets found at the roosts of snowy owls and skuas.

Calcium deficiency in growing chicks is a problem for vultures and other scavengers which feed on the carcasses of large animals. They tear off the flesh, which contains little calcium, and cannot cope with the calcium-rich bones. Griffon vulture chicks are fed a meat diet and grow only slowly, although the growth of their bones is helped by the parents bringing bone fragments with the meal. Marabou storks and bateleur eagles of Africa, and the wedge-tailed eagle of Australia, switch from scavenging to hunting small vertebrate animals when feeding their chicks, the bones from the whole prey providing them with calcium. Although marabous are common through East Africa they breed only in a few places where they can capture sufficient fish and frogs to rear their young. The effect of a diet of calcium-deficient squid on the breeding regime of albatrosses is described on p. 97.

A diet that is adequate for maintaining the adult bird but insufficient for rearing a family is also a problem for seed-eating birds because seeds are deficient in some of the amino acids (the constituents

massive mortality of chicks which have an almost wholly insect diet.

The problem of a poor diet for growing young has been solved in different ways by two vegetarian groups of birds. Goslings leave the nest shortly after hatching and feed themselves. Like their parents they feed on grass and other leafy vegetation and they need to eat large quantities. They are able to eat 10% more than adult geese because they are guarded by their parents and so do not waste time keeping watch for danger. The young, or squabs, of pigeons are fed in the nest by their parents who both manufacture a special food similar to the milk of mammals. A few days before the pigeon squabs hatch, the lining of the parent's crop thickens and is thrown into folds. The

*Having used a precious supply of body calcium in manufacturing eggshells, a female ostrich recoups the loss by eating the shells after the chicks have hatched.*

*The favorite food of the palm nut vulture (center) is the fruit of the oil palm, but it supplements its diet with small animals and here it is eating the remains of hatched crocodile eggs.*

of proteins) which are essential for growth. Consequently many seed eaters enrich the diet of their young with insects because they contain two to four times as much protein and a better balance of amino acids.

Queleas in Africa are fed on insects for the first week of life before being given the adult diet of seeds, and some adult European finches continue to eat seeds themselves, while bringing the brood a mixture of seeds and insects. The disappearance of grey partridges in Europe is probably due to the destruction of insects by pesticides, thereby causing a

outer layer of cells sloughs off to form a thick fluid called "pigeon's milk". It is very rich in protein (46% dry weight) fat (26%) and various minerals. The newly hatched squab receives nothing but pigeon's milk at first, but this is supplemented with an increasing amount of solid food when it is half grown. The only other birds known to do this are flamingos, which feed their young on milk when they are first hatched, and the emperor penguin, whose egg is incubated by the male alone. He waits for the female to return with food for the newly hatched chick, but if she is delayed he will feed it on milk for the first few days of its life.

*Flamingos (above) and emperor penguins (far left and center) feed their chicks on 'milk'. Note the spines on the penguin's tongue which help it to seize slippery prey.*

# DRINKING

*A marabou stork pants in the hot African sun. Birds usually keep their water loss very low, but in hot weather they keep cool by panting, which allows water to evaporate through the mouth.*

*Most birds, such as this Australian magpie-lark (right), drink by taking a mouthful, and then raise the head to let the water run down the throat. Pigeons (below right), along with sandgrouse and buttonquails, can suck up water without raising their heads.*

*Namaqua sandgrouse gather from a wide area to drink at a pool (far right). Drinking together helps to reduce danger from predators. When nesting, the males soak their breast feathers to carry water back to the chicks (right).*

Water is essential to a bird's well-being. It is continually lost as vapor in the breath and through excretion, and it has to be made good by drinking. Compared with mammals, however, birds lose little water because their high body temperature reduces the need to evaporate water to keep cool and they excrete uric acid in their urine, instead of the urea of mammals. Uric acid can be excreted in a highly concentrated form, and the urine of birds is a thick, whitish liquid that is deposited with the droppings. Despite these adaptations, drinking is still a regular need, depending on the amount of water in the food and the amount of water used for keeping cool.

Finding sufficient water poses few problems for most birds. Canopy-dwelling birds of forests find water trapped in the foliage while swifts and swallows, and the fish crow, drink by dipping into the water while on the wing. Problems occur only in harsh environments. In winter, birds must resort to eating snow. This may be hazardous for small birds because heat is needed to melt the snow and warm the water to body temperature, and they could already be having difficulty in keeping warm.

In arid regions, large flocks of birds gather at regular drinking places. Sandgrouse fly to water either in the early morning or evening, according to species. Thousands, or even tens of thousands, of birds gather from all around at the same time each day, making an impressive spectacle at the drinking place. On one occasion the regularity of the flight to water saved the life of the explorer Richard Burton. When almost dying of thirst in the Sudan, he spotted a flock of sandgrouse and followed them to a waterhole.

Desert birds can prolong the time they spend without drinking by being economical with their body water. Water is lost in hot weather through the process of evaporation which helps to reduce the body temperature. Unlike mammals, birds have no sweat glands and they lose water by rapid panting, or by

fluttering the bare skin of the gular pouch under the chin. A panting budgerigar raises its breathing rate from around 100 to as much as 300 breaths per minute. Reducing this evaporation and conserving body water can be achieved by allowing the body temperature to rise during the day, as in the mourning dove which can survive a rise in temperature that would be lethal to other species.

One problem facing small birds is that they have a relatively large surface area compared with their bulk and so will heat up quickly. Gray's lark of African deserts overcomes this by building an elaborate, well insulated nest under the shade of a tuft of grass or overhanging rock. By relying on insect food, it gets sufficient water and never has to drink. The very much larger ostrich heats up more slowly by virtue of its greater bulk and relatively smaller surface area, but it, too, saves water by reducing its exposure to the sun. If no shade is available during the hottest part of the day, it faces the sun with its wings held out from the body so that the long, loose plumes give it shade. This position also exposes the naked flanks which can then act as radiators, giving off excess heat.

The problem of obtaining water becomes more intense when birds have nestlings which are dependent on them for all their needs. If there is insufficient fluid in the food, it must be supplemented with water. The roadrunner of North American deserts holds an insect or other prey in the tip of its bill and, when the nestling gapes to receive it, the adult regurgitates water into the nestling's mouth before releasing the insect.

Delivery of water to the brood is found in other species, including storks and cormorants, but sandgrouse have the unique habit of carrying water in their feathers. The breast feathers of male sandgrouse have barbules which are not hooked together so that the water-shedding properties are lost and the feathers act as a sponge. When taking their daily drink, male sandgrouse wade into the water and crouch to soak the breast. They then fly back to the brood and, despite evaporation losses from flying in the hot desert air, enough water remains for the chicks to drink by sucking the damp feathers.

Seabirds and birds living in salt marshes and salt lakes face the problem of the Ancient Mariner: "Water, water everywhere, nor any drop to drink." The body fluids of vertebrate animals have a salt concentration less than one third of seawater, and drinking seawater raises the salt in the blood to dangerous levels. Drinking quantities of salt water is fatal for most animals but birds living in a salty environment have a means of coping with the extra salt taken in when they drink or eat. Zebra finches dwelling in salt marshes have kidneys which are capable of excreting the extra salt safely, and seabirds and flamingos use a pair of salt-excreting glands just above the eyes. These secrete a salt solution stronger than seawater, which trickles down the nostrils and accumulates as a "dewdrop" at the tip of the bill. Petrels blow it away as a fine spray but other birds flick it off with a shake of the head.

*Painted storks deliver water to their nestlings by carrying it in their crops and then dribbling it down their bills.*

# CHAPTER 5
## DIET AND WAY OF LIFE

Birds eat an enormous range of foods – from the microscopic diatoms which flamingos filter from shallow water to the floating carcasses of whales on which seabirds gather to gorge – but every species is restricted to a diet consisting of only a part of the food available. The snail kite, or Everglade kite, which eats nothing but large freshwater snails, has one of the most restricted of all diets, but even specialists are flexible enough to vary their diet within certain limits. Crossbills use their overlapping mandibles for extracting seed from cones, but they take berries and insects as well, and hummingbirds that sip nectar through probe-shaped bills regularly eat insects and spiders found among the flowers.

Other birds have feeding habits which give them a wide choice of food. Gulls are essentially fish eaters, but the herring gull, among other gull species, has become a hunter of smaller birds, a pirate robbing others, a ground feeder that can dig for crabs and worms, and an exploiter of humans that follows fishing boats and plows, or scavenges on refuse dumps. In some birds there is a regular change in diet over the year, as with the shorebirds which rear their young on insects and other invertebrates in the Arctic, sometimes switch to berries to fatten up before migration, and then spend the winter on the coast feeding on marine invertebrates. Some birds even undergo a physical change in their digestive systems, correlated with a change in diet. The reedling, or bearded tit, moves from insects in the summer to seeds in winter. As its diet begins to change in the early fall, it develops the thick, muscular gizzard of a

seed-eating bird. When starlings switch from a diet of insects to one of plants, the gizzard enlarges and the intestines lengthen.

Every species of bird is, then, adapted to feed on a wider or narrower range of food, which is determined by the constraints of both physical form – bill shape, legs, wings, size and so on – and behavior. Only rarely do they break out of these constraints, as in the case of the European kestrel, seen eating apples during a severe winter, and the sharp-beaked ground finch of the Galapagos, which normally feeds on seeds but has formed the habit of pecking holes in the skin of nesting boobies and sipping their blood, probably as a way of getting liquid.

Within any community of birds each species has its individual way of earning a living which is known as its "ecological niche". It is one of the basic tenets of ecology that no two species have exactly the same niche because, if they did, one species would inevitably do better and the other become rare or disappear entirely. According to this theory, whenever a community of animals is examined, it will be found that its members are not in direct competition with each other for food. Their niches may overlap a little, but there is sufficient contrast for them to eat different things, especially at a time of shortage. This is well illustrated by four owls found in the prairie country of the mid-western United States. The great horned owl, the largest species, hunts the widest variety of prey and catches animals up to the size of a hare; at the other end of the scale, the diminutive burrowing owl eats large numbers of insects as well as rodents and

*For the reedling, and probably for many other birds, a seasonal change in diet is accompanied by a change in the structure of the digestive system.*

*Red crossbills are specialist feeders, using the crossed mandible tips to open cones, but they occasionally take other food, such as mountain ash berries.*

*It is not unusual for the sexes to have slightly different diets but the trend was taken to an extreme by the extinct huia, one of the New Zealand wattlebirds. Both obtained insects from timber but the male had a stout bill for chiselling wood and the female a long bill for probing.*

*Some birds have a very varied diet. The jungle myna, one of the starling family, is seen here pecking at the sore on an Indian rhinoceros (below) and taking nectar from a kapok flower (far right). Its main foods, however, are fruit and insects.*

the occasional frog or small bird. The medium-sized long-eared and barn owls take much the same prey as each other and both hunt on the wing at night, mainly for small rodents, but the barn owl captures a wider variety of animals. The niches of the four owls overlap to some degree, but they are mostly eating different proportions of prey. Competition will disappear during a glut, as they all exploit a plague of rodents, for instance, but it is intense in times of shortage and the contrasts in diet then become important.

Differences in feeding behavior may exist even between males and females of the same species. One sex may be larger and capable of tackling larger prey. The female European sparrowhawk hunts thrushes and starlings, occasionally larger pigeons, jays and grouse, while the male, half her weight, takes smaller songbirds – finches, sparrows and buntings. This trend is often more marked in birds living on islands, where there are fewer species to compete with and the sexes can spread their diets. The bill of the male Hispaniolan woodpecker is 20% shorter than the female's, and he spends more time gleaning insects living on the surface of plants, while the female uses her larger bill for excavating insects from cracks and crevices. Overlap is not completely abolished between the two sexes in these woodpeckers, though it apparently was in the huia of New Zealand which sadly became extinct around 1907 before its feeding habits had been properly studied. Males and females had completely different bills and are supposed to have had different feeding methods. The male's straight bill is said to have been used woodpecker-fashion for chiselling grubs from timber whereas the female's long, slender, curved bill was used for probing into crevices. As there is only a single account of this behavior from one pair of huias kept captive in 1864, we shall never know whether the sexes' habits were as exclusive as these observations suggest.

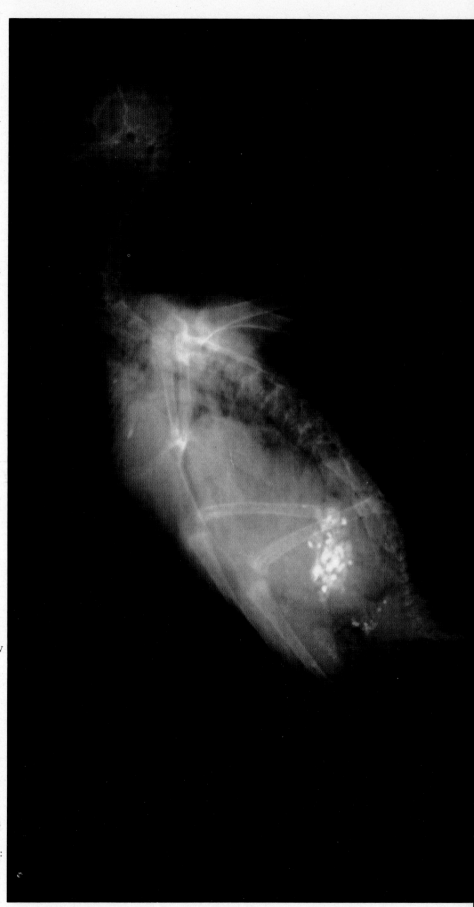

*An X-ray of a 25-day old pigeon clearly shows grit in its gizzard as a mass of bright spots. This bird was still in the nest and it had been fed the grit by its parents.*

For most vertebrates, plants are poor food compared with the flesh of animals. They contain large amounts of cellulose, a material which animals cannot break down without the help of bacteria, and as a result they are hard to digest and low in energy content. The exceptions are a plant's storage organs, in the form of tubers, bulbs and rhizomes, and its seeds and fruits, which are mostly rich in starch or sugar. Most plant tissues, other than seeds, are also poor in proteins, which diminishes their food value. Nevertheless, many birds feed extensively on fruits (pp. 80–1), although they often switch to animal food as a richer source of protein when rearing their young. On the other hand, carnivorous birds may turn to energy-rich fruits when laying down a store of fat for migration or when animal food is scarce in winter. Nectar is another energy-rich plant food which is used by some groups of birds (pp. 82–5). Seeds give a much more balanced diet, and they are the main food for a great many birds (pp. 78–9), but green plant material is far less important: in contrast to the mammals, very few birds have exploited its nutritional possibilities.

The problem of dealing with cellulose has been solved by ruminating mammals – cows, sheep, deer and others. They rely on bacteria in their complex stomach system to break down the cellulose into a form which they can assimilate, and aid this digestive process by "chewing the cud". Other grazing mammals, such as rabbits, have similar bacteria in the gut and eat their droppings so that the material passes through the gut a second time, allowing the nutrients produced by bacterial breakdown of cellulose to be absorbed. Birds have failed to evolve a comparably efficient system and the only essentially leaf-eating birds are the swans, geese, grouse, some of the ducks and the kakapo. Pigeons, coots, gamebirds, and the ostrich and its allies are mainly leaf eaters, but they supplement this diet with fair quantities of other plant and animal food. Some of these birds have bacteria in their intestines which break down cellulose, and allow them to gain some nourishment from it, but other species rely solely on the plant's sap for sustenance.

Lacking teeth, leaf-eating birds use the muscular gizzard, aided by quantities of grit, to pulp the plant tissues and release the nutritive sap. Grit is also used by birds with different diets, and some species ingest other hard objects instead of grit. Starlings, for instance, eat small snail shells, and fruit eaters use the stones of the fruit to crush the pulp. For plant eaters grit is essential, and willow ptarmigan must travel in search of it when their normal supplies are covered with snow. Most of the grit is retained in the gizzard as the food is passed on, but some is voided and needs replacing. The size of the particles is related to the diet: the tougher the vegetation, the coarser the grit. Some remains of the extinct moas are so well preserved that the contents of the gizzard lie undisturbed in the skeleton. They show that the moas ate grasses, twigs, leaves and berries, which were pulped in the gizzard by up to 7 pounds (3 kilograms) of stones. Captive ostriches are renowned for swallowing strange objects, from beer bottles to padlocks, but in the wild they swallow pebbles. An early study of ostrich migration involved relating the types of stones in gizzards to the geological map, and in Burma a ruby mine was discovered as a result of finding a ruby in a pheasant's gizzard.

Merely grinding plants and releasing the cell sap is an inefficient method of feeding. Waterfowl have to eat vast quantities of food and pass it rapidly through

Efficient digestion of plants by bacterial action in the manner of mammals is difficult for birds because it involves carrying large volumes of food for a long time while it is processed in an elaborate digestive system. The extra weight would make flying difficult but the problem has been partially solved by grouse, which carry out bacterial digestion in two caeca (blind tubes leading from the bottom end of the large intestine). Compared with geese, grouse are even more selective feeders, choosing carefully what they eat and restricting their intake. Emus, ostriches and, probably, the kakapo, also make use of bacteria. The kakapo is unique for the way that it eats grass by taking

*When grain and other seeds are not available, woodpigeons have to turn to less nutritious food such as the leaves of Brussels sprouts.*

*Far left: a blue-naped parrot of the Philippines holds a leaf with one foot while it snips off chunks and eats them.*

*After roosting by day under a boulder or tree stump, the flightless kakapo wanders through the forest by night. It follows regular trails which are marked by the remains of grass leaves which it has chewed and sucked dry.*

the body. When grazing, a flock of geese spends virtually the whole day feeding, pecking at rates of around a hundred times per minute. Grasses are plucked off with a jerk of the head, or clipped by the "nail" at the tip of the bill, and then ground by grit in the gizzard. The resulting mush passes through the intestine in about two hours, with little digestion and assimilation having taken place, so that continuous meals are needed. To make the most of the poor diet, geese choose the best grasses, avoiding shrivelled stems and selecting succulent, green shoots which are not only the easiest to pluck but also have the highest protein content.

a blade in the bill and chewing it without severing it from the plant. The juices are sucked out and the blade is left as a bundle of tangled fibers, which dry white, showing where the kakapo has been feeding. A third bird which may be digesting cellulose with bacteria is the hoatzin, which grinds its food in the crop – normally a storage pouch – rather than in the gizzard. It may be no coincidence that the emu, ostrich and kakapo are flightless and therefore not so concerned with weight problems, and that the hoatzin is a clumsy flier. When its crop is full, it becomes top heavy and balances on a perch by leaning on its breast, which is provided with a hard callus.

# SEED EATERS

In contrast to the few birds feeding on green plant food, there are a great many seed eaters, and some gather in huge flocks to feed on crops of ripe seeds, becoming serious agricultural pests when they invade fields of wheat, millet or rice. The edible kernel of a seed is normally protected by a husk, or shell, which must be removed before it can be digested, and the smaller finches, weavers and similar birds, including the house sparrow, process seeds by removing the outer covering before swallowing them. These seed eaters typically have stout, conical bills and strong jaw muscles for crushing seeds. Larger birds swallow seeds whole and rely on grit in the gizzard to remove the husks and crush the seeds.

Removing the husk from a seed is a task requiring considerable skill. The finches of the Old World are assisted by the structure of the bill, in which the sharp edge of the lower mandible fits into a groove on the edge of the upper mandible. The seed is fitted into the groove on one side of the bill, and held by the edge of the lower mandible, being placed nearer the corner of the mouth to get a better leverage if it has a tough husk. If the seed has a suture making a weak point, it is aligned with the lower mandible to make splitting easier. A squeeze cracks the seed, as if in a nutcracker, and the lower mandible is worked into the split. With the help of the tongue, the seed is revolved and the husk peeled off.

*The Eurasian bullfinch feeds on the seeds in berries, among other things. It removes the flesh of the berry by rotating it against the edge of the lower mandible. Small snails are treated similarly to remove their shells.*

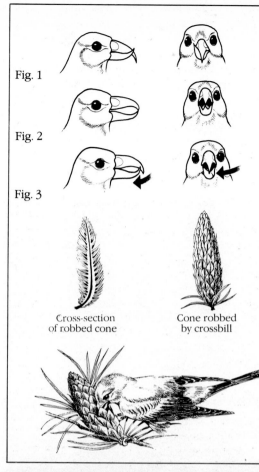

Fig. 1

Fig. 2

Fig. 3

Cross-section of robbed cone

Cone robbed by crossbill

*A male parrot crossbill (below) feeding its nestlings with seeds. Their bills will not cross until they have left the nest. Fig. 1 (left) shows the bill at rest. To feed, the crossbill pushes the partly open bill (Fig. 2) behind a cone scale. A sideways movement of the lower mandible, and a twist of the head (Fig. 3), raises the scale and splits it vertically. Then the seed is worked free with the tongue.*

The hawfinch has the most powerful bill and jaw muscles and, while its main food is the soft seeds of elm and hornbeam, it can deal with the stones of cherries and olives. The bill has four rounded knobs at the base, two on each mandible, and by placing the stone between them, the force for cracking it can be shared equally by the muscles on each side of the head. Nevertheless, the force required to crack an olive stone, even with the suture arranged to split easily, is nearly 50 pounds (23 kilograms), a remarkable force for a small bird.

Members of the crow and titmouse families deal with pine cones, nuts and other hard seeds by holding them down with one foot and hammering with the bill until the shell cracks or, in Eurasian jays eating acorns, biting and levering. Nuthatches do not use their feet but instead wedge nuts in crevices to hold them steady for hammering. The great tit can deal with such stout shells as hazelnuts, and these nuts are the favored food of the European nutcracker. It splits the shell using the sharp edge of the bill like a finch, except that the groove is on the lower mandible.

Seed crops are seasonal and the birds which feed on them are faced with alternating periods of abundance and scarcity. The crop eventually disappears when the seeds germinate – in spring for temperate latitudes, or in the rainy season in the tropics. Several options are possible when the seed crops run out. The birds can change to another diet: queleas eat swarming termites and other insects between the time that the grass seeds germinate at the start of the rains and the ripening of the next crop a few weeks later. Some birds store food, as described on p. 64, others can move away from the famine-stricken area. Some species migrate regularly each year but others, like the crossbills, erupt irregularly.

In any particular area there are good crops of cones only once in every few years, and crossbills move to take advantage of them so that a place with large numbers of crossbills feeding on a good crop in one year may be devoid of them in the next. Red crossbills in Europe nest between summer and spring, when the various crops of cones are growing. There is a big movement of birds in early summer after the seeds have been shed from the cones (the crossbills being unable to pick them from the ground because of their overlapping mandibles) and before the next crop sets. In North America, most seeds are shed in the fall, and crossbills move at this season.

In Britain, bullfinches become pests of fruit crops when a shortage of seeds in winter forces them into orchards to eat unopened buds on the fruit trees. The natural winter diet is made up of the seeds of ash, birch, nettle and dock, and the fruits of privet and brambles. When these run out, the bullfinches turn to eating the buds of trees and shrubs. They take only the parts that will later develop into fruit, but there is so little food value in them that, when the days are short, the birds cannot survive on buds alone despite eating up to thirty per minute. The switch to buds depends on the size of the seed crops, especially of ash. Ash trees seed well only in certain years and, in general, there is a good crop every other year. Invasions of orchards follow the years when the ash crop fails.

*Eurasian nuthatches deal with hard-shelled nuts by wedging them in crevices and hammering them until the shells split.*

*A northern cardinal shows the typical conical bill of a seed eater. It is adaptable enough for use on insects as well as buds.*

Only in the tropics, where an even climate allows plants to flower and set fruit the year round, can birds survive on a diet solely of fruit. The tropics are the home for several families with fruit-eating members: the toucans and araçaris of America and the hornbills of the Old World with their outsize bills, the cotingas and oilbirds of tropical America, the fruit pigeons, barbets, touracos, mousebirds, caciques, oropendolas, cassowaries and parrots. The palm nut vulture is an unusual bird of prey whose distribution coincides with that of the oil palm, its greasy fruits being the bird's favorite food.

In climates with a cold winter season, the fall crops of fruit and berries attract many birds, including thrushes, orioles, waxwings, warblers, grouse and finches, and they continue to feed on them until the supply is exhausted. Shorebirds fatten up on berries before migrating south, woodpeckers eat berries on occasion, and the tree swallow feeds on bayberries when cold weather prevents it from catching sufficient insects. Ivy is unusual in that it flowers in the fall and provides a late crop of berries for woodpigeons and thrushes in winter.

There is an important difference between a carnivorous and frugivorous diet. Animals avoid being eaten: they take flight, hide or defend themselves when attacked. Insects, in particular, have evolved stratagems of camouflage or distastefulness to avoid being found and eaten by birds. Fruits, on the other hand, "want" to be eaten because birds will assist with the dispersal of their seeds. They are often brightly colored, grow in masses where birds can easily reach them and provide easy meals.

Although some parrots and finches eat seeds and drop the flesh (the seeds being more nutritious than the fruit), the general rule is for fruit eaters either to regurgitate the seeds or pass them through the body unchanged so they fall to the ground at a distance from the parent tree. In some instances, the seeds are too hard to be digested, like the woody seeds of palms, or they are poisonous, so ensuring that the bird does not eat and destroy them. Hornbills in South-East Asia eat the fruits of nux vomica and avoid cracking the seeds, which contain the poison strychnine, but how the knysna touraco of South Africa survives eating the red berries called "bushman's poison" is not known. Parasitic mistletoe plants rely on birds to spread their seeds to other host trees. The mistletoe berries have very sticky flesh which adheres to the bird's bill, so it has to wipe it off, usually on a tree branch where the seeds lodge and germinate.

In parallel with the evolution of fruits to attract birds and promote seed dispersal, the birds have become adapted to dealing with fruit. Oilbirds, bellbirds and trogons pluck fruit in flight. Trogons also eat insects and they pluck fruit in the same way as they pick insects from foliage, hovering momentarily while tearing the fruit off its stalk and then bearing it back to the perch. Other fruit eaters are agile at clambering among foliage. Fruit pigeons hang upside down like tits to reach hanging fruits and the long bills of hornbills and toucans could perhaps be an adaptation for reaching awkwardly-placed fruit.

One species of imperial pigeon can stretch the base of its bill and swallow whole nutmeg fruits 2 inches (5 centimeters) in diameter – larger than its own head – whereas mousebirds tackle large fruit by pecking holes in the skin and removing the flesh inside. In general, however, the size of the bill

*The chestnut-eared araçari is one of the toucans of South America. These birds are mainly fruit eaters but they also prey on small animals. Their young develop very slowly as is often the case with fruit-eating birds.*

*Fallen apples are a valuable food for many birds in winter. Here a Eurasian redwing tries to defend its food supply. This may be worthwhile in some circumstances, but it is unnecessary if there is a glut, and impossible if there is a shortage and too much competition.*

*The figbird is an oriole living in New Guinea and Australia. As the name suggests, it regularly eats the fruits of wild figs and helps to spread the plants by excreting the seeds, unharmed, in its droppings.*

controls the size of fruit which can be swallowed. In the lowland forests of New Guinea there are eight species of fruit pigeon living together with little competition because each takes fruit appropriate to the size of the bill. The smaller pigeons are also able to feed on the outer branches of the trees where the larger ones are unable to perch.

The intestine of fruit eaters is short and the remains of fruit can be voided as little as five minutes after it has been eaten. Fruit pigeons have wide intestines which enable them to pass nutmeg seeds 1 inch (2.5 centimeters) in diameter; in contrast feral pigeons, which are not specialist fruit eaters, have to regurgitate cherry stones. Fruit pigeons rasp the flesh away from the seeds in the gizzard, which is provided with horny knobs or plates. The phainopepla, one of

*The phainopepla eats some small insects, but mistletoe berries are its staple food and it has special adaptations for digesting them. In these pictures the male (top) and female (below) are feeding their nestlings on the berries. Note those visible in the neck of the nestling being fed by the female.*

the silky flycatcher family (a mis-named group that feeds mainly on fruit), lives largely on the berries of mistletoe growing on mesquite bushes in the deserts of Mexico and the south-western United States. Other birds lose weight if they are kept on a diet of mistletoe berries but the phainopepla survives on about 250 berries a day. Its digestive system is adapted to dealing with the berries by stripping off the skin in the gizzard and, like other fruit and nectar eaters, passing the pulp through the digestive system in a matter of minutes.

Fruit crops form a supply of food that is both abundant and easily gathered. In the tropics this gives birds plenty of time for the other activities. Male birds can devote their time to elaborate courtship routines, as in the cotingas and manakins, with only a fraction of the day needed for feeding. However, fruits are deficient in protein and other nutrients and most frugivorous birds feed their young on insects. They would grow slowly on a fruit diet and consequently spend longer at risk from nest predators. The oilbird is one exception which feeds its young exclusively on fruit. Since it nests on ledges deep in caves beyond the reach of predators, its chicks can afford to grow slowly, taking a hundred or more days to fledge. The bearded bellbird, one of the cotingas of Trinidad, also feeds its young on fruit but the fledging period is only thirty-three days, perhaps because the chick is given fruits from the plant family Lauraceae which are particularly rich in protein, although still not as proteinaceous as animal food.

Because so much fruit has to be eaten to provide an adequate diet (waxwings eat three times their body weight of *Cotoneaster* berries each day), birds can cause great damage to fruit crops. In temperate countries opportunist feeders may become pests by turning to fruit as crops ripen. Gulls are attracted to the important crop of wild blueberries in New England and normally popular songsters such as the American robin and European blackbird temporarily lose favour by attacking cherries and soft fruits. Flocks of starlings can also inflict heavy damage, having the particularly infuriating habit of arriving just as the fruit is ripening. Apparently they discern ripeness by the color of the fruit.

Gluttonous fruit-eating can also be detrimental to the birds, when they flop helplessly on the ground after becoming intoxicated on the fermenting juices of over-ripe fruit. There is a record of an ostrich lurching, with legs crossing and long neck wobbling, after gorging on fallen fruit.

NECTAR DRINKING AND POLLINATION
Flowers and flying insects evolved together: bright colors and nectar attract insects that then transfer pollen from stamens to stigmas as they fly from one flower to another. In later ages, the energy-rich, sugary nectar was sought by birds, as well as other animals, and some flowers have turned from insects and evolved relationships specifically with birds.

A wide variety of birds are casual collectors of nectar. In Europe, warblers and titmice have been recorded as sipping nectar on occasion, while in

North America the list includes mockingbirds, tanagers, flickers and verdins. It seems likely that nectar drinking was developed by birds that searched among flowers for insects, and there are now members of eight families specializing in drinking nectar. These are the hummingbirds and honeycreepers of the Americas, the honeyeaters of Australasia and the islands of the western Pacific, the sugarbirds of South Africa, the sunbirds of Africa, southern Asia and Australia, some of the Hawaiian honeycreepers (only distantly related to the South American birds known as honeycreepers), some of the flowerpeckers of India, South-east Asia and Australia, and the lorikeets of Australasia.

Nectar specialists have a mainly tropical or subtropical distribution and live where the climate allows a long flowering season. A few hummingbirds have penetrated North America, and the rufous hummingbird nests as far north as Alaska, but they migrate south for the winter. Only in low-lying tropical forests can birds rely on a supply of nectar all the year round, as the even climate allows a continual succession of plants to come into flower. Where the climate becomes more seasonal with increasing latitude or altitude, nectar eaters supplement their diet with insects and spiders. The honeyeaters also eat fruit and berries, becoming a pest in Australian orchards. However, the nectar season can be extended by the birds becoming nomadic and following a succession of flowering plants. In the western United States, for instance, hummingbirds move up and down mountain slopes to take advantage of the delayed flowering at high altitudes. An alternative strategy used by some hummingbirds is to defend a feeding territory when flowers become scarce and deny other hummingbirds access to their private supply.

Co-evolution of both birds and flowers has led to specialization, in which the bird is adapted for collecting nectar from the bottom of a long tubular corolla and the plant has made itself attractive to the bird. Nectar drinkers have tongues with finely divided

*The Cape sugarbird is very dependent on* Protea *bushes. It nests in them when they are in flower, so that there is a good supply of food close by. The flowers not only provide nectar but the sugarbird also searches for insects living in them.*

*A rainbow lorikeet on* Banksia *(left) and a scaly-breasted lorikeet on* Erythrina *(far left). Nectar is the main food of these small parrots. The parrot and honeyeater families are the most important pollinators of flowering trees and shrubs in Australia.*

*The bill of the sword-billed hummingbird is as long as the rest of the bird. It is used for probing long tubular flowers to reach the nectar.*

tips forming a "brush". Except in the lorikeets, the tongues are very long and the edges roll inwards to make a narrow tube, or scoop. At one time it was thought that nectar was sucked up the tubes as through a drinking straw, but in fact the tongue does no more than hold the nectar by capillary action while whipping rapidly in and out.

Even where there is an assured supply of nectar, many of these birds supplement their diet with small insects and other invertebrate animals as a means of getting protein. The nestlings, in particular, are fed largely on animal food, although the stitchbird (one of the honeyeaters) appears to feed its nestlings on nothing but nectar. It has been calculated that two honeyeaters – the stitchbird and the New Holland honeyeater – use as much energy in hawking for flying insects as they derive from digesting them, which suggests that they are taken only when the birds need an extra source of proteins and minerals. Other honeyeaters and some hummingbirds pick insects off leaves which is less strenuous. Hummingbirds, however, frequently hawk for insects, and pluck spiders and their insect prey from webs. They have a better design for hovering than other nectar drinkers and this is reflected in the way that hummingbirds typically hover in front of flowers, while other nectar drinkers usually perch when feeding.

COEVOLUTION WITH PLANTS

The different families of nectar drinkers and their similar tongues are an example of convergent evolution, whereby unrelated groups of animals have acquired similar adaptations for the same habit. Within these families there have been further refinements in which the birds have become adapted to feed at particular plants. This is demonstrated by the shape of the bill. Small-billed hummingbirds compete with insects at open flowers, and they can visit a wide variety of flowers, but within the hummingbird family there is a trend for specialized bills to fit more elaborate flowers. The sword-billed hummingbird, whose bill is longer than the rest of the bird, can reach the nectaries of long tubular flowers,

*A white-bellied sunbird hovers like a hummingbird in front of a flower, about to sip some nectar. The sunbirds' brilliant plumage makes them the Old World equivalent of the hummingbirds, but they usually feed while perching.*

*Far right: The yellowish honeyeater is a nectar-drinker, but it feeds its nestlings on insects to give them a protein-rich diet.*

while other hummingbirds have curved bills which fit curved corolla tubes . Similar specializations occur in the Hawaiian honeycreepers, a family which has evolved to fill many different niches in the isolation of the Hawaiian islands in much the same way as Darwin's finches have done on the Galapagos Islands. It is a great loss that one quarter of the twenty or so species of Hawaiian honeycreeper have become extinct through the destruction of the islands' forests.

Plants have "encouraged" the nectar-drinking habit in birds by providing such copious supplies of nectar that a bird can subsist on this source alone. The flowers are colored so as to attract birds, and some even provide perches for visitors in the form of rigid parts extending beyond the mouth of the flower. The benefit accruing to the plants is that the birds carry pollen from one flower to another. For pollination to take place, pollen must be transferred from stamens to stigmas of the same species. The chances will be slim if the birds fly haphazardly from one plant species to another. However, birds tend to forage at one kind of flower at a time, perhaps through a search image (p.63), and their choice is automatically restricted because only limited kinds of flowers are open at one time and in one place.

Co-evolution between plants and birds increases the chances of pollen reaching the right destination. The long corolla tubes keep out insects and, as already described, limit the bird visitors by the size and shape of their bills. Some African mistletoes will not even open without the aid of a pollinating sunbird. At one mistletoe the sunbird slits open the corolla with its bill and is showered with pollen as the stamens spring forward. Later, the stigma bends down and receives pollen from subsequent visitors. Plants may also be specific in the way they daub pollen onto the bird's plumage. In Arizona there are a number of bird-pollinated plants which are very alike but which have different arrangements of the anthers and nectaries, so that their pollen is deposited on a specific part of the bird's head. For example, the beard-tongue *Penstemon barbatus*, a member of the snapdragon family, puts pollen on the bird's forehead, while the sky-rocket *Ipomopsis aggregata*, a type of phlox, deposits its pollen on the bird's chin. When the bird visits another flower of one or the other species, its stigma removes pollen from the appropriate spot and the risk of it being pollinated by a plant of another species is minimized.

The interdependence of flowers and birds has led to cheating on both sides. The cardinal flower *Lobelia cardinalis* secretes no nectar but mimics other plants, so it is pollinated by birds visiting its flowers in the hope of finding a meal. On the other hand, sunbirds and flowerpiercers (species of American honeycreeper) poke holes in the bases of flowers and drink the nectar without picking up pollen. The flowerpiercers hook the curved upper mandible over the base of the flower corolla to hold it steady while the straight lower mandible pierces a hole in the side for the tongue to enter.

The insects are one of the most successful animal classes. Like the birds, they have mastered flight and invaded almost every conceivable habitat in every corner of the world. There are more species of insects than all other species of animals put together, and many insects occur in huge numbers, so it is not surprising that they form a major source of food for birds. Some birds are specialist insect eaters like the swallows and swifts that pursue flying insects, while others eat insects on occasion. Birds of prey frequently take insects along with larger prey, and many birds switch to an insect diet at particular times. Insects are rich in protein and other nutrients, and many plant-eating birds feed their young on insects, so permitting a rapid rate of growth. On the other hand, some birds which are well known as insectivores, such as titmice and woodpeckers, have a surprising amount of vegetable food in the diet. The term insectivore is in many ways inappropriate, for most such birds also eat invertebrate animals other than insects, including spiders, crustaceans, molluscs and worms. A swallow feeding on flies is unlikely to pass the opportunity of snapping up spiders floating in the air on their threads of gossamer.

The insect-eating birds collect their food in a number of ways, which is reflected in the shapes of their bills. The titmice and warblers have short, slender bills, used like tweezers for picking small insects off leaves and twigs; vireos and shrikes have stouter bills, hooked at the tip, for dealing with larger insects, but bee-eaters and jacamars have long, slender bills for the same purpose. The swifts and swallows have a short bill with a wide base so that the mouth opens into a broad gape, strengthened by expanded bones in the palate, for scooping up flying insects. A similar bill is seen in the unrelated wood-swallows of Australia and Asia. These are passerine birds that hawk insects in flight and look remarkably like stockily built

*Earthworms provide a very good meal for a song thrush when they come to the surface. A rapid stab with the bill – too fast for the camera to freeze – catches the worm before it can retreat. Then it is repeatedly pecked and squeezed to subdue it. At intervals the thrush drops the worm and looks around for predators.*

swallows, an example of convergent evolution. The nightjars and their relatives, the potoos and owlet frogmouths, have an even wider gape for catching night-flying insects. Woodpeckers and woodcreepers have strong, chiselling bills for exposing insects in wood. Plovers, towhees, chats, gamebirds, thrashers and others pluck insects from the soil with short bills; longer-billed shorebirds probe for insects lying underground as do starlings and meadowlarks, which push the tip of the bill into the earth, then force it open and peer down the hole.

Insects have adopted many stratagems to avoid being eaten. Camouflage is a common insect defense, but many species have adopted the opposite tactic and are brightly colored to advertise the fact that they are dangerous or unpleasant tasting. While both camouflage and warning coloration have evolved because they increase the survival of individual insects, neither defense is perfect. Moths matching a tree trunk or caterpillars imitating twigs stand a good chance of passing undetected, unless they become so populous that the chance of a bird stumbling across one by accident is increased. Once the bird learns their identity, it has a search image for them, and the insects' protective camouflage is useless. Looking like a twig or leaf is then no advantage because the bird will start pecking at twigs and leaves in the hope that they are camouflaged insects, and it continues doing so for as long as a sufficient number prove, in fact, to be disguised insects. When the proportion of insects drops and the bird finds itself pecking too many inedible objects, it loses interest: the search image wanes and a new prey is sought.

Birds that prey on small animals are likely to meet some that are armed with powerful jaws or pincers, irritating hairs, venomous bites or stings, or contain poisonous chemicals within their bodies. A repellent poison in the tissues can save an individual

insect, and it has the additional advantage that the bird will avoid similar insects in future. Chickadees remember distasteful insects as much as a year after the encounter. Sometimes there is an instinctive tendency to leave insects with warning coloration alone; young reed warblers avoid wasps, presumably recognizing their bold black-and-yellow stripes.

However, this defense is not absolute, and many birds have been recorded as occasionally feeding on bees and wasps, perhaps after learning how to deal with them. The honey buzzard eats grubs and adult wasps, while some shrikes and the bee-eaters specialize in eating stinging insects. The honey buzzard seems to be little troubled by the attentions of angry wasps as it tears open a nest to get at the grubs, and it is probably protected by its stiff, close-fitting plumage. The plumage of smaller birds is less of a defense, and bee-eaters and shrikes handle their prey carefully, rubbing them firmly against the perch to squeeze out the venom. Bee-eaters' recognition of insects is so precise that they treat stingless males with less respect than the stinging workers.

In North America, monarch butterfly caterpillars feed on milkweed, which has cardenolide heart poison in the leaves. The caterpillars store the poison in their bodies, and it is retained when they are transformed into adult butterflies. The adults migrate to spend the winter in a few sites in Mexico, where millions of butterflies cover the trees to make a magnificently colorful spectacle. The resting butterflies are protected by their poison from most insect-eating birds, but two species of birds are undeterred. Audubon's oriole treats the monarch butterflies with care and eats only parts of the body containing small amounts of poison. It is sick if it ingests too much, whereas the black-headed grosbeak eats the butterflies indiscriminately. How it is immune to the cardenolides is still unknown.

Large and heavily armored insects have some immunity from attack because small birds find them difficult to handle. This cuts down the rate at which they can be caught, and the birds may choose to leave them alone if there is easier prey. While in general it is more profitable to hunt larger prey, there is a limit beyond which the bird wastes time processing it. Large insects need to be subdued by repeated pecking or thumping against the perch, continuing, if necessary, until the body is pulped and easy to swallow. Similarly, removing the stings of bees and wasps, or the long legs of grasshoppers and crickets, slows the rate of feeding. This situation may change when there are nestlings to feed and large "packages" of food are more economical for carrying back to the nest. At this time chickadees select large caterpillars for their brood, but while searching for them they quickly snap up small ones for their own sustenance.

Snails are protected by their shells and, like difficult insects, even small snails derive some protection from being hard to handle. In Europe, the song thrush deals with medium-sized to large snails by smashing the shell on an "anvil" – a convenient stone or a concrete path. One snail provides a large meal but the preparation takes time and energy, so song thrushes switch to eating snails only when other food is hard to find.

INSECTS ON THE WING

The majority of insects are caught while they are settled, but specialist birds catch insects on the wing. They take advantage not only of the large, actively flying insects – butterflies, bees, dragonflies, hoverflies and the like – but also of the myriad small insects such as thrips, aphids and small flies which float through the atmosphere, more or less passively, as "aerial plankton". The aerial plankton is exploited by the fast-flying and maneuverable swifts and swallows. These birds are most abundant in the tropics, where flying insects are available all year, but some migrate to temperate regions to rear their families on the summer crop of insects. Although superficially similar, the swallows (including the martins) are passerines, while swifts are classes in the order Apodiformes with the hummingbirds. Both have the curved, slender wings typical of fast fliers, and some species in each group have forked tails for

*A pied flycatcher with insect larvae for its chicks. Although better known for its habit of flying out to catch insects on the wing, it also hovers to pluck them from leaves.*

*Center: the European robin eats a variety of insects. These are mainly picked up from the ground or plucked from vegetation, but here it is jumping to catch a fly which it has disturbed.*

*When dry weather makes other small animals hard to find, song thrushes switch to eating snails. Only then is it worth the time and effort of smashing the shell on a stone to extract the flesh.*

*A streaked spiderhunter at banana flowers. This is a species of sunbird which mainly eats insects and spiders found in flowers but also takes some nectar. It is thought that the true nectar-drinking birds evolved from insect eaters in this way.*

extra maneuverability. The swifts are more adapted for an aerial existence, gathering nest material and even mating in flight. Their method of feeding is to speed through the air with bursts of flickering wingbeats interspersed with glides, often at a considerable height, while swallows are slower but more maneuverable, following an erratic track with frequent wingbeats, and opening and closing of the forked tail, closer to the ground.

The flight of the two types affects their feeding strategies and breeding habits. The swallow's flapping flight uses up more energy but its rewards are greater, as the bird can twist and turn after large insects. The swift's rapid glides are economical in terms of energy used but it catches mostly small, weakly flying insects, so its feeding efficiency (as measured by comparing energy gained from food to energy expended in gathering it) is only a little over one-quarter of the swallow's. It is not surprising that barn swallows arrive in Europe over a month before common swifts, when insects are still scarce. They lay larger clutches of eggs and often lay a second clutch, which the swift never does. By way of compensation for inefficient feeding, swifts can cope with a spell of heavy rain or low temperature which removes their food supply. Adults abandon their nests temporarily and flocks stream spectacularly in search of better conditions. In Sweden, 27,000 swifts once passed the island of Öland in one day. In the northern hemisphere the wind in a depression spirals counter-clockwise so, by heading into the wind as it approaches, swifts pass around its rainy southern edge and quickly enter the dry zone behind it. Meanwhile, their nestlings become torpid and drop their body temperatures to conserve energy until their parents return. The swallows continue to hunt in the rain, finding insects under trees and very close to the ground where some remain active.

By night, these insect eaters are replaced by the nightjars and, to some extent, the owls. Nightjars feed mainly by pursuing insects with a swallow-like, erratic flight. Their usual food is large insects such as moths, beetles and craneflies, which are easy to pick out in dim light, especially when they are silhouetted against the sky, but smaller flying insects are also taken.

Some nightjars also hunt, flycatcher-fashion, from a perch. The fiery-necked nightjar of southern Africa, the pauraque of Texas and Mexico, and the related potoos of Central America are examples. Terrestrial insects and other small animals are also seized on the ground by many nightjars, including the European nightjar, and the frogmouths feed almost exclusively in this manner. Unlike other nightjars, they fly only weakly and have a large hooked bill.

At one time it was thought that nightjars caught insects almost at random by flying around with their large mouths opened wide. Hunting by chance would be very wasteful of time and energy, and it is now known that nightjars pursue individuals which they have spotted and snap them up. The rictal bristles, which are modified feathers surrounding the mouth, have been supposed to aid feeding. They are a feature

*Black drongos catching insects flushed from their hiding places by a bush fire. Many kinds of birds, including kites, storks and swallows, are attracted to fires because they disturb prey which can easily be caught.*

Large insects can be difficult to swallow. This lilac-breasted roller is crushing a grasshopper to make it an easier mouthful.

A blue-throated bee-eater with a dragonfly which it has caught in flight and carried back to a perch to kill and dismember.

A pair of tawny frogmouths (far left) demonstrate their incredible camouflage as they roost during the day. At night, they hunt from perches and drop to the ground to seize insects and other small animals, up to the size of mice.

*Many kingfishers hunt for insects rather than fish. This buff-breasted paradise kingfisher has a praying mantis in its bill.*

of many insect-catching birds, including swallows, flycatchers and some, but not all, nightjars. Other suggestions are that the bristles are sensitive to touch and somehow help detect prey or, most likely, that they are merely a guard to protect the eyes.

### KINGFISHERS AND WOODPECKERS

Despite their name, the majority of the eighty-seven species of kingfishers do not catch fish. They hunt for insects and other small animals over land, and the shoe-billed kingfisher of New Guinea digs for earthworms. Those that do catch fish mainly hunt over freshwater, but the pied kingfisher of Africa and Asia and white-collared kingfisher of Asia hunt over the sea, as will the European kingfisher, especially when fresh waters are frozen in winter.

Their hunting technique is approximately the same over land or water. The kingfisher watches from a perch and flies down to seize its victim before returning to the perch. The prey is then beaten into submission and pulped for ease of swallowing. Some species, including the pied kingfisher, the belted kingfisher of North America and occasionally the European kingfisher, also hover over water like terns.

Insects hidden under the bark of branches and trunks are sought out by the creepers and woodcreepers which probe crevices or pry off the scales of bark, but the woodpeckers use their stout

*Shrikes are like miniature falcons with sharp, hooked bills. They hold their prey in their feet while they tear at it. This fiscal shrike is about to feed on a bush cricket.*

bills for chiseling deep into the wood to uncover insect grubs. The skull of a woodpecker is strengthened, and the brain cradled and cushioned to withstand the repeated shocks of hammering into wood. The long tongue is supported on a Y-shaped bone which, when retracted, runs from the back of the mouth, behind and over the top of the skull to the base of the bill or even into the upper mandible. The tongue is extended by the bone being thrust forwards through muscular contraction. The tip of the tongue is provided with a covering of sticky mucus and often has fleshy barbs for picking up insects. It is mobile enough for great spotted woodpeckers to rob nests of birds in cavities or nestboxes; after drilling a hole in the side, the tongue is used to maneuver the eggs or chicks within range of the bill. The green woodpecker and the piculets raid ants' nests by wiping up the swarming inhabitants with their tongues.

Some North American woodpeckers have turned to a partially vegetarian diet, such as the flickers which eat seeds and fruit, in addition to ants and other insects, and attack avocado and orange crops in California. The acorn woodpecker and red-headed woodpecker eat acorns, and the sapsuckers drill rows of holes into the soft phloem layer under the bark of trees to feed on the oozing sap, also taking the insects that are attracted there.

*The red-billed scythebill of South America is a woodcreeper which uses its long, curved bill to probe for insects. Like other birds which forage on tree trunks, it uses the stiffened tail as a prop.*

*A yellow-bellied sapsucker at a hole in a tree, which it has drilled to collect sap. This sugary liquid is a useful source of energy in winter and a mixture of sap and insects are fed to the young.*

# WATERBIRDS

The distinction between seabirds and freshwater birds is rather arbitrary since several groups of birds are to be found in both fresh and seawater. Loons and grebes nest by freshwater and move to the sea after the breeding season, while terns, gulls and cormorants, which are generally considered as seabirds, often live in freshwater, and herons fish along the seashore.

The ducks as a group find their home in salt or freshwater, and on land, and have a wide variety of feeding habits and diets. Most species are mainly vegetarian, but others specialize in catching invertebrates or fish. It is often possible to see several species feeding on one stretch of water but there is little competition between them because they are subsisting on rather different diets.

The "dabbling", or "surface-feeding", ducks are largely omnivorous. Their bills are lined with three sets of horny or rubbery comb-like plates, known as lamellae, one along the inner side of the edge of the upper mandible and one on each side of the edge of the lower mandible. Water is pumped in and out of the mouth, and food is retained by the lamellae.

The size of the gap between the lamellae varies and is related to the size of food taken. Shoveler and teal have close-packed lamellae and feed on the tiny seeds of rushes and plantains, and the smaller freshwater crustaceans. Mallard and pintail, with more widely spaced lamellae, take a wider variety of seeds and animals.

The "diving" ducks may feed at the surface, but they more frequently dive to search for food. Many of these species, such as the oldsquaws, the scoters and eiders spend the greater part of their lives at sea. They feed on a variety of molluscs, crustaceans and echinoderms, and slow-moving fish which are pulled off rocks or grubbed from the sand. The "sawbills", including smew, red-breasted and common mergansers, have bills with serrated edges enabling them to catch active fish and crustaceans. They put their heads below the surface to look for prey and then dive after it. It is not unusual for a flock to

*Shelduck sift their food from shallow water or mud. Water can be seen flowing from the side of the bill as this immature bird feeds (right). Tracks in the mud (far right) show how a shelduck sweeps its bill from side to side as it walks forward. It had evidently found a good place to feed as it has walked in tight circles.*

*A hammerkop, or hammerheaded stork, swallowing a frog. Prey is usually swallowed headfirst so that it will slip down easily.*

feed together, like cormorants and pelicans, apparently to increase their chances of a catch.

Long-legged, long-necked birds such as herons, storks and ibises feed in shallow water or on land for any small animals they can seize. A few sometimes catch their prey by swimming or diving, but their usual technique is to use stealth. Herons stand stock-still for long periods or wade slowly forwards with a fluid movement that reduces the chance of alerting potential victims. An alternative strategy to stealth is to scare prey into giving away its position. Some herons and storks flick their wings, stab at the surface or dash through the water to disturb small animals. Green-backed herons, snowy egrets and others, stir up hiding animals by raking through the mud with one foot, and some green-backed herons use "bait" to attract prey (p. 58). Another strategy is to shade the water by spreading one or both wings and holding them forward to form a canopy over the head, which either reduces dazzle from the water surface or acts as a lure for fish that like to gather in the shade.

The spoonbills, yellow-billed stork and wood stork feel for their prey, relying on the sensitivity of the bill to touch. The wood stork gropes with an open bill, and the open bills of the other two sweep rapidly from side to side and snap shut on any suitable object that comes between the mandibles. The similarly long-legged, long-necked flamingos live in shallow lakes and lagoons rich in animal or plant life, but feed on much smaller items, some of microscopic size, which they filter from the water with their strangely shaped bills. They wade or swim slowly forwards with their heads down and their bills held upside-down in the water, sweeping from side to side. The tongue works to and fro like a piston, alternately drawing water in and forcing it out through the sides of the bill. These are lined with two sets of bristly lamellae, which act as filters for straining out small organisms.

The three smaller flamingos – the Andean, James' and lesser flamingos – have fine lamellae which collect diatoms, minute algae and other such items. The greater flamingo has coarser lamellae; it feeds on small snails and crustaceans, as well as finer organisms, plunging its bill into the bottom mud. The difference between the two diets allows the greater and lesser flamingos to feed together in East Africa.

*A black heron spreads its wings over its head to make a sunshade. This cuts out the glare on the surface making it easier to spot prey. It may also attract some kinds of fish. Once the heron has scanned the water in front of it, it snaps the wings shut, takes a few paces forwards and repeats the exercise.*

## SEABIRDS

The oceans cover 70% of the Earth's surface and are the home of nearly 300 species of birds, from the albatrosses and penguins which spend their whole lives at sea – except when breeding – to the osprey and certain herons which sometimes hunt in coastal waters. Occasional marine feeders include some of the South American ovenbirds and the South Georgia pipit, which sometimes search for crustaceans on floating masses of kelp.

The sea can produce as much food as the land when conditions are right, but the fertility of the sea is very patchy. The production of phytoplankton – microscopic floating plants – depends on the level of nutrients in the water, and is greatest where the nutrients are brought up to the surface from the seabed by upwellings. High productivity is consequently found where currents meet and mix, where they swirl around headlands and islands or rise over shallow banks. This is where concentrations of seabirds are to be found. Elsewhere, the nutrients sink from the surface water, phytoplankton production is low and seabirds are scarce.

Seabirds exploit the ocean from the surface to the bed in shallow waters, and to depths of 330 feet (100 meters) or more in open water. Yet none are vegetarian, the phytoplankton and seaweeds being left to other animals. All forms of marine animal life are eaten, however, and the available food is divided among the seabirds by virtue of their different feeding habits. Within the range of seabird species, there are four major categories of foraging behavior: picking food from the water while in flight, catching food while swimming on the surface, plunging to catch prey underwater and pursuing prey by swimming underwater. Each requires physical and behavioral specializations, but many birds are adaptable enough to feed in more than one way. Birds which feed while flying are least adapted for an aquatic existence but are, nevertheless, superbly adapted for extracting food from one medium, while traveling in another. The frigatebirds are among the most aerobatically skilled of all birds, and they use their precision flying to lift prey from the surface of the sea or to catch flying fish. They rarely come to rest on the water and when they do they may have difficulty taking off because their plumage is easily waterlogged.

The skimmers have a totally different approach to catching prey at the surface. They rely on touch rather than eyesight and fish by flying with the lower half of the bill plowing through the water. This lower mandible is elongated for the purpose. As soon as it touches an object, the bill snaps shut and is lifted clear of the water. Skimmers can feed only in calm water and they are restricted to inshore waters, lagoons and rivers, but they can feed at twilight or at night when most other birds have to stop feeding and when many more fish are near the surface.

*A flock of African skimmers feeding at dusk, demonstrate precision flying as their lower mandibles plow through the water. They are relying on touch to find their prey.*

Other birds which pick up food while airborne include some of the terns, such as the noddies and white terns, some of the gulls and some of the storm-petrels. They hover or fly slowly forwards into the wind, and storm-petrels, like Wilson's storm-petrel, maintain an even height above the water by pattering over the surface on their long, spindly legs. In this habit lies the origin of the name "petrel", an allusion to St Peter walking on the water.

The second group of seabirds settles on the surface to feed, and prey such as crustaceans, squid, fish or carrion are seized singly. This group includes the albatrosses and gulls which will also tip up, or plunge underwater. Petrels, such as fulmars and cape petrels, peck rapidly at the surface like chickens but other petrels, the prions, filter small animals from the water. These birds were once called whalebirds because they fed in much the same way as the baleen whales that inhabit the same Antarctic seas. While some species of prion with narrow bills seize prey by quick grabs, the broad-billed and dove prions have transverse plates along the margins of the upper mandible and "hydroplane" – paddling forward with the wings outstretched and the open bill thrust underwater. Water flows through the bill, and small crustaceans are retained by the plates as they are by the baleen plates of whales. Filtering on a much grander scale is carried out by the pelicans. Contrary to popular myth, their pouches are not for carrying

fish but are used as nets. When a pelican opens its bill underwater, the lower half turns into a large scoop. The horny sides bow out to form a stiff loop and the skin stretches to make a deep bag in which fish are trapped. On surfacing, water is ejected but the prey is retained and swallowed.

The remaining two categories of foraging involve catching prey well below the surface so that the hunting range is effectively increased. The "plungers" dive from a height and use the momentum from their fall through the air to carry them below the surface. These birds have no particular specialization for underwater swimming: their wings are large and their bodies are buoyant. Having plunged as far as their momentum will take them, they sometimes swim after their prey but soon bob back to the surface.

The greatest exponents of plunge-diving are the gannets and boobies. These birds sometimes plunge from 100 feet (30 meters) or more above the water, and 330-foot (100-meter) dives have been estimated for the masked booby, but they are carried only a few yards below the surface. The plunge is a carefully controlled maneuver: the wings, tail and feet are used to keep the flying gannet or booby on target as it plunges towards the fish and at the last moment the wings are swept back to avoid injury as the bird penetrates the water with a spurt of spray. The immense impact of hitting the water is taken on the head, which is protected by air-sacs under the skin

*A flock of dove prions (with some cape petrels) feed along a tide rip. They are swimming forward with their bills open underwater to filter out tiny crustaceans which have been gathered by the swirling currents.*

*Cape petrels feed on crustaceans among the giant kelp that surrounds the shores of South Georgia.*

*After taking a large scoop of water in its extensible bill, a pink-backed pelican carefully lifts it to drain the water out and leave fish behind. Then it tips its head back and swallows them (far right). Like most pelicans, this species is found on both coastal and inland waters.*

*An Arctic tern hovers while looking for small fish or crustaceans swimming near the surface. It plunges into the water to catch them but never pursues its prey underwater.*

and by a strengthened skull. The full force of the impact is reduced by the stout conical bill acting as a cutwater. The nostrils are permanently blocked, as they are in cormorants, and the birds breathe through the corner of the mouth. This must be a useful adaptation for birds which hit the water head first at speeds in the order of 100 mph (60 kph). Similar plunge-diving is used by brown pelicans, tropicbirds, some terns and gulls and sometimes albatrosses, but they do not dive from as high nor plunge as deep as the gannets.

The most highly adapted of the seabirds are those which actively pursue their prey underwater (pp 26–9). They include the penguins, cormorants, alcids, diving petrels, some of the shearwaters, diving ducks, loons and grebes. Most of these species feed on fish, squid and crustaceans, which they chase through the water, but some of the diving ducks, cormorants and alcids forage on the seabed for shellfish and bottom-dwelling fish.

It is not easy to study the details of how such seabirds catch their prey, except when they are feeding close to the shore or a boat and stay near the surface. Some advance has been made recently

through the use of instrument packs strapped to the birds' bodies. Depth gauges attached to chinstrap penguins, which feed on Antarctic krill, showed that they feed near the surface, three-quarters of the dives recorded being shallower than 70 feet (20 meters). The fish- and squid-eating king penguin dives deeper, and half the dives recorded went below 160 feet (50 meters). Calculations from the food brought back to their chicks suggest that only one in ten dives results in the capture of a fish or squid. Compared with a gannet or brown pelican, which prospects from the air and plunges only when it spots a victim, usually capturing it, the penguins must make many speculative dives until they find a shoal to exploit. Another type of recording instrument attached to gray-headed albatrosses has shown that they feed mainly after dark. Indeed many seabirds are thought to be nocturnal because the crustaceans and squid on which they feed come to the surface at night.

These four categories of foraging behavior help to reduce competition between species of seabirds, but there are many finer differences which allow species to live together. On the subantarctic island of South Georgia there are huge numbers of seabirds of

*The great skua (top) is a relative of the gulls and is basically a fish eater but it also becomes a hunter, especially in the summer when young birds are easily caught.*

*Trawlers provide seabirds with easy meals and now that fishing fleets visit the Antarctic, albatrosses (bottom) and cape petrels are attracted to scavenge behind them.*

twenty-five species, breeding in colonies and feeding in the extremely rich seas around the island. The twenty-five species, include penguins, albatrosses, several petrels, a cormorant, a gull, a skua and a tern. Within these groups the competition between related species is alleviated by their diverse feeding habits. Two small penguins, the gentoo and the macaroni, feed in different places: the former remains within 19 miles (30 kilometers) of the colony, while the latter travels farther out to sea.

Nesting in burrows on slopes above the penguin colonies there are two species of diving petrel which are so similar that identification is not easy, even with birds held in the hand. Their nesting times are staggered so that the common diving petrel is rearing its chick, and hence requiring the most food, six weeks before the South Georgia diving petrel. The two also have differences in diet, although both eat several kinds of crustaceans: the common diving petrel catches mainly large shrimp-like krill and the South Georgia diving petrel has a diet predominantly of tiny copepod crustaceans.

Between two of the species of albatross found on South Georgia there are differences in diet which

have a significant effect on their breeding biology. The gray-headed and black-browed albatrosses are almost identical except for the characteristics which give them their names but, when their breeding was investigated, the former was discovered to rear only one chick in alternate years, while the latter reared a chick each year. The difference appeared to lie in the forty-day-longer fledging period of the gray-headed albatross. Further studies showed that gray-headed albatrosses eat mainly squid, with some fish and krill, but the black-browed eat mainly krill, with some fish and squid. Now, squid is deficient in both calcium and calories when compared with fish and krill, so the growth of gray-headed chicks is slowed. By the time they have fledged, the winter decline in food supplies in subantarctic seas has taken place and their parents are unable to regain condition until the following summer, which is too late for nesting. Black-browed albatrosses launch their chicks soon enough to feed well before winter sets in and are in condition to breed again next spring. But in some years the krill swarms disappear and black-browed albatrosses have a disastrous nesting season, while the gray-heads, with their squid diet, are unaffected.

*Giant petrels are seabirds which have become part-time scavengers. As well as catching prey at the surface they gather to feed on carcasses. Some of the Wilson's storm-petrels are showing their habit of pattering over the water.*

*Giant petrels feeding on a dead seal display aggressively at each other (bottom) in an attempt to monopolize the food source.*

# SHOREBIRDS

There are about 135 species of birds which are known in North America as shorebirds and in Britain as waders. Both names recall the principal lifestyle of the group: unlike the distantly related gulls, terns and alcids, these birds rarely swim but are commonly seen on the shoreline of the sea or inland waters. They are running and wading birds, and some have very long legs. The families include the oystercatchers, the avocets and the stilts, but 90% of the species are in two families – the plovers and sandpipers.

Many shorebirds are long-distance migrants and alternate between two very different habitats and food resources each year. Those that migrate to the Arctic regions spend the summer breeding season inland, where they feed on a wealth of insects. Every visitor to the Arctic is familiar with the swarms of biting flies that plague people and birds alike (a bird sitting on its eggs is denied the luxury of using a foot to scratch its head!), yet the greatest mass of insects comes from non-biting chironomid midges and craneflies. The adult flies are mostly caught as they crawl on the ground or while they sit in grass or flowers, and larvae are taken from muddy banks or in the shallows of streams and pools. There is an ordered sequence of change in the diet through the Arctic summer. In Alaska, dunlins feed mainly on cranefly larvae when they first arrive in spring. Later they turn to midge larvae in pools and then back to craneflies, while their chicks, fresh out of the nest, are eating adult midges and so do not compete for food with their parents.

The winter habitats of shorebirds and the places where they stop on migration are mainly shores and estuaries, especially where there are extensive mudflats, and lakesides of temperate and tropical countries. Shorebirds escaping from the Arctic freeze-are joined by birds which had remained in more temperate latitudes to nest. The diet now switches to crustaceans, molluscs and worms.

Feeding on mudflats gives shorebirds access to an extremely rich food supply. A survey of the Ribble estuary in northern England gave the following densities (in numbers per square meter) of potential food for shorebirds: clamworms *Nereis* 596, sandworms *Arenicola* 128, the amphipod crustacean *Corophium* 22,000, shore crabs *Carcinus* 10–12, laver spire snails *Hydrobia* 47,000 and cockles *Cardium* 132. In the fall, when the migrants are passing through, numbers of intertidal invertebrates are at a peak. During the winter many invertebrates die in cold weather, and those that survive are inactive at low temperatures, so it is hard for the birds to find them. As a result, many shorebirds go hungry during a cold spell in late winter. Invertebrate numbers have dropped to their lowest point by the spring, but the survivors have grown in size, so although the birds encounter fewer prey, each one they find makes a larger mouthful and foraging is still economical.

The size and shape of the bill are related to the feeding behavior of shorebirds. Essentially, the sandpipers have long bills and probe into mud or soil, while the plovers with short bills peck at prey on or near the surface. A few species have particular feeding habits. Avocets sweep their upturned bills from side to side in shallow water to catch small animals between their parted mandibles; turnstones and the wrybill plover, with its laterally curving bill, lever stones over to expose animals underneath. The phalaropes feed while swimming and pick up small insects and other aquatic invertebrates on or just below the surface. They have the habit of spinning round in circles while feeding, which seems to be a way of stirring up and concentrating the prey.

The plovers typically have large eyes and find their prey by sight; banded and semipalmated plovers, for instance, forage by a series of fast runs. They start with a visual search of the surroundings, then, spotting a target, race towards it and abruptly halt to seize it. Their prey includes sandhoppers and flies which live on the surface, especially around washed-up seaweed, and the plovers watch for a movement before dashing across to seize a victim. Worms, crustaceans and molluscs are other important prey. These live just beneath the surface but they too are detected by sight either from marks in the mud showing where the animals are buried or from their movements.

The sandpipers sometimes forage by sight, using the same watch-run-peck method of the plovers, but they more often feed by probing. Dunlin and red knot, for instance, feed by "stitching", rapidly probing the ground like the needle of a sewing machine and leaving a line of tiny holes in the mud. Probing allows the birds to feed on animals living in deeper burrows, and the sandpipers have bills provided with large numbers of touch-sensitive Herbst's corpuscles at the tip to feel for prey.

Having located a mollusc or worm deep in its burrow, the sandpiper has to extract it. Small animals can be swallowed without the bill being withdrawn, but larger types need to be pulled out and dealt with at the surface. The long-billed members of the sandpiper family – the curlews, snipe, woodcock, dowitchers and godwits – have relatively strong bills and powerful jaw muscles for thrusting deep into soil, sand or mud. They are aided by the ability to open the tip of the bill while the rest remains closed: movement of bones in the front part of the skull pushes the bone that runs the length of the upper mandible forward, causing the flexible tip to bend upwards. This helps the bird to feel for a deeply buried animal, take hold of it and pull it out without having to force the whole bill open against the resistance of the soil or sand.

Shorebirds feeding on the shore face various problems in the winter. Their food is available only when the tide is out, and the weather can make

All over the world there are birds which specialize in scavenging, from the ivory gulls that feed on the remains of polar bears' kills in the Arctic, to the giant petrels, skuas and sheathbills that feed on dead seals and penguins in the Antarctic.

In addition to the specialists, omnivorous birds, such as crows and gulls, often act as scavengers, and many hunting birds include carrion in their diet from time to time. All predators are "lazy" in that they choose prey which through illness or accident is easy to catch. If the victim is helpless or even dead, so much the better. Many predators use the chance of scavenging to save both energy and the risk of injury, and birds of prey that are persecuted for lamb-killing, or similar crimes, are often only feeding on animals that have succumbed to accident, cold or neglect.

A number of raptors include carrion as a major component of their diets. Kites are especially well known as scavengers and have an important role in clearing up refuse in parts of the world where waste disposal in human settlements is inefficient. In Elizabethan London red kites were protected for their value to public health, although there must have been a strong temptation to flout the law because then, as now, kites were famous for their bold thefts from market stalls, and they even stole bread from the hands of children!

A scavenger makes use of a source of food that is normally scarce and scattered and, with the exception of human activities, only a natural disaster will create an assured supply of carrion. The ability to roam widely and survey a large area for the chance of a meal is therefore a necessary part of a true scavenger's way of life. The vultures are most adept at this. Soaring in

*Common ravens rely on the remains of other animals' kills, especially in winter when the soil is snow-covered.*

thermals enables them to patrol at a high level and cover great distances; the area of ground searched in this manner is increased by the vulture taking note of the behavior of other vultures. If one bird abandons its circling and drops down to a dead animal, it will attract other vultures who could see it only as a speck above the horizon and would have had no chance of spotting the carcass for themselves.

The result is that a dead animal soon becomes the center of a crowd of vultures. On the plains of East Africa, white-headed and lappet-faced vultures usually arrive first because they fly at relatively low altitudes and actively search for food, while white-backed and Rüppell's vultures are high-level soarers that react to the behavior of other vultures or hyenas. The lappet-faced vulture is the most aggressive and can keep others from the carcass, but the spoils are generally portioned by the feeding habits of the six species.

White-backed and Rüppell's vultures rarely feed anywhere except at carcasses. They have long, naked necks which they thrust deep into a carcass, and they

*The lappet-faced vulture (top) is a powerful bird which gets first turn at a carcass. It can drive others away and its bill is strong enough to tear open the body. Rüppell's vultures (bottom) have long, naked necks for rummaging deep inside. Here they are fighting for precedence at the carcass.*

*Ivory gulls remain in the Arctic throughout the long polar winter whereas most other birds migrate southwards. Scavenging on the kills of polar bears helps them to survive.*

*A herd of wildebeeste watches from a distance as vultures and marabou storks gather around the bodies of their dead companions, drowned while crossing a river.*

*Kleptoparasitism is often a feature of opportunist feeders, such as gulls. As soon as this sacred ibis pulled a fish out of the water, a grey-headed gull arrived to see what it could steal or scavenge.*

may even climb inside, to rasp gobbets of soft flesh with tongues that are set with backward-facing spines. The remaining species have feathered necks and also hunt live prey. Lappet-faced and white-headed vultures have powerful bills for twisting and tearing meat from bones, but the two smallest species, the hooded and Egyptian vultures, peck scattered fragments or pick at the scraps left on the bones.

When the vultures have finished with a carcass, only the bones are left, and the lammergeier of southern Europe and Asia is the only bird capable of dealing with them. In the same way that crows and gulls drop molluscs to break their shells, the lammergeier drops bones, and sometimes tortoises, on to rocks to split them open. By using the updrafts at a cliff face, it can lift and drop a bone repeatedly with little expenditure of energy until it succeeds in breaking it.

## PIRATES OF THE AIR

Another alternative to finding and catching prey is to steal it. Robbing another species is called piracy or kleptoparasitism. The habit is rather rare in mammals – lions may drive hyenas from their prey, for instance – but it is widespread among birds. They sometimes rob other kinds of animals, like the hummingbirds which steal insects from spiders' webs, but most cases are of birds robbing other birds. The least aggressive interactions are in those associations which occur when one bird takes advantage of prey which has been flushed by another (p.66), but this can turn to theft, as when the house sparrows which follow American robins switch from picking up fragments they drop to snatching food from the robins' bills.

Kleptoparasitism is sometimes an opportunist form of feeding employed only occasionally or locally. In some parts of the Antarctic, skuas steal from blue-

*Birds of prey sometimes turn to piracy if hunting proves unsuccessful. Here a black kite makes swooping attacks on an egret, hoping to force it to drop the eel that it has just caught.*

eyed cormorants, whereas in other places they ignore them entirely. At one island it is Dominican gulls which rob the cormorants as they bring fish to the surface. The gulls have to carry the large fish to the shore to deal with them, where skuas are waiting to drive them off and get a meal at third hand.

Piracy becomes a regular habit where the victimized species breeds or feeds in a concentrated area and carries large amounts of food. Perfect situations are seabird colonies where birds stream in with food for their young, or where seabirds are feeding on shoals of large fish which they have to bring to the surface before they can be swallowed. Regular piracy is found in the skuas, jaegers and some large gulls. These birds are powerful, often predatory, birds, which harry other gulls, terns, alcids and gannets by relentless chasing until they drop their food in order to get away. Often they will regurgitate

their last meal, a reflex reaction to danger which lightens the body and improves the chances of escaping from a predator. Taking advantage of this, a jaeger will swoop down and eat the lost food.

Habitual piracy is also a feature of the frigatebirds, in the tropics, and the sheathbills in Antarctica. Frigatebirds have evolved spectacular aerobatic skills at the expense of swimming ability, and are better adapted to steal marine food than catch it for themselves, while the sheathbills are probably dependent on penguin colonies for their survival in some places. These white, pigeon-like birds, which are distantly related to the shorebirds, scavenge on corpses and abandoned eggs but also steal food from penguins as they feed their chicks. As the penguin passes food into the bill of its chick, the sheathbill flies up and frightens them and they jerk apart, scattering food for the sheathbill to pick up.

# CHAPTER 6
# COMMUNICATION

One of the attractions of birds is that they are conspicuous, noisy and easy to observe, and these features also make them rewarding subjects for the study of animal communication. Birds communicate by means of visual signals and vocalizations (songs and calls), as befits animals with well developed senses of vision and hearing. Since these are also the dominant human senses, birds are particularly simple to study, compared with mammals, for whom scent is all-important.

Communication involves a signal passing between two individuals. The meaning of the signal depends to some extent on the context in which it is given, so that the same signal can convey different messages depending on the motivation of both sender and receiver. Bird song, for instance, may signal two messages, depending on the listener: rival males are warned to keep away, but unmated females are invited to approach. In some species, song also brings females into breeding condition after the pair has formed. To observe a bird singing in only one of these situations would lead to an incomplete interpretation of the function of song.

The "language" of birds, in the form of calls, songs and visual displays, is not like a human language. Rather than a series of words ordered by rules of grammar to give specific meanings, birds have a language of intentions and of emotions, like our crying, laughing and interjection. They tell what the bird will do next and convey messages of aggression, warning or willingness to mate. The messages may be simple but the communication system is often extremely sophisticated, more so than immediately seems to be necessary, with the development of large repertoires of songs or intricate displays supported by spectacular plumages.

## VISUAL COMMUNICATION

The movement of a flock of dunlins or starlings is a marvel of coordinated precision-flying that surpasses the spectacle of a drill-team display. The birds take off, wheel and alight, apparently without a leader or any sort of command, yet collisions are extremely rare. The secret is that each bird is watching other birds in the flock, and from their slightest movements it anticipates their actions, so that a maneuver spreads through the whole flock in a smooth wave, taking only a fraction of a second. When the flock changes direction, birds watch those ahead of them and time their reactions to create a wave of movement. It is too rapid for the human eye to catch what is happening but it is possible to see what occurs when a small flock of starlings takes to the air. As each bird prepares to take off, it crouches slightly, then leaps into the air and flies away. The crouching action that precedes

*The maguari stork accentuates its display by fluffing out the feathers of its neck and breast.*

take-off is known as an 'intention movement", and by watching these 'intention movements" of flight all the members of the flock are brought into a state of readiness.

Woodpigeons use similar intention movements in a different way. Provided that each pigeon makes the intention movements before taking off, the others ignore it, but if one spots danger and does an emergency take-off, the others interpret the absence of intention movements as an alarm signal and the whole flock rises into the air. Another simple signal is the attitude of alertness that conveys a warning among flocks of geese. They are quick to notice one of their number standing with its neck stretched after spotting a possible danger.

In these examples, the birds are reacting to the behavior of others but the behavior is not primarily a signal. More specific forms of communication have evolved through such behavior patterns being modified into deliberate signals. These signals are called displays, and they are common to all members of a species, forming a kind of sign language which conveys the mood of the bird. The most common displays are those concerned with conflict and courtship. Displays are used, often in conjunction with calls or songs, to advertise a territory, repel a rival, attract a mate and, in some birds, to reinforce the bond between the mated pair.

As with song, it is rare for a display to have a simple, unequivocal meaning. The display of the European robin, in which it shows off its red breast to a rival by a tilting back of the head, is the result of conflicting emotions and its actual message depends on the context. In hostile encounters, a bird is not being wholly aggressive: in facing up to a rival, it runs the danger of being attacked and defeated, so there is an element of fear expressed in the display. Displays which express a mixture of aggression or threat and fear or avoidance are called "agonistic".

A common threatening display of gulls is the "upright", in which the bird approaches another with its neck stretched and bill angled downward, and the wings held out slightly from the body. The angle of the bill is an intention of attack and the wings are like raised fists – ready to strike. The upright display shows that the gull is in a hostile frame of mind but that it is not aggressive enough to actually fight. The situation may not be serious enough for a physical dispute or the bird's aggression may be held in check by fear of its opponent – it is difficult to separate the two in practice. The balance between them is affected by circumstances. When gulls are feeding on carrion, a dominant bird can stride boldly forward, in the upright display, and "elbow" others aside to get at the food. Another gull which would normally be submissive may be driven by starvation to behave aggressively and risk a fight. After the urge to assuage their hunger has abated, each will become less aggressive and be displaced by birds more hungry than itself.

Such displays reduce the chances of actual fighting by signaling the bird's motivation, and they are especially valuable in social species where contact between individuals is frequent, or if the birds are well-equipped to fight. Among the lovebirds, the more solitary species fight only rarely but are very violent

*This display may be used to drive away rivals or attract a mate. Here it constitutes a greeting between a pair of storks, when one lands near its mate. The male, on the left, raises his wings and displays more vigorously than the female.*

when they do so, whereas the social species, such as the peach-faced lovebird, have replaced fighting with harmless bill-fencing. In another group of parrots, the lorikeets, there is a gradation in the size of body and bill and this is accompanied by a parallel range of social behavior. The smaller-billed lorikeets can only pinch the skin of an incautious human hand, while the larger ones easily draw blood and even splinter wood. The latter have the potential to do each other serious harm in a hostile encounter, but they are effectively prevented from doing so by possessing a greater variety of agonistic displays for settling disputes.

The threat of violence in a particular encounter could of course be simply avoided by one bird fleeing and putting an end to the dispute, but if birds have to live together, this becomes impractical and time-wasting. So a lack of aggression is signaled by displays which inhibit or reduce aggression on the part of the other bird. These displays often involve actions which are the opposite of hostile displays. The plumage is sleeked down, the head is withdrawn and the bill – the main weapon – is averted. Some gulls have a "facing away" display in which the bird turns its head and the offensive bill is hidden from the other bird. This has three possible functions: it can appease the other bird's hostility, or allay its fear, or it could decrease the displayer's own tendencies to attack or flee by removing the stimulus from its line of vision. In courtship, the sexual drive has to overcome the aggression or fear that result from two birds coming close to each other. Consequently, courtship displays often show elements of attack and flight behavior which have become transformed into stereotyped signals, and now help to bring the partners together.

Displays consist of a set of movements, which, although they may seem very different from the bird's ordinary behavior, have their origin in a number of simple types of movement involved in locomotion, feeding or nesting. Intention movements have been one major source of the actions used and other sources are displacement activities and redirected behavior. These are types of activity which take place when there is a conflict of motivation as, for instance, when we scratch our heads in perplexity. The action of scratching the head is for comfort, and is clearly irrelevant to the problem facing us, but it gives an outlet for the frustration we experience. During equally contested disputes between domestic poultry, the participants may break off and eat or drink, or merely go through the motions of eating and drinking. This is a displacement activity whereas redirected behavior is seen, for example, when a gull in a prolonged, inconclusive boundary dispute with a neighbor turns aggressively on its own mate.

During the course of evolution, actions such as these have become "ritualized" into specific signals. Even without ritualization, these actions convey information: a bird can gauge another's motivation and predict its next move by watching its intention movements, displacement activities or redirected behavior. With ritualization, however, the original

When sulfur-crested cockatoos display, the raised crest is made more conspicuous by bobbing and swinging the head. These actions are used by the male in courtship but flocks of cockatoos often display together. Here a lone male gives an unusual upside-down display.

Two common grackles in dispute stand side-by-side, or facing up to each other, with bills raised. Rituals like this take the place of fighting, thereby saving time, energy and possible injury.

action is exaggerated, simplified or repeated, to enhance its communication function. For example, the male grey heron has a "stretch display" in which it points its bill vertically and sleeks its feathers. This is an exaggeration of an intention movement to take off that has become a signal that the heron is rather frightened of a more aggressive male and is about to retreat. Simplification of movement is also seen in the courtship of some cage-birds in the finch family. Many birds wipe their bills on the perch after feeding, but the zebra finch also does so as a displacement activity during courtship because there is a conflict between sexual attraction and the hostility evoked by another bird coming too close. In the related striated finch and spice finch, the bill-wiping action of courtship has become simplified into a ritualized "bow" which is held for a few seconds. Not only has the form of the action changed but the basic motivation and function of bill-wiping have shifted from feeding to courtship.

The signaling effect of displays may be further enhanced by crests or long plumes, patches or flashes of colored plumage, or areas of bare skin. Signals can be switched on and off by exposing a colored flash, by spreading wings and tail, raising a crest, or inflating a pouch, like the balloon under the chin of the male frigatebird. Some male ducks have a patch of color on the wing, known as the speculum, which is probably a specific recognition mark that is shown

*A great frigatebird displays by inflating his throat pouch into a scarlet balloon. At the height of the display he flaps his wings and rattles his bill against the pouch. The female, on the right, lacks the red throat.*

*The only difference in the plumage of male and female yellow-shafted flicker is the black "moustache" of the male (left). If a moustache is painted on a female she is treated as a male. The gilded flicker (below) has a red moustache, but this is not a sufficient difference to prevent interbreeding. Hybrids may have a black moustache on one side and a red one on the other.*

*Displays may be used to warn another bird not to approach too close, as with the threatening raising of the bill by this spot-billed pelican.*

while in flight. The speculum may also be used to make displays more conspicuous. A number of species have incorporated preening into their courtship displays and some, such as the mallard, make ritualized preening movements behind the wing, which is lifted to show off the speculum. The mandarin's display is highly ritualized and it does no more than touch the secondary feathers which are raised permanently, like sails.

The function of these signal-enhancers has been studied by artificially altering them. Female chaffinches with their breast feathers dyed pink like a male usually become dominant over other females and occasionally hold their own against males. The pink breast clearly highlights threatening displays. The male red-winged blackbird's red epaulets similarly enhance displays used in defending territory. If they are blacked out with dye, the male is likely to lose his territory, although his ability to attract and retain a mate is not directly affected by his changed appearance.

### SEXUAL SELECTION

In other species the male's plumage does serve to attract females and, as the female makes the choice of mate, there is competition between rival males for her attention. If the female chooses her mate on the basis of certain features of the male's plumage, possessing these features will be an advantage and in time they will become more and more exaggerated (unless

*Like many tropical, fruit-eating birds, touracos can devote a great deal of time to courtship. Almost all touracos have a pointed crest, which is raised during displays, and may help the birds recognize members of their own species. The crest is seen in both male and female birds.*

*Both sexes of the Victoria crowned pigeon possess a fine lacy crest but only the male performs the "bowing" display, used mainly in courtship, in which the crest is shown off.*

*A male crested wood partridge shows its elaborate head decoration of plumage and colored skin. As with other members of the pheasant family, the female is drably colored. She alone incubates the eggs and since the nest is on the ground she has need of good camouflage, unlike her mate.*

*Many parrots can raise the feathers of head and neck but the trait is best developed in the red fan parrot (left). This is a generalized display, used both in courtship and aggressive encounters.*

*The sky-pointing display of the blue-footed booby is used in courtship, to attract a mate and to maintain the pair bond. It has distinct similarities to the sky-pointing of the closely related northern gannet, shown on p.123, but both the form and meaning are slightly different.*

some other form of selection, such as predation, keeps them in check). This is known as sexual selection and it differs from the normal process of natural selection because it operates solely on the individual male's ability to sire offspring rather than his own chances of survival. Species where a gaudy male far outshines a dowdy female are examples of what has been called "evolution run riot" because the bright colors and bizarre plumes appear far more elaborate than necessary. Examples include the birds of paradise, lyrebirds, cotingas and pheasants.

The process of sexual selection has been demonstrated in the long-tailed widowbird. The male of this African species is black with red flashes on his wings and a tail of loose plumes, twice the length of the body. He displays by flying low over open grassland with his tail dangling below. In an experiment, the tail feathers were cut off one group of widowbirds and glued to the tails of another group. Those with extra long tails proceeded to attract twice as many females into their territories.

A male with more elaborate plumage will be a greater attraction for the females, and will father more offspring, but why the female should benefit by mating with a pretty, but otherwise apparently ordinary, male is not obvious. The reason is that her male offspring will be similarly attractive, so her genes will prosper through them. This does not explain why bright plumage or a long tail should be attractive in the first place. Neither are assets in themselves, and

*Female blue-footed boobies dispute ownership of territory while a male stands by. They point aggressively with their bills and nod their heads vigorously up-and-down as a threat. The nodding display is probably derived from nest-building actions.*

indeed can be a positive liability as the former will attract predators and the latter hinder escape. One possibility is that the trend starts through enhancing communication between males, as in the red-winged blackbird, and that, once females start to favor well-endowed males, their special eye-catching characteristics will be an asset simply because they improve a male's success at mating and hence his chances of fatherhood.

## VOCAL COMMUNICATION

In few other groups of animals has the production of sound reached such a peak of variety and technical skill as in the birds. Yet we are only half-aware of the versatility of bird voices, since the complexities of bird song are beyond our ability to resolve. The description of bird sounds and the interpretation of their meaning has been assisted by the invention of the sound spectrograph, first developed in the 1940s. This apparatus translates sounds into movements of a pen and reproduces the exact form of the song as a "sonagram", a graph which relates the pitch of the sounds to a time scale. The sonagram is a picture of a sound and it can be used to analyze the physical form of a song and compare songs of different individuals and species.

Vocal communication in birds is divided rather arbitrarily into calls and songs. Calls are simple notes, often not musical, and they are produced by both sexes at any time of the year. Song may be defined by its function of advertising the ownership of a territory.

*The extravagant plumes of the superb lyrebird have evolved by the process known as sexual selection. Its display takes place on a mound cleared of leaves and is accompanied by an equally elaborate song that includes many mimicked sounds. Both display and song are advertisements to rival males and prospective mates.*

*Male black grouse gather in spring at traditional leks, where they call and display, to advertise the ownership of territory and attract females for mating. Like other lekking species, black grouse show the effects of sexual selection very markedly, and the male's elaborate plumage contrasts sharply with that of the dull brown female.*

It is usually, but not necessarily, elaborate and musical. The harsh repeated calls of a herring gull – its "long call" – or the monotonous metallic notes of several tropical birds (called "brain fever birds" because of the maddening regularity of their call throughout the heat of the day) have a similar function to the melodious outpourings of a warbler, even though they would touch the imagination of only the gloomiest poet.

The messages contained in bird sounds are not always easy to construe. The herring gull, for example, is said to give a "food-finding call". This is based on the observation that a gull calls when it joins a group that is already feeding and more gulls arrive in response to the call. In view of their aggressively selfish behavior when feeding, it seems odd that one gull should invite others to join its meal. An alternative suggestion proposes that the call is a cry of fear that perhaps makes competing gulls pause and look for danger long enough for the food to be swallowed or carried away. The fact that gulls do not call when feeding alone tends to confirm this, but the notion would be very difficult to substantiate. Deciding which explanation, if either, is likely to be right, would depend on laborious observation of the call in different situations.

The sounds of birds are produced by a different mechanism from the human voice, which emanates from the larynx at the junction of the throat and trachea, or windpipe. Birds have a larynx but this is concerned with the regulation of airflow in breathing. The voice comes from the syrinx at the junction of the bottom end of the trachea and the two bronchi. Sound is produced either by air rushing over membranes which are set in vibration, or by vortices forming in the airflow, but the exact mechanism is not known.

The essential differences between the voices of men and birds are that the avian syrinx has two separate sources of sound, one in each bronchus, and that the tongue and mouth are not used to modify sounds. The control and variety of birds' utterances depend on muscular control of the syrinx mechanism. This is more complex in a group of over forty families of passerines called the oscines, better known as the

*Black-headed and mew gulls gathering to feed. The sight of one gull landing when it has found food acts as a signal to others and their calls attract even more birds to the scene, but why gulls should give a "food-finding call" remains a mystery.*

*The "long call" of the black-headed gull is a long-distance threat. The gull's aggressive intent is also shown by the slightly raised wings.*

*The limpkin, a relative of the cranes, is renowned for its eerie, wailing calls. It has been called the "mourning widow" or "crying bird" because the calls sound so sad, and one legend is that they are made by "small boys lost forever in the swamps".*

songbirds. Sound production reaches its peak in species such as the reed warbler and brown thrasher which sing two tunes at once with different notes coming from each half of the syrinx at exactly the same instant. At one point in its song, the brown thrasher actually utters four different sounds at once, but it is not known how this feat is achieved. And there is a similar mystery with the Gouldian finch, also called the rainbow finch from its gaudily colored plumage, which maintains a bagpipe-like drone over two independent songs.

Sounds can also be modified in the trachea or airsacs to make deep, resonating sounds. The whooping crane, trumpeter swan and the trumpeter manucode (an Australian bird of paradise) produce trombone-like calls in long, coiled tracheae, and an extra loop in the trachea of the male plains chachalaca gives it a call one octave lower than the female's. Male prairie chickens inflate yellow pouches, formed from airsacs, in the neck as part of their courtship display, and use them as resonators to generate loud "popping" calls.

Vocal music is supplemented or replaced by "instrumental music" in some birds. The drumming, or tattooing, of woodpeckers is made by rapping a branch or trunk with the bill at a very rapid rate. The great spotted woodpecker drums at about twenty times a second to make a hollow rattling. Snapping the mandibles together produces the "clappering" of storks and the hollow click that the wandering albatross uses in courtship. The display of the wood-pigeon includes a loud "slap" which is produced by clapping the wings on the top of the upstroke and elaborate wing noise is a feature of the "drumming" of ruffed grouse. The male stands on a log, leaning back and bracing himself with his tail, then cups his wings, beating them forwards and upwards to strike the air and give a "thumping" sound. As the tempo of wingbeats increases, the thumping changes into a drum roll which can be heard at over 500 yards (450 meters). Common snipe produce a "drumming" or "bleating" with two stiffened tail feathers. As the bird dives, these are swung out and the wingbeats "chop" the airstream, eleven times a second, so that it hits the

*A pair of black-necked storks greet each other at the nest. Their display is accompanied by various vocal calls and the sound of their bills being repeatedly snapped shut. This "clappering" is common to all storks.*

*The greater prairie-chicken is one of the grouse family that courts and mates in leks, known as booming grounds. When not displaying, the male is similar to the female in appearance (right), but in display (below) the neck epaulets and the tail are raised, the wings drooped and the yellow airsacs are inflated. The resonant, popping noise produced by these airsacs sounds like a continuous booming when several males are calling in chorus.*

feathers in short blasts and they vibrate to produce a muffled throbbing, like someone blowing in quick puffs across the mouth of a bottle.

## CALLS

Bird calls are overshadowed by the more attractive songs, but the honking chorus of geese, the nocturnal hooting of owls or the cooing of doves on a hot day can be just as evocative as the melodies of songbirds. Some songbirds have a considerable repertoire of calls, as well as their songs, the chaffinch having fifteen and the song sparrow seventeen basic calls, plus many variations. By contrast, other birds have few calls but each can have several meanings depending on the context in which it is given. An example is the *kitter* call of the eastern kingbird, one of the tyrant-flycatchers. The kingbird is an aggressive species that attacks hawks and even low-flying aircraft. Pairs of kingbirds often squabble between themselves. The *kitter* call is heard when a hawk is being driven away, or when a kingbird is about to give chase. It is also given by a male when patrolling his territory, by both sexes when approaching each other and by fledglings when approaching a parent who may well attack them. These are very different situations on the surface but the underlying motivation seems to be similar in that the kingbirds are showing hesitation and uncertainty. It is the context which gives other kingbirds the appropriate message: warning of an approaching predator, hostility towards a rival male, or appeasing an aggressive mate or parent.

In general, calls are given in three main situations: between members of a flock or mated pairs, when predators are threatening, and during the rearing of the family. These are situations when the behavior of two or more birds has to be coordinated and one bird needs to "tell" others of its intentions or feelings. Because the language and the response are stereotyped there will be a quick and positive reaction from the birds hearing it.

Contact notes which serve to keep birds aware of each other's position are a feature of birds which live in flocks. They are familiar sounds in woods and forests as small parties of songbirds work their way through the foliage, feeding as they go, or when birds gather at a crop of seeds in the open. After an interval of searching in one small area, the flock streams on. In flocks of finches, the movement is started by one bird which begins to call. The others stop feeding and join the calling until they all take off. If one is left behind and lost, it flies up, calling loudly and looking around, until it makes contact with its fellows.

Some of these flocks are made up of several species, and sonagrams show that the calls of each are remarkably similar. The particular form of these calls is short bursts of sound spanning a wide range of frequencies. Both characteristics help to pinpoint the source of the sound. The sharp start and stop of each call make it easier to compare the time of arrival at each ear (p.48) and the range of frequencies make for easy comparison of loudness.

While contact calls are recognizable by all other members of the species and may even cut across species barriers, breeding calls need to be individually recognizable so that mates, or parents and offspring, can keep together. Sonagrams have shown that the contact calls of a pair of American goldfinches

*A ruffed grouse "drums" to advertise his territory. He beats his wings at 20 times per second to produce a muffled thumping sound.*

*A sooty owl, of eastern Australia and New Guinea, clicking its tongue. As with the related barn owl, this sound is used in courtship and to intimidate predators when the bird is threatened.*

are virtually identical but different from those of other pairs. This is achieved by the male learning to imitate the call of his mate during courtship.

Individual recognition is especially valuable for birds such as gannets, gulls, terns and black-legged kittiwakes, which live in crowded colonies where the ground immediately around the nest is fiercely defended. When gannets return to their nests, which are no farther apart than is necessary to keep sitting birds away from each other's bills, they give a landing call to identify themselves to their mates, who become alert and ready to greet them. All the other gannets ignore the returning bird unless it lands in the wrong place. The value of a landing call may be to warn the bird on the nest not to attack its mate as it suddenly drops down beside it.

For Manx shearwaters, recognition calls are used as homing beacons. The males return to the colony first, at the start of the breeding season, and reoccupy the nesting burrows. When the females arrive they call from the air and the males call back from deep underground. Recognition of calls from last year's mate guides each female to the right burrow. The emperor penguin also has to be guided to its mate but in this case there is no nest. The adults shuffle about with their eggs on their feet and continually change position within the colony. When an emperor penguin returns to the colony, it calls with loud brays and its mate comes out of the group to meet it. Similarly, young Sandwich terns wander around the beach and parents returning with fish call as they circle overhead. The chicks recognize their parents and the excited reaction tells the adult which is its offspring.

*When a northern gannet lands at its nest in a colony (far right) it calls to identify itself to its mate who recognizes its voice. There follows a display of sky-pointing, a ritualized intention movement, that precedes taking off. The incoming bird may sky-point if it intends to leave again immediately, but the display is usually made by the bird on the nest. If both gannets wish to go, they sky-point together (right) until one "wins" and departs.*

A Eurasian coot holds food for its young and calls for them to come and eat.

The male snowy owl advertises his territory by hooting and displaying, with his tail cocked and wings lifted. Hooting is also used to warn his family of approaching danger.

Urgent calls by a fledgling superb glossy starling (far right) entice its parent to drop food into its gaping bill.

Domestic chicks run for cover when their mother gives the drawn-out "squawk" that warns of danger overhead, from a bird of prey. A rapid clucking would tell them that the danger is due to a ground predator, such as a fox or weasel.

Recognition signals between adult and chick can start even before hatching. Common murres pack together on cliff ledges but do not build nests. Each chick has to maintain contact with its parents while it is on the ledge and later when it flutters down to the water and swims out to sea with them. It starts to call several days before hatching and at the same time it learns the parents' call. Thereafter, it responds only to calls from its own parents if it becomes separated on the ledge, and later the parents use a special "water call" to find their own chick among the crowd of juveniles in the sea below the cliff at fledging time.

When the bird spots danger it may, if it is in a flock or has young nearby, give warning calls to alert other birds. Among small birds there are two types of alarm calls which are distinguished by their acoustic properties and their functions. "Chat" calls, abrupt and harsh, have similar properties to contact calls and are easy to pinpoint, at least by the human ear. "Seet" calls, by contrast, are thin and high-pitched. They have a narrow range of frequencies and the volume rises and falls. One feature of both "seet" and "chat" calls is that they are very similar across a variety of species so that a warning by a cardinal will alert catbirds, wrens, chickadees and sparrows.

"Chat" calls are used in the presence of a cat or other ground predator, or when an owl is being mobbed in the daytime. The object seems to be to draw the attention of other birds within earshot to the predator's position and so ruin its chances of a stealthy approach. The caller, being alert, can escape attack and there is evidence that predators recognize this and give up when they hear these alarms. "Seet" calls, on the other hand, are used when a falcon or hawk passes overhead. The bird calls from the safety of the foliage, where it cannot be spotted, and to human ears it is difficult to pinpoint its position. This suggests that the raptor would be unable to locate the bird either by sight or sound. Unfortunately for the theory, experiments using recordings of alarm calls played to captive pygmy owls and goshawks have shown that these birds are capable of locating "seet" calls: the raptors turned to stare at the loudspeakers. But whether such an artificial situation is a fair imitation of a bird calling from cover remains to be proven. The pure, 7–9 kiloHertz tone of a "seet" call attenuates rapidly in foliage, so it could alert other small birds nearby without being heard by the raptor flying above.

BIRD SONG

The melodious utterances that we call bird song are such a feature of the countryside at certain seasons that it is easy to forget that only a small proportion of the 8,600 species of birds are songsters. Song, in the sense of musical vocalizations, is a characteristic only of the oscine group, or songbirds. A few of these, the crows for instance, are far from melodious and there are other passerines outside the songbird group, such as cuckoos, cotingas and tyrant-flycatchers, whose calls are musical enough to be called songs.

Despite the interest that bird song has aroused over the centuries, there is much about it that is

*The* klee-yer *call of the yellow-shafted flicker is used by young birds in the nest to attract their parents' attention, and it later helps to keep the family together.*

*When fledgling birds, such as this shrike tyrant, have left the nest but have not mastered flying, they call to let their parents know where to bring food.*

puzzling and the greatest mystery is why these elaborate outpourings should have evolved in the first place. While the songs of some birds are no more than a repetition of simple notes, others have lengthy and varied repertoires which seem to be unnecessarily elaborate for any likely function.

Many birds sing most persistently at the start of breeding but continue throughout the nesting period; others become quiet or totally silent after pairing. The sedge warbler ceases to sing completely after pairing but the reed warbler continues, and in the European blackbird, song actually increases while the female is incubating. For thrushes, wrens and others that raise a second brood, there is usually a second but smaller peak of singing between the two broods. After breeding, at the end of summer, the general rule is to molt and during this period birds become very quiet. This is followed, in the fall, by an "Indian summer" of song, apparently due to a renewed but short-lived secretion of sex hormones. This song is not normally related to breeding activities and Old World warblers,

turns the black of night into grey. The birds will have wakened a few minutes earlier and preened and stretched before flying from the roost to a singing post. The silence is broken by scattered snatches of song, then the volume and tempo increase and the countryside becomes a babel of sound, which lasts at peak intensity for about half an hour.

The start of the dawn chorus is related to light intensity and is earlier on fine mornings, especially following a moonlit night, than on overcast days. It is modified by the stage of the breeding cycle, being earlier when courtship is at its height. There is a general order in which different birds start to sing, with species that eat insects and worms starting before seed eaters. Despite the detailed documentation of the timing of the dawn chorus and proof that it is triggered by light intensity, there is no good explanation for its occurrence, although several suggestions have been put forward. One is that sounds travel farther in the still air of early morning and that a bird that sounds as if it is nearby will be more

*Yellow-necked francolins start to call at dawn, sometimes with male and female duetting. Although they are a territorial advertisement, these calls are said to be difficult to pinpoint because they have a ventriloquial quality.*

*A western meadowlark sings at daybreak. The eastern and western species of meadowlark are very similar in appearance and their ranges overlap in the central United States and Central America but the two species have completely different songs, which helps them to avoid interbreeding.*

American sparrows and others sing, not only before setting out for their winter quarters, but also at stopping points on the migration route, and they may continue in their winter quarters.

Among those birds which remain behind, there are those that continue to sing during the winter because they defend territories throughout the year. These include the European robin and tawny owl, and the American mockingbird, cactus wren and wrentit. Other species occasionally sing during the winter, especially on clear days when they give the impression that spring is just around the corner. In regular winter songsters, the female may sing as well as the male, either to defend a territory jointly with the male or to defend her own individual territory. An annual cycle of continuous song, with the female equally vocal, is more common in tropical countries where both territory and pair bond are maintained throughout the year.

As well as varying through the year, bird song fluctuates through the day. The peak comes in the "dawn chorus" shortly after the first glimmer of light

threatening, or will attract females over greater distances. Another is that there is an advantage in a communal "beating the bounds" in which birds let each other know their whereabouts at a time when "homeless" birds are most active in looking for somewhere to settle.

Song continues through the early morning, dies away in the middle of the day and increases again in the afternoon. In the evening there is a second chorus, of lower intensity than that at dawn, before the birds go to roost. Snatches of song by late retirers like the European robin are heard in the dusk, and some song can, unexpectedly, be heard in the hours of darkness from birds which are not normally active at night.

The amount of song is affected by the weather. Birds sing less in the wind, although the mistle thrush has been nicknamed the "storm cock" for its habit of singing from an exposed perch during gales. Warm weather encourages song and the number of song phrases uttered per minute by a pied flycatcher is directly proportional to air temperature.

It has long been realized that bird song is a form

of advertisement. It is usually loud and far-carrying and the song is frequently delivered from an exposed perch or in a "song-flight". The function of this advertisement is less obvious. If ornithologists can identify species by their songs, clearly birds should be able to, and each bird's voice could be distinctive enough for individuals to be recognized, but the problem is why birds should spend so much time proclaiming their identities.

For many years the object of bird song was held to be for "the charming of females", to use Darwin's words. Then, in the 1920s the significance of territory in the life of birds began to be better appreciated, and the underlying motivation of song was seen to be aggression, so that the sounds which are so charming to human ears were viewed as a "message of hate" directed at intruding males. It has now become apparent that bird song serves both functions simultaneously and conveys messages of both "love" and "hate": attracting females and repelling males. Deciphering the messages contained in bird song has

blackbird relies on the specific final trill of its three-phrase "*conc-a-ree*" song. If the first two phrases are edited out of a recording, the trill alone elicits aggressive reactions on playback.

Individual variations on the basic song pattern may be useful in giving each bird an audible "identity card". Recognizing the individual voices of neighbors is an asset to a bird because it saves time and energy which might be spent on aggressive encounters and can be better directed towards other activities. When territories are being claimed, the song of one bird provokes a response from neighbors and, if they are near the boundary, aggressive displays, chasing or fighting may result. After a few days a neighbor's song is often ignored because the boundary between the territories has been settled and each bird knows its own place. A familiar song coming from usual singing posts is no longer a threat, but the unfamiliar song of an intruding stranger immediately sounds the alarm and a returning burst of song from the resident bird acts as a first line of defense.

*The whitethroat fluffs out the feathers of its head and throat when it sings. It normally delivers its song from a hedge or bush but sometimes flutters up to sing while airborne.*

*The song thrush is one of the species which can sometimes be heard in full song during the winter months.*

been achieved by the analysis of sonagrams and by "playback experiments" in which birds are exposed to recording of songs.

The European robin has a complex, warbling song. Each burst of song, or strophe, is made up of about four different phrases, or motifs, but a single robin has a repertoire of several hundred phrases which it uses in different combinations. Nevertheless both humans and other robins recognize these infinitely variable songs as coming from a robin, as they are based on a set of "rules". By chopping up recordings of songs and playing them to robins, three main rules of composition were discovered: consecutive strophes must be different, in each strophe all motifs must be different, and consecutive motifs must be alternately high and low pitched. Artificial songs made by an electronic sound generator, and conforming to these rules, elicit the same aggressive reactions from a territory-owning robin as a recording of a real robin song. So for the European robin, the pattern of notes in a song is important for recognition. By contrast, the red-winged

A bird's song is, therefore, an acoustic beacon which tells other birds of its position and identity. Unmated females are attracted and rival males, and females in species where the female also sings, are warned to keep away. The relative importance of these two functions varies between species, but it is not easy to distinguish between them in practice, except in a few species, where there are different songs for territorial defense and courtship.

A common pattern to the singing behavior of birds is that the intensive, day-long bouts of singing that herald the start of the breeding season are reduced as soon as a female takes up residence and the pair is formed. Singing then becomes restricted to the dawn and dusk choruses. If the female disappears for some reason, the full intensity of singing is resumed. So there are sexual and territorial components in the information conveyed by the song. In the sedge warbler the song is concerned only with courtship because, once the pair has formed, the song of rambling chatters and trills is no longer heard. Border disputes are settled silently, with displaying and fighting, and there is none of the singing which accompanies confrontation among other warblers.

It is not easy to demonstrate what effect song has on the female's behavior once she has been attracted to the male. In some laboratory experiments the sexual message of bird song has been found to continue after pair formation as it brings the female into breeding condition and triggers her nesting behavior. Female ring doves need the "cooing" of males to stimulate the development of their eggs and female canaries do more nest building, and lay more eggs, if they can hear a complicated canary song, as compared with a simplified song.

The use of song to maintain and defend a territory is easier to observe because the response of other males to a singing bird is obvious when compared with the unseen physiological changes and the unobtrusive behavior of females. Male birds show their reaction to song by breaking into song themselves and approaching the source of the sound. In great tits, the song is used for territorial defense rather than attracting females. When all the territory-holding males in a small wood were removed and some territories were fitted out with groups of loudspeakers broadcasting great tit songs, new males invaded territories with no loudspeakers almost immediately, but the barrage of recorded songs kept them out of the other territories for over two days before the effect wore off.

Duetting, in which both sexes sing together, seems to be a form of territorial song but may also help the pair to keep together in dense undergrowth. It is found in several tropical birds including motmots, barbets, ovenbirds and shrikes. The notes of male and female may be so well coordinated that it is impossible to tell that they are coming from two birds except when standing between them. The Australian whipbird, a relative of the babblers, is named after the notes of the male which start with a pure note that increases in intensity and ends with a sharp whip-crack. The female then replies with two or three notes. In common with other duettists, whipbirds maintain a pair bond throughout the year. They live in the undergrowth, staying close together, which suggests that the far-carrying, easily-located notes are for signaling their position to other whipbirds, which cannot see them, rather than in keeping the male and female in contact.

The brief, jingling call of the chickadee or the cheeping of house sparrows under the eaves appear to convey as much information as the diverse outpourings of the most musical of the thrushes, wrens and warblers. In communication terms, the signals of songsters exhibit redundancy, since sections can be cut out without reducing the information content, as in the experiment with the red-winged blackbirds. The birds are, in effect, saying the same things in many different ways, and it is difficult to see what advantage there is in this. However, as with commercial advertising, it may be that the same message repeated too frequently leads to habituation: the impact is lost and variety is needed to renew it. There is some evidence, in great tits and mocking-birds, that variety in the song repertoire of an individual is more effective in driving off rivals than a set, stereotyped pattern. The same experimental

*A pair of d'Arnaud's barbets sings together. These birds are members of a tropical family named after the bristles around the bill. When birds sing in duet they are usually so well coordinated that it sounds as if only one bird is singing.*

system of removing great tits from a wood and replacing them with loudspeakers playing songs, showed that areas "defended" by a single, reiterated song were almost completely reoccupied in eighteen hours, at which time areas "defended" by a more varied repertoire of songs were still virtually empty. This has been called the *Beau Geste* effect, from an incident in the novel of that name, when dead legionnaires were propped up behind the battlements of a desert fort to deceive the attacking Arabs into thinking it was still well-defended. By changing the song pattern after each singing bout, a male tit misleads others looking for somewhere to settle, into thinking that they are in an area already crowded. A further finding was that the great tits with the largest song repertoires (the average number of song types is three to four) are more likely to survive for over one breeding season and tend to produce more young. This is probably because a large repertoire of songs enables a great tit to occupy a high-quality territory where there is plentiful food.

The hard-pressed defenders in *Beau Geste* deceived their enemy by running to and fro behind the battlements and firing the rifles of their dead comrades to create the impression of numbers. The avian equivalent is for birds to sing from inconspicuous places as they move about the territory. Mimids, however, since they sing from regular, exposed perches, would not fool the opposition with a large repertoire and an alternative explanation for varied songs needs to be sought. It may be that they are singing more to attract females than for territorial defense against other males. If females discriminate

between different individuals' songs, as they are known to do in some species, at least, the forces of sexual selection will lead to a "runaway" evolution of extensive song repertoires in the same way as they have led to highly elaborate plumage. So the complex melodies of some songbirds can be seen as the acoustic equivalent of the peacock's train which makes such a dazzling display when it is courting the female. Females attracted to males with larger song repertoires would be choosing those with the best territories and most breeding experience. This has been found in the red-winged blackbird, which sometimes has more than one mate. Males with the largest territories and the greatest breeding experience are those with the richest song repertoires. These birds attract the most females to nest in their territories. Such a link between song repertoire and attractiveness to females will lead to the evolution of ever more elaborate songs, beyond the level of variety needed for successful territorial defense, as males compete for females.

## MIMICRY

Over-elaboration of song through sexual selection could help to explain the puzzling phenomenon of vocal mimicry by birds, although there is as yet no proof. Among cage-birds the best known mimics are the parrots and mynas, yet no one has ever been able to find them using their powers of imitation in the wild. Nevertheless, many other wild birds do mimic naturally. These include jays, starlings, catbirds, thrashers, birds of paradise and lyrebirds. The mockingbird's scientific name, *Mimus polyglottos*, means the "many-tongued mimic", and its burbling,

*For a small bird, the European winter wren's song is surprisingly loud and can be heard at over 550 yards (500 meters). Some parts of the song are above the range of human hearing.*

*A red-winged blackbird singing and showing off its scarlet wing patches. Only the final trill of the song is needed to identify it to other red-winged blackbirds, but males with a rich repertoire of song have greater breeding success.*

rapidly-changing song includes snatches of other birds' songs as well as mammal calls and mechanical sounds, such as the tinkling of a piano. Bowerbirds have been recorded as imitating cats, dogs, axes chopping wood, motorcar horns and fence-wires twanging, as well as many kinds of birds. One bowerbird is said to have mimicked an eagle so well that it caused a hen and her chicks to run for cover.

One champion mimic is the marsh warbler, a European species whose varied musical songs of trills and chirrups are composed of the notes of other birds. The full range of its plagiarism was only realized through a study made in Belgium. Analysis of sonagrams revealed that probably the entire repertoire was made up of mimicry. Not only were the songs of nearly a hundred European species recognized in the sonagrams but also those of over a hundred African species, which the marsh warbler would hear in its winter quarters.

seems to be that mimicry is not exact and the warbler changes the songs it imitates to produce a specific pattern of song elements.

LEARNING TO SING

Birds need to recognize songs of their own species and ignore those of related species. This is especially important for species which have almost identical plumage, such as the willow warbler and chiffchaff. Birders often talk of "willow-chiffs" because of the problem of identifying them by plumage alone. Presumably these Old World warblers have the same problem, but their songs prevent them from choosing the wrong mates and interbreeding. Experiments show that they not only ignore songs of other species but that they discriminate against the slightly different patterns of song from other populations of their own species. Female German chiffchaffs which have been reared in isolation and have never heard their species' song, respond, with an increased

*The mockingbird is a well-known mimic, and one tenth of its burbling song may be made up of mimicked sounds. These are changed at intervals, as the mockingbird picks up new sounds and drops others.*

*The first four sonagrams on the right show the development of chaffinch song, from the quiet subsong of the young bird to the full adult song, complete with terminal flourish. The final sonagram shows the simple notes of a bird which has been reared in isolation.*

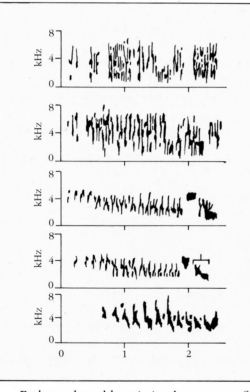

Each marsh warbler mimics about seventy-five other species and its repertoire is complete within its first year of life and probably shortly after its first arrival in Africa. This gives a clue as to a possible function of mimicry. Many birds, as will be described below, learn their songs during a critical period in their youth. On reaching maturity they imitate the songs of their fathers and neighboring males which they heard as chicks. Imitating other species could be a quick way of increasing the song repertoire, thus gaining a *Beau Geste*-type advantage over other males and developing an extensive range of song to impress females. But with every bird singing its own collection of imitations there is the problem of how one marsh warbler recognizes another by its song. The answer

heartbeat, to songs of German chiffchaffs but not to the rather different songs of chiffchaffs from Spain and Portugal.

In these species, birds instinctively recognize the correct song, but how do the males come to sing it? In those species which have been tested, the song develops through a combination of instinct and learning. The chaffinch has a distinctive song with a regular pattern of repeated, emphatic notes descending the scale and ending with a terminal flourish. Each male has up to six variants made by changing the number of notes. Young chaffinches start with a subsong shortly after leaving the nest. This is a quiet, rambling and very variable collection of chirps and rattles which probably has no function and is merely practicing. After its first winter, the young chaffinch sets up a territory and starts the subsong again, but now it gradually becomes replaced by versions of the true song until the full adult song is regularly repeated.

Chaffinches which have been reared in isolation fail to develop the complete song. All they can utter is a simple series of notes lacking the terminal flourish. This "instinctive song" is an outline sketch or framework which will be filled out by copying other chaffinches. The young chaffinches first remember the songs of their father and his neighbors while in the nest, and later on they listen to their neighbors when perfecting their songs at the start of the first breeding season.

The learning process in chaffinches is such that they are sensitive only to the songs of other chaffinches. Other birds are less specific and will learn the "wrong" song. If the eggs of zebra finches are

*The sedge warbler's song is a medley of musical and chattering phrases. It is used by the male solely to attract a mate, and once he has paired all singing stops.*

Learning song from parents and neighbors leads to the development of dialects, as it does in humans. Local populations of chaffinches sing very similar songs, which differ noticeably from those farther afield. White-crowned sparrows, which have a single song are, like chaffinches, able to learn only the song of their own species. They are sensitive to the songs of their father and neighbors during a critical fifty-day period after hatching and so learn the local dialect which is transmitted from generation to generation. Male Carolina wrens have large repertoires averaging thirty-two song types but neighbors hold many song types in common. As the distance between two wrens increases, the number of song types shared decreases. Nevertheless, Carolina wrens from all over North and Central America respond to each other's songs.

Following the progress of song-learning in wild birds from generation to generation is not easy but it has been achieved in a population of saddlebacks on a

*Analysis of the contact calls made by American goldfinches shows that members of a pair have very similar notes, as a result of the male mimicking the female's call. They can recognize each other and so keep together.*

incubated under a Bengalese finch, the young zebra finches grow up to sing the Bengalese finch songs. They are sensitive only to the voice of the male which fed them and ignore the songs of zebra finches which they may hear while in the foster nest. Canaries are undiscriminating and will copy anything, which makes them so popular as cage-birds. Their vocabularies can be improved with lessons or by keeping them with "tutor-birds" of another species. There is the famous example, from the early 1900s, of the Eurasian bullfinch which had been taught to whistle "God save the King". A canary in the next room learnt the tune over the course of a year and, when the bullfinch hesitated too long at the end of the third line, the canary would chime in and finish the tune.

small island off New Zealand. These are almost flightless birds that form permanent pairs and maintain territories throughout the year. It transpired that the tiny island population of twenty-eight pairs is divided into groups, each of which shares a small number of song-types making up its dialect. A young male establishing a territory for the first time learns the songs of his new neighbors, rather than those of his father. If he has settled on the borders of two dialect regions, he chooses both song types, and when a male moves his territory or a new neighbor moves in, he alters his song to match. Sometimes new dialects arise through a note being changed, lost or repeated by one bird which makes a mistake when learning its song.

# CHAPTER 7
# SOCIAL LIFE

The evening flight of starlings to roost starts in late afternoon while there is still plenty of light. Birds from over a wide area leave the fields and gardens, where they have been feeding in small groups, and fly together, straight and fast, to a staging point. There they join into larger flocks until a swarm of starlings floods into the roost, in a reed bed or wood, or on the ledges of buildings in a city center, where they twitter on their perches before settling down for the night. Other birds behave in a similar fashion, and red knots, rooks, queleas, galahs, cattle egrets and swallows all perform spectacular mass aerial evolutions. Much less obvious are the flocks of small birds, which often include several different species foraging together. In temperate woods they consist mainly of finches and chickadees, but, around the world, there are many other associations of insect-, seed- and fruit-eating birds. The flocks can be so well spread out – birds may be over 50 yards (meters) apart – that their existence is not always obvious, except that their members are following the same line of travel and are keeping in touch by calling.

Whatever its composition, a flock of birds is more than a formless collection of individuals. It is bound by practices that prevent collisions in the air and reduce squabbles on the ground. When birds in a flock are feeding or roosting together they keep apart from each other, usually by a minimum distance. If one bird comes too close to another, a jab of the bill or a hostile display forces it to retreat. This behavior can be seen among starlings feeding on the lawn, swallows perching on telephone wires before they migrate and gulls standing along a roof or sea wall. The spacing between two birds is called the individual distance, and it varies with the species and according to the situation. For black-headed gulls, individual distance is about 1 foot (30 centimeters), and for herons it is several yards. Individual distance is reduced to zero among the most sociable of birds and they huddle together, shoulder to shoulder. This is how lovebirds, a group of small parrots, got their name and their aggression is probably reduced by preening each other. Red avadavats spend up to two-thirds of the daytime in clumps. They perch side-by-side and lean against each other so that the end bird may have to use one wing as a prop. When an avadavat approaches the clump it adopts a submissive posture and peaceful relations are established by the birds preening each other's heads, as mated pairs do in less sociable species (p. 148).

*A shoal of fishes has brought a yellow-billed stork and a pink-backed pelican into temporary dispute. Each understands the other's threatening gestures so they will move apart, and avoid spoiling each other's fishing.*

*A male great tit displays at two blue tits in an attempt to claim a good source of food. In general, species that have regular contact understand one another's signals, but here the blue tits are undeterred.*

*Herring gulls neatly spaced out on a roof illustrate the importance of individual distance. Aggression keeps them apart and gives them space to take off without colliding.*

Among less sociable birds, keeping a distance serves a practical purpose. Rooks feeding together must keep well spaced so that they can make a stealthy approach on earthworms which vanish down their burrows when disturbed. In other circumstances spacing can be ignored. Woodpigeons feed in dense flocks on clover leaves or spilled grain which, unlike worms, cannot escape. A particularly good concentration of food, as in a field of clover or stubble, is sometimes such an attraction that individual distance is temporarily waived, and gulls jostle at the carcass of a drowned animal or pelicans feed cooperatively on a fish shoal. Another reason for keeping apart is that jostling and squabbling reduce the time that can be spent feeding. Sometimes one bird is able to defend a limited food supply and keep its fellows away; a starling keeps others away from a crust on the lawn, but it may be so busy chasing other birds that it barely has time to feed. Such aggression is most severe in short-lived gatherings of birds which have come together solely to exploit food. In a stable flock, a regular order of precedence is established and, because the amount of fighting is reduced by every bird knowing its place, the birds take turns to feed in a more or less orderly way.

The order of precedence in a flock is called a peck order or dominance hierarchy. In some flocks there may be only one or two dominant individuals lording it over the rest, who make little distinction between one another. However, in a flock of barnyard chickens there is a definite hierarchy which includes all the birds and is expressed by one bird taking precedence at food or in a roost, by means of a sharp peck and the flustered retreat of the subordinate.

A peck order can become established only where a permanent flock is formed, as in the barnyard. The birds learn to recognize each other individually and have the chance to settle the order of precedence. The consequence is that the amount of fighting is reduced because the birds know and accept their place in society. If one steps out of line, it is quickly reminded by its superiors. One common hierarchy has a straightforward order of ranking, with bird A, the superior chicken, pecking all others who step out of line. Bird B pecks all others except A, bird C pecks all except A and B, and so on down the line. The lowest bird is not only harassed by the rest but has to be content with the leavings after the others have fed, so it is often undernourished and in poor condition. If food is short, the lowest ranks die first.

The order or dominance may also be set by social factors. Jackdaws mate for life and the female takes her husband's rank, while in Canada geese, pairs with young take precedence over pairs without young. Barren pairs dominate their superiors' young, but single adults are inferior to the young while they are still with their parents. In the colonial Steller's jay, the peck order changes as the flock moves in search of food. When they stop to feed, the dominant male is the one from the nest nearest to the food. When the flock moves on, this bird loses its dominance in favour of another which is now nearer its home.

*Under certain circumstances individual distance is abolished for a while. This generally occurs when there is limited access to a resource, as with these ring-necked doves crowding onto a boulder to drink.*

*A flurry of aggression in a flock of domestic geese as the dominant bird asserts itself. The junior birds usually retreat without fighting back, unless one is prepared to contest the senior's authority.*

*In some species, individual distance is reduced to zero. Here, a pair of cinnamon-chested bee-eaters huddle together on a perch. Antagonism between them has been completely overcome.*

At night, the majority of birds find a perch where they are sheltered from the weather and predators. The nest is often used as a roost and some woodpeckers and sparrows make a special nest, used solely for roosting, outside the breeding season. Wrens do the same, but they will also make use of other birds' nests, nestboxes and similar cavities. Brown creepers hide behind flakes of loose bark or excavate roosting holes in the decaying wood of dead trees or the soft, fibrous bark of living redwoods.

Birds which feed in flocks commonly retire together into roosts, but some solitary feeders also gather to roost communally in the evening, especially in winter. European robins may even leave their winter territories to roost with others. Those birds which have been feeding sociably during the day, such

The second possible benefit of communal roosts for birds which also feed sociably is to act as "information centers". During the day parties of birds will have spread out to forage over a very large area. When they return in the evening some will have fed well but others may have found little to eat. Although there is no definite proof, it seems that when the birds set out again next morning, those birds which did not feed well on the previous day will follow those that did, perhaps by noting the confident way in which the latter set forth. Some circumstantial evidence for this comes from the behavior of common and lesser kestrels in Africa. The common kestrel hunts vertebrate animals in a small, familiar hunting ground, whereas the very similar lesser kestrel feeds on insects over a large area. The common kestrel roosts and

*Flocking helps birds to keep warm, especially if they huddle together. Here a cloud of steam hangs over a colony of emperor penguins as they incubate their eggs. The temperature in the center of the mass of birds is raised by as much as 20°F (11°C).*

*When mallards roost in a flock, each bird opens its eyes at intervals which makes it difficult for a predator to surprise them. The birds are more vigilant when they are roosting in a potentially dangerous place, but a frozen pond is fairly safe.*

*Three Eurasian spoonbills roosting on a sandy beach. The open space makes it difficult for a predator to creep up unseen.*

as shorebirds, gulls and finches, travel to the roost in parties, but solitary feeders, like robins and blackbirds, arrive singly. Some roosts are huge: in recent winters blackbirds, grackles, starlings and robins have assembled in roosts of up to 70 million birds in the mid-southern states.

The reasons for roosting communally are not always obvious, but there are three likely benefits. In winter especially, it is important for birds to keep warm at night and conserve precious food reserves. One way to do this is to find a sheltered roost. Solitary roosters shelter in dense vegetation or enter a cavity – horned larks dig holes in the ground and ptarmigan burrow into snow banks – but the effect of sheltering is magnified by several birds huddling together in the roost, as wrens, swifts, brown creepers, bluebirds and anis do. Body contact cuts down the surface area exposed to the cold air, so the birds keep each other warm. Two kinglets huddling were found to reduce their heat losses by a quarter and three together saved a third of their heat.

hunts alone, but the lesser kestrel roosts and hunts in flocks, so one bird can learn from others where to find insect swarms.

Finally, there is safety in numbers at communal roosts since there will nearly always be a few birds awake at any moment to give the alarm. But this increased protection is partially counteracted by the fact that mass roosts attract predators, and are especially vulnerable if they are on the ground. Even those in trees can be attacked by birds of prey. The birds on the edge are at greatest risk and bird banders, like predators, find it easier to catch small birds perching at the margins of a roost. Entering or leaving the roost is particularly dangerous and this may be why starlings, finches and others enter roosts in dense, fast-flying formations. Starlings that arrive later appear to be anxious, judging from their calls, and their erratic flight may help to confuse predators. A safe place is a great advantage, so gulls, terns and pelicans are found roosting on sandbars or small islands, and coots and ducks on open water.

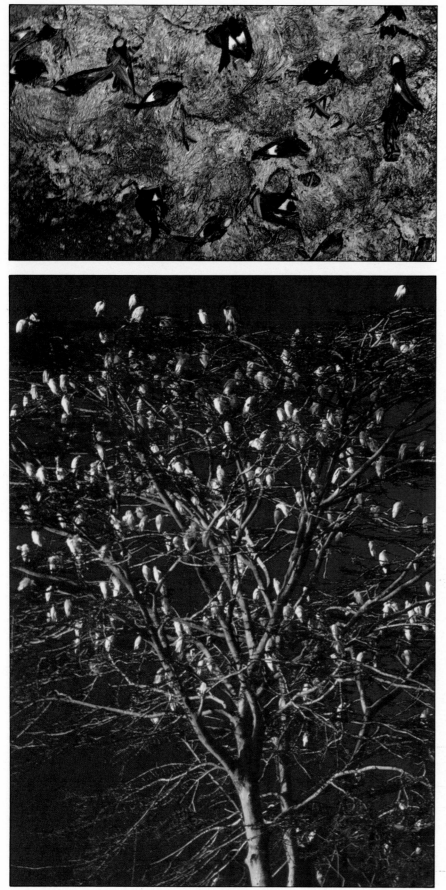

## THE BENEFITS OF FLOCKING

Some birds that spend the night in a communal roost disperse at dawn, but others stay in a flock during the day. Birds would not do things together unless there was an advantage to be gained and flocking has several important functions. Like communal roosting, it can give birds a measure of protection from predators, and it can also help them to find or catch food.

Calculations based on watching a merlin preying on wintering shorebirds showed that a bird is three times more likely to be killed if it is alone than if it is in a flock. An experiment with captive starlings showed that a group of ten reacted to the appearance of a model hawk, on average, one second quicker than did a solitary bird, an interval which could be sufficient to give them time to escape. Periods of vigilance in a flock are usually uncoordinated, although jungle babblers and cockatoos apparently employ sentinels which perch in a tree while the remainder feed on the ground below.

The protection afforded by being in a flock has the further advantage that it allows more time to be devoted to feeding. Geese, titmice, starlings, herons, sparrows and ostriches have been shown to spend less time on the look-out for predators when in flocks than when feeding alone. Birds feeding with their heads down are vulnerable, but when in a flock, signals of alarm from their companions will give them early warning of attack. An ostrich feeding alone has its head up and is looking around for predators 35% of the time. When with a companion this drops to 21% and the food intake increases by 14%. If there are three or four ostriches together, each spends 85% of the time feeding. Starlings in a flock of ten spend 10% of their time being vigilant, while a solitary bird spends as much as half its time looking around.

As well as providing an early warning system, the flock gives safety in numbers. Sometimes the flock can turn the tables and mob the predator to drive it away, or the predator may be confused by the numbers of potential prey and put off its strike. Furthermore, it can only kill one bird at a time so, for any attack, each member of the flock is statistically less likely to be caught than if it is on its own. The typical reaction to a bird of prey is for the flock to gather in a tight formation, and circle or fly erratically, rather than try to make an escape by speed. The defensive formation makes it harder for the predator to strike a victim without risking a collision with other birds. Even a slight injury can be fatal to a bird of prey in the long run (p. 104) so they are wary of accidents. Faced with a flock flying in defensive formation a raptor's only chance of a safe meal is to single out a straggler. The more vulnerable birds on the edge of a flock are noticeably more vigilant.

Depending on the diet of the species, spending the daylight hours as a member of a flock can also lead to greater success in feeding. As might be expected, birds that gather to feed on crops of fruit or seeds are more likely to feed in flocks than those which eat scattered insects or warm-blooded prey. However,

*House swifts roosting at their nesting place, in a sea cave on the Kenyan coast (far left). Communal roosts provide a safe place for the night, and may also act as information centers, helping hungry birds to find the best feeding places.*

*A mass roost of cattle egrets and sacred ibises in a tree (far left). It is an advantage for an individual bird to roost in a flock because it stands less chance of being the unlucky victim if a predator strikes.*

insectivorous birds can often improve their feeding rate by working together to disturb or drive prey, as described on page 66, and by watching each other to determine where to find food. A study has shown that a flock of chikadees is more likely to find a source of food than a solitary bird, presumably because several pairs of eyes are better than one. Moreover, when one chikadee has found food, the others tend to gather at that spot to search more intensively and also start to look in similar places.

herons did not catch anything after about three and a half minutes, they would give up and fly off. So the size of the flock is regulated according to the food supply. When prey is plentiful, the herons are catching fish every minute and more birds keep arriving to swell their numbers, but if prey becomes depleted and herons find themselves waiting too long for a catch, departures exceed arrivals.

The social behavior of herons has a significance for fish farmers. When herons are feeding alone on a

*A small flock of ravens harries a Himalayan griffon vulture. Mobbing a possible predator is a dangerous business but the risk is reduced by several birds acting together.*

The discovery of a good source of food brings birds together from all around to make a temporary flock while it lasts. Great blue herons feed both solitarily and in flocks. When food is patchily distributed, as shoals of fish in shallow water are, the herons feed in flocks. As the size of the flock increases, the number of fish caught per minute rises until the herons start to interfere with each other's hunting. One set of observations showed that if any of the

limited resource, they are able to defend it against other herons, so installing a realistic model heron by garden ponds is a practical way of keeping real herons away from the goldfish. The technique was tried at commercial fish farms, where dense shoals of valuable fish are reared in shallow pools, but the experiment was disastrous. With such a mass of food available, herons were attracted in large numbers and the models only served as a signal.

The rivalry that exists between male birds during the breeding season and the intolerance one bird shows for another of the same species coming too close was familiar to the English naturalist, Gilbert White of Selborne. In 1772 he wrote: "During the amorous season such a jealousy prevails amongst male birds that they can hardly bear to be together in the same hedge or field". He realized that this "jealousy" is expressed through songs and displays and understood that the result was to space out most bird species "over the face of the country".

As knowledge of bird behavior has increased, so the concept of territory has become refined but more complicated. This is because territories have a number of uses which makes it difficult even to give a precise meaning to the term. However, a simple definition is that a territory is any defended area,

many birds – European robins among others.

The importance of territory in courtship and pair formation is described later, in Chapter 8. Polygynous species in which one male mates with several females, often have territories which are no more than a stage where the male displays to attract the female. Birds of this type, including some grouse, ruffs and birds of paradise, gather into communal display grounds, known as leks, where the males hold small territories and compete with each other for the attention of the females (p.158).

Where the same territory is used for both courtship and nesting, it confers several advantages. Breeding can proceed undisturbed and the owners may be able to defend a monopoly of food supplies for themselves and their offspring. For a male bird, acquiring a territory is, therefore, almost always a

*The Magellanic oystercatcher uses its territory for courtship, nesting, and often for feeding. Here, the territory holder's aggressive intent is communicated by its erect-tail posture. The intruding bird, on the right, is undecided whether to attack or flee, and is "mock-sleeping".*

which can range from the nest hole alone, for sparrows and starlings, to the hunting ground of an eagle measurable in square miles. The time that a territory is held can last from a few minutes to a lifetime. There are, in general, three uses of territory: for courtship, nesting and feeding.

A single territory may serve more than one of these functions and the most common territories, of songbirds, woodpeckers, birds of prey and others, serve all three. Many other birds court and nest in the territory but disperse to feed, like the seabirds, waterfowl, swifts and swallows, whose food resources are not defendable. There are exceptions, such as oystercatchers nesting a short distance inland, which have one territory for courtship and nesting, and a separate feeding territory on the shore. Feeding territories include the hoards defended by acorn woodpeckers (p.64) and the winter territories held by

prerequisite for breeding, but a closer investigation shows that this rule sometimes breaks down. Great tits, as is usual among songbirds, hold large territories in woodland where they feed and breed. However, despite the resident males spending a considerable part of their time in singing, displaying and chasing interlopers, other pairs can settle in the territory. They behave inconspicuously and claim nest holes where they rear families. This is only a second-best option because they produce half as many fledglings as the territory owners. Holding a territory is expensive in terms of time and energy spent defending it, but it makes possible an increased number of offspring, so presumably territory owners can exploit the food resources much more easily than the intruding pairs.

### ADVANTAGES OF TERRITORIES
The value of a territory depends on the various facilities it can provide. A great tit needs a territory that

*The small territories of the black grouse are used solely for courtship. The males defend their territories vigorously, usually by displays.*

contains a suitable crevice or cavity in which a nest can be built, and a sunbird requires sufficient flowers to provide it with nectar. For birds of open country – gulls, skuas, snowy owls and ptarmigan – a mound where the owner can stand guard and survey the surrounding area is a necessity, while song posts are needed for others. One pair of brown tree-pipits was able to nest on a bare heath because a telegraph pole provided the essential perch from which to launch the song-flight. For the polygynous red-winged blackbird which nests in marshes, cover in which to build a nest is the important consideration, and a male holding a territory with plenty of cover will attract more females than one with poor cover.

Where a territory is used for feeding, it may be possible to measure the resources provided by the territory with some accuracy and so estimate its value to the owners. The North American ovenbird feeds on the forest floor by picking invertebrates from the surface of the leaf litter. The male sets up the territory in spring and later both male and female collect food

difference between territorial behavior in summer and winter. During the summer, pairs defend an area around the nest and hunt farther afield over ground shared with other pairs. After the breeding season, individuals defend their hunting territory against other kestrels. Where prey is plentiful, these winter territories are smaller and the density of kestrels is greater. This is due, not to kestrels selecting smaller territories, but to the good hunting attracting more kestrels, including newly independent young and immigrants. Defending a large area in these circumstances would be expensive in time and energy, and the kestrels apportion the space so that returns from hunting are not rendered uneconomical by too great an expenditure on defense.

Defending a territory can alternate between being advantageous and disadvantageous according to circumstances. From October to March, some pied wagtails, especially adult males, defend riverbank territories. They spend nearly all the daylight hours walking up one bank and down the other, picking up

*An adult white-bellied sea eagle attacks an immature bird (below). Young birds of prey are unwelcome in the territories of established birds and cannot settle until they have found an unoccupied area.*

*Hammerkops use a hippopotamus as a perch during a dispute. Standing on the back of its mate is a common, if rather odd habit of hammerkops. It may help to strengthen the pair bond during territorial disputes.*

for their chicks within the same area. There is a relationship between the density of invertebrates in the litter and the size of the territory: where food is more abundant, the area held by a pair of ovenbirds is found to be smaller.

A link between food resources and territory size has been established for several birds, as in hummingbirds where territories vary in size enormously but usually contain about the same number of flowers. In an experiment with a rufous hummingbird, half the flowers in a territory were enclosed in bags. Within a day, the hummingbird had enlarged its territory to restore the number of flowers it was defending. When the flowers were exposed again, the territory reverted to its original size. In general, however, territory size seems to be determined by competition rather than by the birds assessing their needs. In Eurasian kestrels there is a

insects which have been washed ashore. The size of the territory provides enough riverbank for the supply of stranded insects to be replenished by the time the wagtail comes back again. Intruding birds – pipits, and skylarks, as well as other wagtails – will disrupt this well-adjusted cropping of insects and deplete the resource, so they are driven out. However, if the food supply is so great that the presence of intruders does not affect the owner's feeding, it tolerates them and does not waste time chasing them. On the other hand, if food is so scarce that the supply is not replenished quickly enough, the wagtails abandon their territories and gather to forage in flocks, returning at intervals to check the food supply in their territory and prevent intruders from taking over. Sometimes a territorial wagtail compromises and allows a "satellite" wagtail to occupy the territory. In return for a share of the food, the satellite helps to defend the territory.

*Territorial disputes among coots (above center) can be violent, especially when the boundaries are first being established. One bird charges the other and a fight may develop, the birds striking with their feet and stabbing with their bills. Here, the weaker bird is being forced onto its back.*

Pied wagtails defend renewable resources since insects are always being washed up. Hummingbirds and sunbirds are doing the same thing because they feed on nectar which is replenished by the flowers. By progressing around the territory nectar drinkers allow the resources to recover, but fruit eaters depend on resources which are non-renewable. Once a tree is stripped of its crop, it must be abandoned until the following year. Mistle thrushes, and to a lesser extent other members of the thrush family, eke out fruit crops by adjusting their territorial behavior. They feed on the berries of holly, hawthorn, buckthorn, ivy and the like, and when possible they defend berry-bearing trees and bushes against other thrushes. A holly tree with a good crop of berries can support a mistle thrush throughout the winter but it will last longer because the thrush also feeds on undefended berries or on the ground. So the defended tree is partly a reserve larder, for use when other food is short. However, when the weather is really severe and snow locks up many sources of food, the owner is swamped by flocks of hungry birds and the resource is impossible to defend.

There are other aspects of a territory, apart from food supply and a place to court and breed, which are very difficult for a human observer to evaluate. Any bird with a "patchy" food supply, that varies in time or location, is likely to benefit from familiarity with its territory, and the same is true of a bird hunting wary, secretive prey. The bird learns the habits and movements of its prey and adjusts its behavior accordingly. Kestrels, for instance, hunt in several bouts during the day that coincide with the activity cycles of voles. It is also possible that familiarity makes life less dangerous because the bird can learn the whereabouts of safe roosts and places where predators may lurk.

## SETTING UP THE TERRITORY

Except in a few species, it is the male which sets up the territory at the start of the breeding season. In migratory species, he usually returns first, or may spend the winter in the breeding area, while the females and young fly away (p.196). Some resident birds maintain territories the year round. It is clearly an advantage for the male to take up territory before rivals can claim all the available space. In some species, especially long-lived ones, birds claim the same territory each year. This is a time of intense advertisement through song and display, as well as actual fighting where a boundary is being hotly contested. Once the territories have been settled and neighbors have learned each other's dispositions, this activity dies down. Disputes are most vigorous where the population is dense and territories are pressed together, but where there is plenty of room, there can be a "no man's land" between them. The birds defend

*The dancing display of crowned cranes. Pair formation and territorial disputes start before the flock breaks up in spring.*

only a core area around the nest or other resources, and boundary disputes virtually disappear.

The process of establishing territory was first described by Eliot Howard, a British amateur ornithologist who made pioneering studies of bird territory. He watched male reed warblers return from Africa in spring and gather in flocks in reed beds bordering lakes and streams. At intervals, individuals left the flock and settled in a patch of reeds where they would sing for a while. The time that they spent away from the flock gradually increased until the flock no longer existed and the territories were held permanently. Similar behavior is found in titmice. Pairs of great tits remain together in the winter flocks and the male defends a small area around the female. Whenever the weather is mild enough, they visit their territory and the male sings, usually in the early morning, before joining the flock in search of food. As spring approaches more time is spent in the territory, but a cold snap stops territorial behavior because the birds must spend more time feeding.

The experimental removal of a pair from their territory provides a good opportunity to follow the process of establishment. If no new pair appears, birds in neighboring territories gradually extend their holdings into the vacant space, but if a new pair gets in first, it will have to counteract this tendency. In a colony of great skuas a vacant territory caused by the death of the original pair was occupied within a day by a new pair which had previously been unable to settle. They kept close together and explored their new home by walking out cautiously from the center until stopped by attacks from neighbors, whereupon they would retreat into the "safe area". The points at which the skuas were forced to turn back became the boundaries and, within two days of settling, the limits of the territory had been drawn and the pair was behaving with full confidence.

A colony of skuas includes a "club," which is an area where birds bathe, preen and rest. Although visited by "off-duty" breeders, most of the occupants are non-breeders and the club seems to be a reserve from which replacements will come when territory-holders die. In some colonies, perhaps where there is a high density of breeders and territories are in short supply, pairs form on the club and eggs are laid.

The rapid reoccupation of territories after they have fallen vacant suggests that there must be a reserve of potential breeders who are constantly monitoring the presence of the territory holders. In a woodland population of great tits, the replacements came from pairs which had been living in the less profitable hedgerows outside the wood, and in red grouse, they come from flocks of non-breeders living a precarious life beyond the heather moorland which provides their main food.

*At the beginning of the breeding season, male little egrets hold temporary territories where they fight and display to win a mate. Later, when they have paired, they defend permanent nest territories.*

*Spectacular with their barred plumage and raised crests, two hoopoes fly up and try to get above one another, as they squabble over the boundary of their territories.*

*In the Arctic, male rock ptarmigan retain their white plumage well into the summer and they are very conspicuous when they make display flights to advertise the territory.*

# COLONIAL LIFE

*Brown noddies nesting on Cousin Island in the Seychelles (far right). Unlike the related terns, which nest in colonies on the ground, noddies nest in trees or on cliff ledges and the spacing of the nests depends on the number of suitable places available to build them.*

About one tenth of the world's bird species breed in colonies. In some colonies, the nests are packed together, usually with enough space between to keep the birds away from each other's jabbing bills, but sometimes actually touching one another. Such colonies are impressive sights, whether they are cliffs packed with gannets and alcids, the pink fringe of flamingos nesting around a shallow lake or swarms of weavers nesting in trees on the African savannah. Other species nest in looser colonies, for example, finches shorebirds and thrushes. The common factor that enables any species of bird to nest in a colony is that it has a small territory, often comprising little more than the nest, and thus seeks its food elsewhere. So, colonial breeding is especially common among seabirds which need to range widely over the water but return to land to nest. To some extent, gregarious nesting is forced upon such birds because there is a shortage of space in which to nest, but this is not the whole reason and penguins, for instance, gather into tight colonies leaving large areas of apparently suitable ground unattended.

One reason for nesting in colonies is that they may act as "information centers" whereby birds can follow each other to the best feeding places, in the same way as members of a roost (p.134). Another is to reduce the dangers of predation through active

*A colony of carmine bee-eaters nesting in the steep bank of a river. The advantage of nesting together can be lost completely when the bank, already weakened by the burrows, is undermined by the stream and collapses.*

defense. Penguins, close-packed on their nests, present a palisade of bills to skuas that try to land among them, and anyone who has walked through a tern colony will know that piercing screams of alarm and thumps on the head can remove any inclination to linger! Such concerted action is most effective in the center of the colony, and nests on the edges of larger colonies, or in small colonies, are plundered much more than those in the middle.

Although group defense can be effective against predators, there are also disadvantages to nesting *en masse*, in that colonies, like communal roosts, will attract predators. Consequently they are often sited in safe places such as islands, cliffs or sandbars, to keep terrestrial predators away. The relative advantages of nesting colonially or in isolation depend on the sort of predators in the vicinity, and some species are flexible in their breeding habits. Eiders, for instance, nest in isolation and rely on camouflage when breeding on mainland sites, to reduce predation by foxes, but gather in dense colonies – two nests per square yard – on islands, where foxes cannot reach them and gulls are a problem.

In addition to active defense in breeding colonies, there is also, as in a flock of birds, safety in sheer numbers, which dilute the effects of predation so that each individual has a reduced chance of being a victim of attack. The "dilution effect" is increased by synchronization of nesting. The majority of pairs in one colony lay within a few days of each other, probably as the result of courtship displays and calls affecting neighbors as well as the bird's own mate. Each bird excites the others and they come into the

*Seabird colonies are often located at traditional sites, some of which have been in use for centuries. These Cape gannets (far left) have not moved despite human presence.*

*A huge colony of king cormorants on the Patagonian coast (far left). The nests are regularly spaced so the birds do not interfere with each other.*

*An altercation in a Eurasian white pelican colony as some birds get out of place and pose a threat to their neighbors (above left). Such fights sometimes result in eggs being kicked out of the nest, where they fall prey to waiting gulls (left).*

correct physiological condition for breeding at the same time. In colonies of herring and lesser black-backed gulls synchronization is greater in larger colonies than in smaller ones.

In the Antarctic, penguins are preyed on by skuas which wait in the colonies for an opportunity to steal eggs or attack chicks. The chicks are especially vulnerable when they are large enough to come out from under the parent but too small to fight off a skua. Predators exploiting the colony can kill and eat only a certain number of eggs or chicks each day so the shorter the period that the colony is occupied, the fewer will be eaten, and it pays a bird, in evolutionary terms, to lay its eggs with the crowd.

There are many advantages to colonial nesting,

but the dense aggregation of birds also brings a number of difficulties. The main problem that needs to be overcome is the aggression that results from territorial birds living close together. This is reduced by the birds being just out of each other's reach and by ritualized displays taking the place of violent conflict (pp.113–4). Where pairs are closely packed, males need to defend their mates from the sexual advances of neighbors and the eggs and chicks will also have to be protected from their depredations. Gulls, skuas and frigatebirds are quick to seize and devour any egg or young chick of their neighbors, which is left unattended for a moment. It is also possible that disease could be spread more easily in a crowded colony: birds are often stained with droppings which

*A packed colony of elegant terns with Heermann's gulls nesting around them (right). The gulls benefit by nesting close to the more numerous and aggressive terns. Although much larger, the gulls are forced to keep their distance (below).*

*Nesting together is a defense against predators but it carries its penalties. Continual vigilance, backed up by threats, is needed to maintain the integrity of the tiny territories around the nest (below).*

have been ejected forcefully by their neighbors. Nest material can be stolen and tropicbird colonies are so short of suitable nesting cavities that there is severe competition and unguarded eggs or chicks are evicted by pairs looking for a home. Murray Levick, who went on Scott's ill-fated expedition to the Antarctic in 1912, neatly demonstrated the problem of theft in penguin rookeries. He placed piles of colored pebbles on the edge of a rookery and watched them being picked up and incorporated into nests, then repeatedly stolen and passed from nest to nest across the rookery.

Aggression between neighbors is a problem for colonial birds. While they are on their nests, they are out of range of each other's bills but disputes can become very severe when the territory is first being claimed. The level of aggression is likely to rise as territories become smaller and the birds are forced closer together. Northern gannets face hard contest for nest sites and they are very aggressive in their defense, with males not only fighting rivals but frequently attacking their mates and young. South African and Australian gannets have more space in the colonies and are less aggressive. They fight less and their displays are of lower intensity. Actual fighting can be reduced by using displays which signal the messages of ownership, as appears to have happened in the weavers. The insect-eating species that live in large territories settle disputes by means of chases, whereas the seed eaters nesting in colonies use displays (p.156).

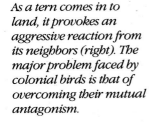

*As a tern comes in to land, it provokes an aggressive reaction from its neighbors (right). The major problem faced by colonial birds is that of overcoming their mutual antagonism.*

*If a chick strays from the nest it will be attacked by other terns in the colony (below left) and a very small chick will often be killed (below).*

# CHAPTER 8
## COURTSHIP AND MATING

The act of mating is the most important event in the life of any bird since it is the means of transmitting its genes into the next generation. For a male bird, the first step in courtship is to advertise for a mate by means of displays and calls or song. As described in Chapter 6, these have the parallel purpose of deterring rivals. Courtship behavior is, indeed, very closely linked with the occupation of a territory and a male bird very often cannot gain a mate without first establishing a territory.

The underlying elements of aggression, fear and sexual motivation are universal in the pair formation of birds. Any animal has a natural reluctance to allow another into its personal space and its reaction to such an intrusion is usually hostile. This must be averted if the intimate contact of mating is to be permitted. Consequently, courtship is a necessary prelude to mating – it brings the sexes together by overcoming their urge to attack each other.

An unmated male black-headed gull has a pairing territory where he spends his time waiting for other gulls to fly past. They are challenged by aggressive calls and displays, with apparently no recognition as to their sex. Passing males take no notice but a female prospecting for a mate will land. Both birds display aggressively and fearfully. An attack may well materialize and the female then flees, but the male often redirects his aggression against neighboring males or pecks at the ground, tearing out grass. After a time, the two birds appease each other's aggressive drives by the "head flagging" display, which hides the aggressive brown hood and the injurious bill.

In the course of pair formation, the female flies off frequently. She may visit a number of males before

*A female lesser kestrel receives food from her mate (below left). His courting has enabled him to enter her personal space and allows the intimate contact of mating (below right).*

*On rejoining his mate (bottom left), a male collared pratincole displays to show off his throat plumage and the chestnut feathers underneath his wings. He also bows with his tail cocked (bottom right). Courtship feeding may take place at this time, with the female bowing (bottom center and bottom right) after she has been fed.*

On the pairing territory, the male black-headed gull displays and waits for a female to land. When she does so, the male (on the right) shows aggression in his upright display, but the female overcomes his hostility by approaching in a hunched appeasement posture.

Periods of circling, standing side by side, turning to face one another and head-bobbing may continue for an hour or so during the courtship of Australian masked plovers (below).

Reddish egrets show off their plumes as they gauge each other's intentions in the preliminaries of courtship (below). In the heron family, the plumes and postures are also important for identifying the right species to court.

making a choice, and she may leave and return to one several times before reaching a final decision. As time passes, the female spends more time in one male's territory and eventually they fly off to feed together. However, each time the two separate and reunite, there is an exchange of hostile behavior, but the level of threat drops and the male no longer attacks. Gradually they become used to each other and vacate the pairing territory for the permanent nesting territory on the breeding ground.

As well as bringing the two birds together, courtship helps to synchronize their reproductive activities so that they are ready for copulation at the same time. Among canaries, for example, the male's song is an important trigger for the female's breeding behavior, while captive female ring doves come into breeding condition as soon as they are courted. The mere sight of a male "bowing" behind a pane of glass is sufficient to stimulate the secretion of sex hormones from the pituitary gland which, in turn, cause their reproductive organs to develop.

COURTSHIP RITUALS

Feeding the female is part of the courtship of many birds. Although called "courtship feeding", the male may not start feeding the female until the pair has settled down together, and it often continues through incubation, until the male has to concentrate on feeding the newly-hatched chicks. For finches, titmice and other birds, it is a means of providing the female with the extra food needed during egg-formation and incubation. In titmice, the male may have to provide all the food the female needs to build up the eggs in her body, and supplying food during incubation is important in birds of prey, where the female alone sits on the eggs, and any time she spends hunting leaves the clutch vulnerable to predation.

The purpose of courtship feeding is not solely to provide nourishment for the female. This is shown by instances of female gulls returning from feeding and begging from a male which has been keeping guard on the territory and has not fed. The amount of food passed between these birds is less important than the cementing of the bond between the pair. This must also be the case for the buttonquail, in which the usual scheme of courtship is reversed. The female courts the male and feeds him, although she has to lay the eggs. Among pigeons, courtship feeding is often ritualized into "billing" in which the pair merely touch bills, or the female puts her bill into the male's without any food being passed.

Pairs of many species – crows, herons, pigeons, parrots, terns and albatrosses – preen the plumage of their mates as part of the courtship ritual. This is called allopreening, and is usually restricted to the feathers of the head and neck, which the bird cannot reach itself. It may, therefore, have the practical function of dealing with lice and fleas and cleaning the plumage, but the social function of cementing the pair bond is likely to be more important. In some species one bird will solicit allopreening by fluffing its head feathers and facing away to present its neck to its partner.

*Courtship feeding is an important part of courtship behavior in a variety of birds. Here an African little grebe (left) and a malachite kingfisher (right) present their females with fish, and a common bee-eater (far right) offers his mate a dragonfly. The extra food probably helps the female during egg-laying and incubation, but the main function of the ritual is to cement the bond between the pair. Hummingbirds (left) are unusual in that the female feeds the male.*

*Like courtship feeding, allopreening has both practical and pair-bonding functions. The partner can attend to parts of the plumage which cannot otherwise be reached, as in these white terns (left) and yellow-billed storks (right) but sometimes both birds preen together, as shown by these Eurasian spoonbills (below left) and blue-eyed cormorants (far right).*

*The courtship behavior of grebes is spectacular in the extreme and western grebes run across the surface of a lake in an amazing display of coordinated behavior.*

It is easy to be anthropomorphic about the courtship and mating of birds, because many appear to be faithfully monogamous, the male attracting a female and the pair settling down to rear a family together. In fact, 90% of bird species are monogamous, far more than in mammals or other vertebrate animals, where courtship and pairing are in most instances brief affairs, and the offspring are either abandoned to fend for themselves, or left to one or other parent to raise.

The reason for the prevalence of monogamy in of the second parent must be enlisted. In only 10% of bird species is it possible for one sex to rear the family alone. For these birds the pair bond may be extremely brief: as long as is needed for courtship to bring the sexes together for mating in some species, although others may stay together at least until the eggs are laid.

Among those 90% of birds where the sexes stay together to rear the brood, the share of duties varies. The chaffinch male, like many others, follows the hen

*At the end of the run, one grebe prepares to dive. It will be closely followed underwater by the other.*

*Inca terns have a more elaborate plumage than other terns. During courtship, the bare yellow skin on the chin, the yellow wattles around the mouth and the white "moustaches" enhance their displays.*

birds is that they are egg-laying and warm-blooded – indeed they are the only animal group to combine these characteristics, other than the primitive monotreme mammals, of which the platypus and spiny anteaters are the only living representatives. The eggs of birds are large in comparison to the size of the parents and they represent a substantial investment of energy. They also need continuous incubation and, in most species, the young must be brooded and fed. The strain of producing eggs and the subsequent parental duties are too much for one bird and the aid

assiduously while she collects material and builds the nest, but gives her no assistance, and then leaves her to incubate the eggs. He does not even feed her, but merely accompanies her when she makes brief forays in search of food. Only when the eggs hatch does the cock chaffinch assume parental duties by bringing some food to the nestlings, but the hen has to provide most of their requirements. By contrast, the male herring gull shares nest-building, incubation and feeding the chicks almost equally with his mate, and the same is true of many other species.

*A pheasant coucal apparently trying to revive its mate, killed by a car. There are occasional reports of birds staying with dead mates, and such behavior shows the strength of the pair bond in some species.*

The diversity of mating behavior – ranging from brief, promiscuous mating to lifelong fidelity and the sharing of parental duties – may seem difficult to explain at first sight. It can best be understood if the relationship between male and female is seen as a "hard bargain", in which each seeks to propagate his or her genes, and to get as much benefit as possible from its partner. A mated pair of birds have come together, often in an uneasy truce, because each needs the other's assistance to help rear their joint offspring. A successful individual is one which leaves a large number of viable offspring to continue its genetic line. Moreover, as producing offspring requires a considerable investment of time and energy, the more

offspring and, in species where parental care is shared, by a male who will be a good support in rearing the family. So she assesses the available males before choosing, with the result that in the early stages of courtship she is "coy" or "playing hard to get", to use two human terms, until she can decide.

In courtship, the male advertises his qualities, and the female assesses them. Older cock chaffinches obtain mates earlier in spring than younger rivals because their songs, displays and pursuits of the females are noticeably more "ardent". It is reasonable to suppose that the hen chaffinch recognizes an ardent suitor as being an older and more experienced bird, who is therefore likely to prove a capable parent for

*When birds stay together to rear their young, the bond between them has to be reinforced regularly, often with displays that echo the earlier courtship rituals. Here a pair of European white storks display to each other on their nest.*

*As a great blue heron rejoins its mate on the nest, a greeting ceremony takes place which helps to reduce the hostile reactions of the sitting bird.*

responsibility taken by one parent, the better it is for the other. Therefore, it is in the interest of each sex to make savings at the expense of its mate.

A male produces uncountable millions of sperm cells in his lifetime, at a small energy cost, so wastage can be tolerated. For the female, reproduction always involves a larger investment because she can produce only a limited number of eggs, and each requires a considerable amount of food for its manufacture. She needs to insure that her eggs are fertilized by a male who can pass on good genetic characteristics to her

her offspring. For a weaver, a desirable male is one that can build a nest that will not fall apart in the tropical rainy season. The male golden palm weaver makes a domed nest of woven strips of grasses or palm leaves. When the nest is complete, he displays by hanging upside down at the entrance, flapping his wings and singing. Females are attracted to survey the nest and, if satisfied, they line it with soft grass, mate and lay their eggs. Their criterion for a mate is that he should have a freshly built nest constructed of strong materials, because this will remain intact.

For other species, the male's ability as a provider of food may be important. At the start of the breeding season, the male tern flies over the nesting ground with a fish in his bill and advertises his availability to the females. When pairs have formed, the males continue bringing fish and give them to their mates as part of the ritual of courtship feeding. At a later stage food brought in by the males can critically affect the pair's breeding success. Just before laying, the female tern remains at the nest while the eggs are being formed in her body, and later, when the chicks have first hatched out, she broods them while the male brings their food. The male's ability to supply food at these times is crucial to the successful rearing of the family, and the female may well be able to judge this in advance from the amount of food she receives in the early stages of pair formation. If she finds this to be insufficient, she can terminate the partnership and look for a new mate before she has become seriously involved with parental duties.

The period between the meeting of the sexes and its consummation is extremely variable. Black-headed gulls mate soon after head-flagging has reduced hostility between them. In the "lek" species such as the sage grouse (p.158), in which the females visit the displaying male solely for mating, copulation follows very brief preliminaries, with the female squatting to solicit her chosen male's attention. At the other end of the scale, there are the albatrosses which pair up one year or more before copulation and egg-laying. For those species where a pair bond develops and lasts at least until the eggs are laid, copulation may be frequent. Grebes mate ten times a day during the two weeks before the eggs are laid. In all species of birds the act of mating is brief, the mounting lasting for only a few seconds as the male perches, rather precariously, on the female's back.

MONOGAMY

In monogamy, a male and female mate exclusively with each other, a situation which may be enforced by the male guarding his mate, or rigorously excluding other males from his territory. Among many ducks the monogamous pair bond only lasts until the female has laid her eggs, and the opportunity for cuckoldry has passed, but in most monogamous species the pair remains together to share parental duties. In such instances, the investment by each sex is large, and both need to exercise care in choosing a mate.

The common moorhen is rather unusual among monogamous birds because of the prominent, and even aggressive, role played by the female. Moorhens live in small flocks in winter and feed together on open ground near water. Pairs form before the birds set up territories and courtship is more often started by the female, who will fight off other females by striking with her clawed toes. The largest females get the pick of the males, but their choice, rather surprisingly, is for small males. The advantage of a small male appears to be that he needs less food to keep healthy and can put on comparatively more fat. A male with a high proportion of fat for his body weight

*Female golden palm weavers select their mates on the basis of nest-building ability. The male (left) will attract a mate only if he displays on a nest of fresh greenery. If it turns brown before he has found a mate, he will have to build a new nest.*

*In Arctic terns, the female assesses a male by the fish he brings. His ability to feed her is important, particularly when the eggs are being formed in her body.*

*In the final stages of a bout of courtship behavior, the female hooded grebe shows that she is ready to mate by crouching (left), and the male is then able to mount (below). In grebes, mating frequently takes place during courtship, some time before the female ovulates.*

can spend more time incubating (because less time need be spent feeding), so a female with a small, fat mate can start more clutches, and replace the losses to predators.

Choosing the best mate is especially important for birds which stay with the same partner for a period of years. For many species, fidelity is more to a place than to a partner, but by returning to the same nesting place they stand a very good chance of rejoining the previous year's mate. However, a genuinely permanent pair bond is found in long-lived birds such as tubenoses, gannets, gulls, swans and geese. Pink-footed geese mate in their second year and thereafter stay together until one dies. They leave the breeding grounds in the Arctic as a family unit and fly south with their brood, the young staying with their parents until the following spring.

Remaining faithful from year to year results in an increased breeding success. This is due, at least in part, to the experience of older birds. Kittiwakes spend the winter at sea and return to the colony at the start of the breeding season. The first to arrive, in February, are older birds. They are followed in March and April by less experienced birds, and kittiwakes breeding for the first time finally appear in April or May. Consequently, experienced kittiwakes tend to pair up and young birds are usually left with each other. As with other birds, breeding early in the season gives the best chance of success. Apart from arriving and nesting early there is also an advantage in experience itself. By retaining the same mate, a female kittiwake lays three to seven days earlier than those with a new partner.

Kittiwakes are not as faithful to their mates as geese or albatrosses, and mates are quite frequently changed. "Divorce" is related to failure in breeding, and in a twelve-year study of kittiwakes nesting on a riverside warehouse in north-eastern England, two-thirds of females who had failed in breeding during the previous year changed mates, whereas only one third that had bred successfully became "divorced".

*The act of mating in birds is always brief, as the female twists her tail to one side and the male turns his down to bring the two cloacas together. The position is precarious for long-legged birds, like the Eurasian oystercatcher (below right) and especially so if the pair is perching in a tree, like these Asian openbill storks (far left). Balance is assisted by flapping the wings. The white terns' mating (below left) is helped by the female squatting, with her breast resting on the branch.*

The reason for failure appears to be an incompatibility during incubation. The pair fails to synchronize shifts on the nest, so that one bird leaves before the other returns to take over incubation, and the eggs are exposed to the cold and predators. So, although there is an advantage in being faithful, there is also an advantage in changing mates if the previous partnership was not successful.

concentrate the defense on the female and this is the reason for the phenomenon of mate-guarding, in which pairs of ducks, finches, swallows and others keep close together in the period before egg-laying.

The finches that follow their mates, apparently so idly, as they collect nest material, and the mallard drakes that walk or swim a length or two behind their duck do so with good reason. In human terms, they

A male bird will be wasting his investment of time and energy if any female he mates with also mates with other males, so he attempts to insure his paternity. Vigorous defense of the territory by singing, displaying and chasing may not be totally effective, especially if the birds have to leave the territory to feed, as in seabirds and swallows. It is better to

are not acting out of any fondness or attachment to their spouses, but out of jealousy. They are there to see that another male does not mate with their partner. Pairs of European black-billed magpies live together through the winter, but as the egg-laying period nears in March, the male follows the female closely. The four or five days before the first egg is laid are particularly important because mate-guarding will insure that the male's own sperm is used to fertilize the eggs. (Fertilization takes place twenty-four hours before the egg is laid and a further two days prior to this are needed for the sperm to travel up the reproductive tract.) During this critical period the female magpie is busy feeding to manufacture the eggs, and the male keeps within about 5 yards

mating with the female. This woke the "guarding" male who rushed to attack.

Although a male bird can try to insure his breeding success by maintaining sole access to his mate, he can raise the number of his own offspring by "cuckolding" other males. In many species of ducks, forced mating or "rape" is a common occurrence. The drake can defend his mate against one male but he

*A wandering albatross (left) spreads its wings and gives vent to a loud scream in the sky-pointing display which is an advertisement by a male in search of a mate. Females circle overhead seeking unattached males. Two have landed by this male, and they will display in return, all three birds wheeling around each other over a considerable area. Such behavior is impossible for the black-browed albatross (right) which nests in packed colonies on clifftops.*

*A mallard chases off another drake who has come too close to his mate. Constant vigilance is needed, especially in the few days before the eggs are laid.*

*When a pair of black-browed albatrosses meet, either for courtship or at nest relief, they point their bills as if fencing in slow motion. A nervous bird turns its head aside (left) or wails loudly (below right). The fencing gradually lowers tension and the albatrosses eventually preen each other.*

(meters) of her; whenever she flies up, he follows her. The need for mate-guarding was demonstrated on one occasion when a male black-billed magpie, following his female, was seen to doze off, so that his head sank out of sight behind the parapet of the wall where he was perched. Within a few seconds, the neighboring male left his own mate and flew over to attempt a

will be brushed aside by a "gang" who chase and overcome the female, sometimes leaving her half-drowned. These attacks take place when the female is at a fertilizable stage and, among mallards, cuckoldry accounts for about one in ten ducklings, as revealed by their developing plumage with characteristics not possessed by their supposed fathers.

# P O L Y G A M O U S   B I R D S

While monogamy is the rule for the vast majority of birds, polygamy is practiced regularly by about 10% of species, and occasionally by others. In most cases, the male mates with two or more females, a situation known as polygyny, but there are also a few species that show the unusual condition known as polyandry, where a single female acquires two or more males.

For male birds, breeding can be achieved very "cheaply" by reducing it to the simple act of mating and leaving all the responsibilities to the female. The male is then free to increase his reproductive potential by seeking other females, but it is a successful strategy only when the female can rear the family alone, or

for the females' rearing of a family. If such resources are distributed unevenly some males will gain an unequal share, and attract more females.

In Africa and Asia there are ninety species of weavers which fall into two groups in their ecology and social life. Those that live in forests are mostly insectivorous. They feed solitarily in a large territory and, as food is evenly distributed but hard to gather, they are monogamous with both parents tending the family. The weavers of the savannah grasslands, by contrast, feed on seeds which have a patchy distribution. The flocks of weavers find plenty of seeds, so there is no competition for food, but there is

*Competition for females has led to the evolution of eye-catching displays in some birds. Here, a Jackson's widowbird is leaping repeatedly into the air, with tail plumes streaming. He attracts the drab female (right) who is so different that she seems to belong to another species.*

with little help. Thus, polygyny is most frequent among birds whose young leave the nest soon after hatching and feed themselves, so that parental care is minimal. It is also a feature of those birds that feed on fruit or seeds, which appear in seasonal crops and allow a single parent to feed the brood with ease.

Even within species usually regarded as monogamous, there are occasional records of polygyny, where a male is maintaining two mates who either lay eggs in separate nests or share a single one. A smaller number of species practice polygyny more regularly. In general, the habit occurs where the male's territory contains resources which are critical

a shortage of trees for nesting and males compete for nest sites. Because females can rear the young on the plentiful seeds, the males are free to defend the limited number of nest sites and concentrate on attracting as many females as possible. The quelea is an exception; it is monogamous because the huge colonies exhaust local crops of seeds and the males' help is needed to bring food from distant sources.

The sort of breeding system which can evolve when there is an unevenly distributed food supply is neatly demonstrated by the orange-rumped honeyguide. Like other honeyguides, this species robs bees' nests to eat the wax and grubs, and the male honeyguide defends a territory around such a nest, fighting off other males. Because bees' nests are not very common, a few males can monopolize this food supply and they are able to mate with the female honeyguides which come to feed on the nests. One male is recorded as mating with eighteen different females in a single season.

Nest sites are another resource that can be patchy, as already seen with the grassland weavers, and a remarkable study on the lark bunting showed how the amount of shade in a territory determined a male's attractiveness. Lark bunting males return each spring to their nesting areas in the grasslands of North America. Some males acquire two mates, others a single mate but about one-fifth fail to get any female. The failures are unable to provide the females' requirement of a nesting place with sufficient cover to

predators or finding food (see Chapter 7). The most familiar bird to maintain a harem is the Asian ring-necked pheasant which has been introduced as a gamebird to Europe, North America, Australia and New Zealand. During the winter the sexes usually live apart, in small flocks. At the end of winter the flocks of males split up and territories of several acres are established. At first, young males may keep company with the territory holders, but they are eventually banished to the edges of the territories. The female flocks take up residence in the territories but the males have no control over their movement and the females may enter or leave, although while in the territory they are defended by the owner. After mating, the females disperse to make nests and, once all have laid, the male soon ceases to defend the territory. However he may, on rare occasions,

*A nesting colony of village weavers. This species eats seeds, which have a patchy distribution, and social nesting allows birds to follow each other in the morning in search of a good crop. Once located, the seeds are plentiful, so females can raise the chicks unaided. This leads to polygyny, with the males competing for the limited nest sites and mating with as many females as possible.*

keep off rain or excessive sun, and to hide the eggs and nestlings from snakes and ground squirrels. Breeding was improved experimentally by attaching crowns of plastic leaves to plants to give extra shade and, by estimating the amount of shade each territory gave, it was even possible to predict which would attract two, one or no females.

Another form of polygyny is to defend a group of females rather than the resource which attracts them. Such "harems" are part of the social life of many mammals, but they are rare among birds because they only occur where the females naturally gather into flocks for some reason, such as detecting or avoiding

incubate the eggs and he often tends the chicks of one of his families.

PROMISCUOUS MALES

The ultimate in polygyny occurs when male birds reduce their investment to a minimum and are promiscuous. There is no bond between male and female and each male mates with as many females as possible but takes no part in rearing the brood. These males defend neither a female, nor a resource for rearing the family, but maintain only a small patch of ground where they can mate with any female that visits them. Their sole contribution to breeding is the act of insemination, and they have the capacity to mate

*Male ruffs show off their magnificent plumage at a lek (below). They defend small courts which they sometimes share with a satellite male, distinguished by his white ruff. When a satellite enters a court there is a sequence of displays which includes the owner placing his bill on the satellite's head (bottom left). Satellites are not always tolerated and may be forced to leave (right), but those that get established on a court join in "flutter-jumping" displays (bottom right) to attract females.*

with a number of females and sire several broods of young with little of the effort required in a monogamous relationship, except in the competition with other males, which is intense. Such birds tend to show very strongly the effects of sexual selection in the development of elaborate plumages (see Chapter 6). This form of mating occurs among a number of families including grouse, sandpipers, hummingbirds, manakins, cotingas and birds of paradise. In these birds, males can be freed from parental duties to concentrate on displaying because their way of life is such that the females can rear the young alone.

In promiscuous species, the competition between males and pairing with the females both take place at traditional display grounds, collectively called "arenas", or "leks" (from the Scandinavian word meaning "play") although there are other more descriptive names used in connection with particular species, such as "booming ground", "strutting ground" and "dancing ground". Within the lek, each male occupies a "court" which may be as much as 10 yards (meters) in diameter for the sharp-tailed grouse or a mere 20 inches (50 centimeters) across in the white-bearded manakin.

The ruff is a sandpiper which shows an unusually complex version of the lek system. Male ruffs are distinguished from the females, once called reeves, by a magnificent ruff of feathers, and an ornate plumage which occurs in a number of color variations. They gather at leks, and are visited by females who will line up to mate with the dominant cocks. How the selection is made is not known, but the unusual feature is that some courts are shared with a satellite male. The females are courted by both males, and sometimes the owner is so busy defending the court against neighbors that the satellite manages to mate. Satellites are distinguished by their white ruffs, so they form a separate genetic strain and never become full court owners.

The sage grouse of the western sagebrush country have a simpler lek system. The males make occasional visits to their leks throughout fall and winter, and start to display there in early spring. They return each day for three or four hours. Standing with tail cocked and white neck feathers raised in a ruff, each cock inflates an airsac in his throat, compresses it by muscle contraction, then suddenly expels the air. The result is a loud "pop".

*Ruffs compete vigorously for the best courts and violent fights may break out (left and below left). The aim is then to attract the females who visit the leks to prospect among the displaying males (bottom left). Females are attracted to certain males (below); they respond to their courtship and are mated (below right).*

For much of the time the cocks are displaying only to each other and the hens visit the lek for no more than about twenty days in April. On her single visit to the lek, a sage hen will mate once and, like all the other females, she makes her way to the center of the lek. The result is that the large majority of matings are performed by only one or two males, and most of the rest do not mate at all. A young cock in his first year establishes a court on the edge of the lek. In following years he returns to the same part of the lek but there is a general shift inwards as young cocks compete for the central courts and take over those of birds which have died. So the cocks which mate are the oldest and, having survived so long, they must be the "pick of the bunch" for the females to select.

## POLYANDRY

When conditions of food resources make it possible for one parent to raise the young and let the other desert, the male stands the best chance of abandoning

doubles the reproductive potential of birds which would otherwise only have time to rear one brood because their breeding season is short. Sanderlings can be double-brooded because in parts of the Arctic there are enormous numbers of insects to feed on. One bird can incubate a clutch without assistance since it can collect food quickly enough to return to the nest before the eggs have chilled fatally; after hatching, the chicks can feed themselves.

True polyandry may have developed out of this type of monogamous system and occurs when the female bird, having laid one clutch, leaves it with the father and seeks another male to fertilize her second clutch. The males are now the resource to be defended. This happens with the spotted sandpiper, whose female is sometimes monogamous but can also lay five clutches, each of four eggs, in one season. Her problem is to find enough males to incubate them, amid competition from other females. Both males and

*A displaying sage grouse looks equally spectacular, whether viewed from behind (right) or from the side (below). Although he displays for several weeks, the females pay only short visits to the lek and he must lose no opportunity to court them.*

*The "balloon display" of male great bustard is a signal to females. When one approaches she may peck the male's feathers by way of enticement. The male's display then intensifies and he circles her until she is ready to mate.*

one mate to seek another. Having fertilized the female, he is free to depart while she must lay the eggs. For this reason polygyny is much more common than polyandry in which one female mates with more than one male. There are certain circumstances when polyandry can occur, however, and the sex roles then become reversed. The female defends a territory, courts the male and leaves him to rear the brood.

The first stage of role reversal can be seen in some monogamous species where food is so plentiful that the female can quickly form a second clutch of eggs after laying the first. The process of territorial defense and courtship is the same as in other monogamous birds, but having laid one clutch, the female leaves it in the care of her mate and lays the second in another nest, incubating this clutch herself. This method, which occurs in the red-legged partridge, swallow-tailed cotinga and sanderling,

females defend territories against members of their own sex, but males are also concerned with defending the chicks against predators, whereas the females have nothing more to do with the brood once the eggs are laid. Females are more aggressive at the time of courtship, when older females get larger territories, more males and hence more offspring.

Polyandry has arisen in fewer than 1% of bird species, spread over a number of birds families, although it does not occur in the passerines. Polyandrous species include tinamous, quails, several shorebirds, buttonquails, jaçanas, and one cuckoo.

The northern jaçana, found from Texas to Costa Rica, is the only species in which the female is known to maintain several males simultaneously. As the water rises in pools and rivers at the start of the rainy season the males set up territories where they can build floating nests, and the females set up larger territories containing the stretches of water where the males will nest. The number of males that a female acquires depends on the size of their territories compared with hers. She usually gets two or three but if the male territories are large, the female may have to be monogamous. She stays with each partner for several days before she lays a clutch, so he can fertilize the eggs. Thereafter she does not visit the nest except to drive away predators such as purple gallinules, and come to the rescue when the male northern jaçana gives the alarm.

The female red-necked phalarope has even less contact with her brood. She is much more brightly colored than the male and, instead of defending a territory, she defends the male and denies other females access. She initiates the courtship with an advertisement flight in which she repeatedly takes off and lands while calling. When a male appears she swims around him, entices him into following her and

*This kori bustard, displaying in his territory, has been approached by a female. He has ceased patrolling his borders and is standing still with neck feathers fluffed and tail lowered.*

continues with the advertisement flights. Eventually, a pairing takes place and the two remain close together. Both construct nest scrapes and the female chooses one in which to lay her eggs.

As soon as the first egg is laid, the male phalarope takes charge of its incubation, and when the clutch is complete the female leaves. The female phalarope is almost always monogamous but if there are any unattached males, perhaps one which has lost its first clutch, she will court and defend him and leave him with another clutch.

An unusual variation of polyandry, based on cooperation by males, occurs in some species. In the Tasmanian native hen, two brothers form a breeding group with one female, and the three remain together for life. The reduction in the number of progeny each male fathers by sharing a female may be offset because his brother's offspring share some of his genes.

*A male turkey dwarfs the female as he mates with her. A difference in size between the sexes is typical of polygynous species.*

*A male spotted sandpiper incubates his eggs. The females can lay up to five clutches by leaving each one with a different male.*

However, the Galapagos hawk establishes trios involving males which are unrelated. The advantage is less obvious but appears to be that, in the limited space on the islands, life expectancy is higher if a territory is held, perhaps because a familiar hunting ground is advantageous (see Chapter 7), so it is worth sharing because a longer life means more chances to breed. In both cases, the advantage to the female is that she gets extra assistance in rearing her young.

COMPLICATED RELATIONSHIPS

When birds of one sex mate with two or more of the other, there is the possibility of complicated relationships in which the advantages to the individuals may be difficult to explain. The mating habits of the ostrich were once a puzzle and there was uncertainty as to whether they were monogamous or

*Flocks of mallards (below) often comprise more drakes than ducks. They display to each other and join in communal courtship activities, the unmated males trying to usurp the ducks of other drakes. Courtship begins in the fall, or even late summer, and then continues throughout the winter, but the drakes leave the ducks once the eggs are laid.*

*Wilson's phalarope is usually monogamous, but it is unusual in that the female (on the right) is more brightly colored and courts the male, leaving him to incubate the eggs (below). Sometimes she lays extra clutches and leaves each with a new male.*

polygynous. Cocks courted several hens yet only one hen was recorded on the nest or leading the chicks. The truth is quite strange.

The cock ostrich defends a large territory and acquires a mate who lays her eggs in a nest scrape. A few days later other hens arrive and also lay in the nest. The first, or major, hen gets off the nest to let them in, but only she and the male incubate the eggs. Eventually there are thirty to forty eggs in the nest and, because one bird cannot cover them properly, some get pushed to the edge. One theory was that this was a means of regulating the temperature of the eggs so that they hatch together. In fact, the exposed eggs are cooked in the sun.

The true explanation is that the major hen can recognize her own eggs (perhaps by the pattern of the

*A group of long-tailed shrikes, or magpie-shrikes (left), display in a tree, to repel another group from its territory. In this species, a pair mates monogamously, but it is assisted in rearing the nestlings by other non-breeding birds. Complex groupings of this type are not uncommon in the tropics and are described on p.190–191.*

pores in the plain white shell) and she rolls those of the minor hens to the edge. There, they form a buffer against predators. A jackal or vulture can only eat a few ostrich eggs, or later chicks, so the extra ones reduce the chances of the major hen's offspring being eaten. The large clutch is, in effect, getting safety from numbers, like a flock of birds. The advantage to the minor hens is that, although they have failed to gain a mate with whom to rear their chicks, by behaving like cuckoos and laying in another ostrich's nest, there is the chance that at least a few of their eggs will survive to hatch.

The dunnock is a common bird of the European countryside, once called the hedge sparrow, although it is not related to the sparrows. Its secretive habits make it easy to overlook, and it is best known for its

overlap two males' territories, with the advantage that both will help her to feed her chicks.

A complication is that a male may share his territory with a smaller, subordinate male. In other passerines, excess males fail to get mates, but dunnocks manage to establish themselves in other males' territories by remaining unobtrusively in dense cover. The dominant, territory-owning male tries to insure his paternity of the eggs by guarding the female as she is approaching laying, and spends as much as half of his time chasing the other male. Vicious fights can break out and the death of the subordinate dunnock may result. However, he may manage to mate when the dominant male has lost sight of the female. She is unselective and will solicit either male, crouching and quivering her wings.

*Courtship displays and song, or distinctively colored plumage, normally prevent interbreeding because they enable a bird to identify members of its own species. This sometimes breaks down, especially among captive birds. Interbreeding between closely related species may result in hybrids, such as these macaws, which have a mixture of their parents' plumages.*

jingling song and exquisite blue eggs. Its breeding habits were believed to be quite mundane until a close study was made of a color-banded population. It transpired that the relationships between the sexes are unusually variable and complicated. These relationships demonstrate, more than in any other species, the conflict of interests between the sexes, and the fact that what is advantageous for one is not necessarily of most benefit to the other.

Male dunnocks set up territories at the beginning of the breeding season, and later the females set up feeding ranges. If a female's range lies within the territory of one male, she will mate monogamously with him, but if her range overlaps two territories she will be polyandrous. The female needs a larger range when food is scarce, and it will then be more likely to

Sometimes she evades the dominant male and flies off through the undergrowth in search of other males. This is, again, to her advantage because a male will help to rear her chicks if he has mated with her. It is a disadvantage for the other male in the duo because, although he has also mated with her, his paternity will be put in doubt and he may have to rear chicks which are not his own. However, the male dunnock has an unusual means of improving his chances of fatherhood. Just before mating, he pecks repeatedly at the female's cloaca and she responds by ejecting a mass of sperm stored from previous matings. By such means he effectively replaces his rival as the likely father of the brood, but because the other male has actually mated with the female, he will still help care for the brood.

# BOWERBIRDS
## AND BIRDS OF PARADISE

In ancient times there was a trade in bird skins between the island of New Guinea and the civilizations of the Mediterranean. Only a very valuable item of trade was worth bringing such a distance, but these skins were of rare and amazingly brilliant-plumaged birds. In this trade lies the origin of the myth of the phoenix, the bird that arose from its own ashes. The skins from the Orient were wrapped in myrrh and scorched leaves for protection and,

their "courts". Males establish courts near one another, although the distance between them in the dense forest may be such that the grouping is not obvious to human eyes. Females visit the courts, select a male, are courted, mate and then depart.

The birds of paradise represent the last word in the development of the ostentatious male plumage seen in other polygynous birds, such as pheasants and grouse, where the pressure of sexual selection has led

*Elaboration of male plumage through sexual selection reaches a peak in the birds of paradise. The emperor bird of paradise (above) has a cascade of loose plumes as well as iridescent neck feathers. It shows them to best effect by shaking them, while hanging upside down at the climax of its display (center).*

according to the myth, this was how the phoenix wrapped its own ashes for transport to the Temple of the Sun at Heliopolis.

Centuries later, when European explorers were penetrating the forests of the Australasian region, they found these birds of paradise in their native home, and in the same forests, there were bower birds which fashioned elaborate constructions of sticks and decorated them with flowers, berries, stones and other objects. These two groups of birds are very closely related and they represent the most advanced stage in the evolution of the lek mating system.

In nearly all bowerbirds and birds of paradise the males play no part in the care and rearing of the family but spend considerable time and energy in display at

to visual effects that seem far more elaborate than necessary (p. 117). Among the birds of paradise, there are spectacular capes, fans, epaulets, twisted wires and pennons, often brightly colored or iridescent, and sometimes augmented with colored patches of bare skin. These special features develop in males at the age of two to five years. The females remain dull as befits birds which must be inconspicuous on the nest. One species, the magnificent bird of paradise, enhances its displays by spending hours plucking leaves from the trees above its court so that its iridescent plumage will be lit by a shaft of sunlight.

Not all birds of paradise are highly ornamented. Both sexes of the paradise or silky crow of the Moluccas are an identical glossy blackish color with

*The magnificent bird of paradise has strikingly colored feet, bill and tongue, and its iridescent plumage shines in the sunlight.*

*Lawe's six-wired bird of paradise (below) is relatively somber but he still outshines the female, whose dull brown plumage provides camouflage during incubation.*

no ornament, and in MacGregor's bird of paradise both male and female have the same orange wattles behind the ear and yellowish primaries. In these and similar species, a strong pair bond is formed and, although the female builds the nest and incubates alone, as in many songbirds, the male remains nearby and later helps to feed the nestlings.

The evolution of the bowerbirds has taken an entirely different and unique turn. Instead of eye-catching plumage, they have taken to making bowers – structures of a complexity and sophistication not found elsewhere in the animal world. These are used only for courtship and have nothing to do with nesting. At first, European visitors to Australia could not believe that these structures were not manmade

around a sapling. The striped bowerbird has a shorter crest and adds a roof to its bower, while the crestless gardener bowerbird is indistinguishable from the female and makes a wide roof decorated with shells, berries and flowers.

The most elaborate bowers are the avenues built by several species. Lauterbach's bowerbird builds four parallel walls of sticks, rather than the two walls of other species. The walls are stuck into a floor of interwoven twigs and the inner walls are lined with fine grasses and decorated with pebbles and berries. Each court is about 3 feet ( a meter) long and 18 inches (half a meter) wide and one contained over 3,000 sticks, 1,000 grass stems and several pounds of stones. Other bowerbirds include a strange collection

*The bower of the golden bowerbird (center) consists of masses of twigs woven around saplings. The owner waits on a perch above the bower and, when a female visits him, he displays by fluttering his wings, jerking his head and carrying sticks and flowers to the bower.*

*A great bowerbird (above) decorates its bower with pebbles, bones, broken glass and other items. The female spends several days at the bower during which time mating occurs.*

and they decided that they were, perhaps, the graves of Aborigines, or places where their children had been playing.

It is thought that bowerbirds evolved from the birds of paradise, probably from species which display in the lower levels of the forest and clear their courts of leaves. In the bowerbirds, this habit has been developed to make the court increasingly conspicuous and, in reverse, the plumage has become dull, with the loss of bright coloring except sometimes as a crest. The correlation between elaboration of the bower and loss of bright plumage is shown by three species of the *Amblyornis* genus. The male MacGregor's bowerbird has a long golden orange crest and builds a simple bower of sticks arranged

of objects for ornament: colored insects, spiders' webs, snail shells and cast snake skins. Near human habitation, broken glass, paper, string and matchboxes are added, and missing articles from the home have sometimes been recovered from bowers. The satin bowerbird uses a twig "paintbrush" to paint the bower with berry juice.

Some people have seen in the constructions of these bowers something approaching human art. When decorating the bower, a male bowerbird will place a berry or pebble, step back and cock its head on one side, then come forward to pick up the object and place it somewhere else. He continues to do this until, to all appearances, he has achieved the desired effect.

*The satin bowerbird (above) paints his bower with the juice of berries, sometimes using a twig as a paintbrush. His bower (top right) is a U-shaped construction carefully built up from small sticks. Mating takes place inside the bower.*

Like mammals, but unlike the majority of other animals, birds devote a great deal of care to their offspring. None abandons its eggs without any provision because birds are warm-blooded and the developing eggs must be maintained at a high, even temperature. This warmth speeds the development of the embryo, so that birds' eggs hatch more quickly than those of cold-blooded animals such as the reptiles. The shorter time taken to hatch reduces their vulnerability because there is less time for predators to find them.

After the eggs have hatched, the young birds go through a period when they are more or less reliant on their parents for warmth, protection and, in most species, food. Parental care usually lasts at least until the young birds are able to fly and forage for

may be very simple or extremely complex.

The simplest nests are depressions in the ground, which may be there already – the water dikkop lays its eggs on hippopotamus droppings and sandgrouse sometimes use large hoofprints – or may be formed by the bird. A scrape is made by squatting on the ground, scraping with the feet and pressing with the breast while slowly rotating to produce a round depression. Scrapes are made by shorebirds, nightjars, gulls and grouse, and they are usually lined with pebbles, shells or scraps of vegetation.

One danger faced by birds nesting in a simple scrape is that they can easily knock the eggs out of the nest, an accident that is most likely to happen when the bird is suddenly disturbed. Getting the egg back into the nest is a tricky maneuver because the ovoid

*The Indian courser lays its eggs on bare ground, without any attempt to build a nest.*

*The eggs of the Australian fairy tern are beautifully camouflaged in this nest of shell fragments, set among weathered coral.*

themselves but maleo and mallee fowls are independent from the moment that they dig themselves out of the nest mound. At the other extreme, large eagles, frigatebirds and geese spend many months – sometimes even a year or more – with their parents after they can fly.

THE NEST

A few birds make no nest at all. The white tern lays its single egg on the branch of a tree and the chick has very strong claws which enable it to cling tightly and even hang upside down. Common murres deposit their eggs on bare rock, and the waved albatross, emperor and king penguins shuffle about with their eggs balanced on their feet. But for most birds, care of the eggs is aided by a nest. This is usually something more than a mere basket for keeping the eggs together, since it also helps to keep them warm and protect them from predators, but the nest structure

shape prevents it from rolling straight. When faced with an egg outside the nest, the sitting bird – goose, gull or shorebird, for example – reaches out, hooks its bill over the egg and draws it in, carefully steering it with delicate movements of the bill. It is very easy for the egg to be deflected and an hour may elapse before it is safely back in the nest.

A more elaborate ground nest is made by bringing a greater amount of material to build a solidly based saucer. Geese collect their nest material by reaching out from the beginnings of the nest, plucking grass and dropping it onto the existing structure. The wandering albatross shuffles backwards to the nest while repeatedly lifting lumps of soil and vegetation and throwing them back over its shoulder until it has piled up a mound, 3 feet (1 meter) across.

If there is no nesting material nearby, it has to be collected on special trips. Grebes and gannets bring in plants, and penguins sometimes have to walk down to the shore to find pebbles, carrying them laboriously back to the nest, one by one, in their bills.

A nest above the ground gives a bird safety from many predators and this is why so many birds nest in trees. Where one species builds in both situations, for example the mourning dove, predation is much greater on ground nests. But tree-nesting has its drawbacks, principally the loss of eggs which fall out of the nest, and the threat posed by climbing and flying predators. These problems can be overcome by building deep cups or enclosed nests, so that the eggs cannot fall out, and by hiding the nest or placing it in an inaccessible position.

The variety of nests in trees is bewildering. They range in size from the tiny delicate cups of hummingbirds to the massive piles of sticks built up over the years by eagles and herons, which may become so heavy that they eventually snap the supporting branches. Some are very simple, such as the nests of pigeons, which are so flimsy that the eggs show clearly through the bottom; but many are

One intriguing problem is how the very first billfuls of material, on which the whole edifice will depend, are secured to twigs and branches to make the foundations. Much presumably depends on choosing a suitable site initially, and wedging or wrapping material in place. A female European chaffinch flies for some time among trees and bushes to prospect for a nest site. She lands on a branch and hops down it to the fork. If there is a deep crotch of two or more branches, she turns around and about, flicking her tail and inspecting it. Then she hops into the crotch and continues turning with feathers fluffed. Several sites will be inspected, and building materials brought to some, before she makes the final decision. There must be some configuration of branches that gives the best support for a nest, and this is recognized even by an inexperienced chaffinch. There is also the consideration of shelter from predators, which will be better in dense foliage. Whatever the criteria may be, once the decision is made, the chaffinch's behavior suddenly becomes more purposeful and she brings a steady supply of material to the site.

*A blacksmith plover excavating a nest scrape. It leans forward and, slowly circling, pushes with its breast and thrusts with its feet to make a shallow saucer.*

marvelously delicate constructions of finely woven materials, securely fastened to a foundation of twigs, and often decorated with lichens and mosses.

The technique for constructing the cup nest typical of so many common birds is essentially the same as that used for building a nest on the ground. The simplest types of tree nest are the shallow bowls built by herons, cormorants, pigeons and others, in which a mass of material gradually accumulates. The bird works it into a compact structure, with a bowl to hold the eggs, by the same action as a ground-nester, scraping backwards with its feet and pushing with its breast. A similar technique is even used for making delicate cup nests; the material is not so much woven as felted by being teased, combed and matted until a firm, compact fabric is produced. The walls of the cup are shaped by lifting material onto the rim and tucking it in with trembling movements of the bill.

The first step is to make some "anchor points" by wrapping strands of spiders' web around the branches. Attaching one end of a strand, she leans around the other side of the branch, picks up the free end and loops it around. From these points, more material is added and a shell of moss and grass is knitted together with more webs, by stabbing and shaking actions of the bill, until the nest is firmly wedged in its foundation. The inside of the shell is then padded with dry grass and a little moss, and worked into shape. This is done by the chaffinch sinking into the cup, fluffing her body feathers, spreading her wings against the sides, and spinning around. She also balances across the cup on her neck and tail and rakes with her feet to comb the material. Finally there is a lining of rootlets, feathers and fur and the outside is decorated with lichens, bound with web.

The peak of skill in nest construction has been reached by the aptly named weaver. As described in Chapter 8, the female village weaver selects her mate on the basis of the nest which he has built. When she has chosen a male she adds a lining of feathers and grass heads to his nest. The male's building materials are strips of green vegetation, taken from fresh grass blades and palm fronds. They are torn off by the weaverbird grasping the leaf-edge in his bill and flying away with it.

Leaves, stems, moss and twigs are the main materials for nest building in most species but mud is make the clay soil soft enough to work. The pair first builds a cup and then raises the walls until it is roofed in. The nest chamber is reached by a porch and the walls are 1½ inches (4 centimeters) thick and reinforced with grass, so the nest provides good protection for the inhabitants.

The swifts use saliva as a mortar for binding nest materials, and their salivary glands increase in size during the breeding season to provide the extra quantities needed for nest building. The European swift gathers feathers, dried grass, scraps of paper and other items that it can find floating in the air, and

*Cliff swallows collect beakfuls of mud, while carefully holding up their wings and tails, to avoid getting wet and dirty (below). The mud is worked into pellets to construct flask-shaped nests (bottom right).*

*A male masked weaver constructing his third nest. The first two have failed to attract a female so, as the nest material withers, he must build a replacement with fresh strips of leaves.*

*A pair of New Zealand robin-flycatchers build a cup of mosses and rootlets, set in a crevice. As with other flycatchers, nest-building is mainly the responsibility of the female. In many species of small birds, the male accompanies the female while she is nest-building but does not help her.*

an alternative used by several birds. Members of the swallow family make cup-shaped or flask-shaped nests by sticking together balls of soft mud collected from the edges of puddles, pools and streams. A firm vertical support is needed and barn and cliff swallows now nest mainly within old buildings and under eaves. Only rarely do they use caves, cliffs or branches which must have been the original sites in prehistoric times. The large family of South American ovenbirds get their names from a few species which build clay nests shaped like primitive ovens. The rufous ovenbird starts building in winter when the rains

constructs a shallow cup nest in roofs, or in holes in cliffs or old woodpecker nests in trees. The saliva is dribbled out in threads and the material worked into a cup with the feet before it sets. The alpine swift and pallid swift make similar nests, but the spine-tailed swifts use twigs, gathered by diving past a tree and ripping them off with the feet. The twigs are worked into cups with saliva, which is strong enough, when set, to glue them to vertical surfaces such as the inside of hollow trees. In the case of the chimney swift, the inner surfaces of disused chimneys are the main nesting sites.

*Ovenbird nests perched on fence posts are a common sight on the South American pampas. They are made of clay which is gathered when the rain has softened the ground. By the time the eggs are laid, the clay has set hard.*

The cave swiftlets are best known for their use of echolocation (p. 46) for finding their way to nests in pitch-dark caves, but they are also the providers of the ingredients for the Chinese dish, "birds'-nest-soup". In these species, the saliva is the main nest material rather than acting just as a glue. Some species mix feathers, leaves and other material with the saliva but the nests most prized for soup-making, such as those of the grey-rumped swiftlet, are made of pure saliva.

A bird's nest offers more protection, against predators and the sun, rain and cold, if it is roofed over. Roofed nests are commonly built by passerines,

sticks cemented with mud, then the walls are raised and roofed over with 3 feet (a meter) of thatch decorated with bones, feathers, snakeskins and other debris. When complete, the nest will contain something like 10,000 sticks and other items, and will be large enough to house the two adults and their young even when they are fully grown. The entrance faces away from the tree trunk so that predators such as genets and snakes will find it very hard to get in, but why the hammerkop should go to such lengths when other storks find an ordinary platform of sticks adequate is something of a mystery.

*The crested tree swift's nest (top center) is a flimsy structure made of feathers and bark, and the single egg is glued to the nest with saliva. By contrast, the gray-backed rufous fantail (below center) makes a deep cup of bark bound with spiders' webs.*

*When there is a shortage of trees, many birds use artificial nest-sites. A telegraph pole provides a good platform for the solid mud nest of an Australian magpie-lark. This bird is not related to the true larks, all of which nest on the ground.*

and they are mainly found in the tropics, where there is a greater danger from nest predators such as mongooses and snakes. Among the few exceptions in temperate latitudes are the black-billed magpie's mass of sticks, the bushtit's domed nest of moss, lichen and leaves, and the woven grass ball that gives the North American ovenbird its name (it is a wood warbler, not to be confused with the South American ovenbird family). Some roofed nests are enormous structures. That of the hammerkop or hammer-headed stork of Africa is an outsize construction of sticks that takes two months to build. First, a platform is constructed of

The many birds which nest in cavities include the kingfishers, trogons, hornbills and woodpeckers, and some titmice, alcids, petrels and parrots. A few, such as the titmice, build a nest within the cavity, but many have a much reduced nest of a few feathers or wood chips, and the kingfishers and petrels lay their eggs directly on the floor of the chamber. The form of the cavity ranges from the gap behind a piece of loose bark used by brown creepers, to extensive burrows dug in a cliff face or the ground. In the case of the rhinoceros auklet of the North Pacific, the burrow may be a seemingly unnecessary 26 feet (8 meters) long.

*A bushtit (top right) manipulates spiders' webs to bind fragments of lichen together. They are built up into a firm but flexible cup-shaped base for the nest. At a later stage, the female (below right) brings feathers to line the almost-finished nest.*

*The brown creeper builds its nest in a natural cavity, often behind the loose bark of a dead tree.*

*The Atlantic puffin (below left) often burrows into soil or takes over the hole of a rabbit or shearwater, but it also makes use of cavities under boulders. Feathers and bits of straw may be brought to the burrow but no proper nest lining is made.*

*A burrowing owl (below center) carries a lump of horse dung to the entrance of its nest, where it may act as camouflage or simply as decoration.*

*A common moorhen (below right) adds to the nest after the clutch is laid. If there is a flood, the nest must be built up to keep the eggs clear of the rising water.*

One of the strangest burrow sites is that of the violaceous trogon, which takes over a wasps' nest, eating the adult wasps and then digging out the comb to make a cavity for its nest.

Natural cavities in trees provide nesting sites for owls, starlings, titmice, bluebirds and sparrows, and a shortage of sites can severely limit the population. The provision of nestboxes has improved the prospects of the eastern bluebird, whose nest sites had either been taken over by tree swallows, house sparrows and starlings, or had disappeared completely through the loss of old trees with hollows.

THE EGGS

After mating, sperm may be stored before fertilization occurs, for a period which varies from a few minutes to several days. The egg is laid about a day later, although it can be retained for several days if conditions are unfavorable. The number of eggs laid in a clutch is related to the ecology of the species. If too many eggs are laid the parents will not be able to feed the young properly and their investment in any that die will be wasted. So in most species, the number of eggs laid has been adjusted, through the process of natural selection, to yield the maximum number of fledged young that the parents are capable of rearing. Some species do not fit this pattern: gannets, which lay only one egg, are capable of rearing two chicks if any extra egg is placed under them, and macaroni penguins lay two eggs but only rear one chick. What happens to the other egg is not entirely clear, but it is lost from the nest before it hatches. Tropical landbirds tend to lay fewer eggs than temperate birds because short days restrict the time they can spend collecting food for their chicks. Within species, clutches become larger with increasing latitude and longer summer days; European robins' clutches increase from an average of 3.5 in the Canary Islands to 6.3 in Scandinavia. Birds of prey relate their clutch size to the availability of food, laying large clutches when food is plentiful and sometimes completely failing to breed in times of scarcity.

Some species lay a fixed number of eggs while others have the capacity to replace eggs which have been lost, as when one is accidentally knocked out of the nest. If an Adèlie penguin's first egg is removed it will lay one extra so that it maintains the full clutch of two. Gulls can lay three or more extra eggs and one yellow-shafted flicker was induced to lay seventy-one eggs in seventy-three days by removing them as they were laid. Once incubation is under way, laying stops, and part-formed eggs are reabsorbed. If the whole clutch is lost, a replacement set may be laid after courtship has been repeated and, in some cases, a new nest built.

## INCUBATION

Birds' eggs must be kept at an even temperature for proper development, and too high or too low a temperature will kill the embryos. Maintaining the correct temperature throughout the period of incubation is a demanding chore for the parent birds: they use up energy in transferring heat to the eggs, and they are also more vulnerable to predators while sitting on the nest.

The sharing of incubation duties ranges from both parents taking equal responsibility, as in gulls, cormorants and petrels (or uniquely, in waxbills, with male and female incubating side by side on the nest), to the duties falling entirely on one sex. This is usually the female, but in polyandrous birds it is the male (p.160). Single-parent incubation is a feature of species where polygamy leaves one parent in charge of the family, although it also occurs in some monogamous species such as swans and geese. Male swans sometimes incubate while their mates are feeding but the eggs are more usually covered by nest material at this time.

When the female undertakes all the incubation she still needs to feed. The nest has to be left untended while she is feeding, and although the eggs may be covered by nest material for warmth and security, they are still at risk. In many birds, the exposure of the eggs is reduced by the male

*The elaborate hanging nest of a yellow-breasted sunbird is a defense against the many tree-dwelling predators that live in tropical forests.*

*Strips of vegetation woven around the stems of reeds make a secure nest for the great reed warbler (below left). The whole structure will sway in the wind without endangering the eggs.*

*The hammerkop (below center) builds an enormous "tree-house" of mud and sticks which is large and strong enough to support the weight of a man.*

*A buffalo weaver (below right) is making a foundation for its nest by wedging acacia twigs firmly into place. The finished nest will be a dome of thorny twigs, lined with fine grasses.*

provisioning the female in an extension of courtship feeding. Tree-nesting hornbills walled into their nests must rely entirely on food brought by their mates and female great tits get 40% of their requirements from the male. Birds of prey also rely heavily on the male provisioning the female, but if prey is scarce, the female may have to hunt for herself and so put the eggs in jeopardy. Among the hawks and eagles, the male calls the female off the nest with a special "food-call" as he arrives to feed her. Harriers have turned this into a display of aerobatics: the female flies up to the male and rolls onto her back with legs outstretched to receive the food as it is dropped by the male.

Where both sexes incubate, the routine is variable. In penguins and petrels, where a long trip to

persuade it to leave by pecking it or pushing it off the nest. The opposite situation, when the sitting bird leaves the nest before the return of its mate, is likely to result in total breeding failure as the clutch is chilled, or eaten by predators.

The incubation behavior of the emperor penguin shows remarkable adaptations to the exigencies of breeding on the coasts of Antarctica. To launch the full-grown chick before winter sets in, courtship and nesting have to take place during the previous winter, so that the summer is free for rearing the chick. Shortly after laying her single egg in June, the female passes it to her mate and walks across the frozen sea, as much as 60 miles (100 kilometers), in search of open water where she can feed. The male now has

*The red-billed hornbill "walls in" his mate with mud, once incubation commences. Here, he feeds her through the opening. The female does not leave the nest until the young are well grown, when she will break out of the nest and help the male with feeding them.*

*Female geese only leave the nest once or twice a day to feed and drink. This blue goose (a color morph of the snow goose) covers her eggs with down to keep them warm and hide them from predators. The males of some species of geese guard the nest while the female is away, but they never incubate the eggs.*

*When both sexes take turns to incubate, they must coordinate their behavior. A female great-crested grebe is reluctant to let the male take over, and he is trying to push her off the nest.*

the sea is needed for feeding, incubation turns last several days and the male takes the first shift so that the female can recoup her reserves after egg-laying. The male starling takes turns with his mate during the day, leaving the female on the nest all night, while the male woodpecker usually takes the night shift and the female the day shift. Female pigeons incubate all night and the males all day; the black male ostrich is on the nest during the night and the female incubates by day when her brown plumage blends in well with the soil.

Changeover of incubation duty may be accomplished very quickly, or with a greeting ceremony. As the relieving bird approaches the nest, the sitting bird gets up and vacates it. For the change to be made smoothly, the drive to incubate needs to be at the correct strength in each bird. If the sitting bird still has a strong urge to sit, its mate may have to

sole care of the egg until it hatches. He carries it on his feet and covers it with a fold of skin hanging from his belly. To survive the sixty-four days incubation period in the worst weather faced by any breeding animal, the emperor penguin relies on his store of fat and conserves heat by huddling with the other penguins (p.135).

There is neither nest nor territory to restrict their movements and space them out, so the penguins can shuffle with their precious burdens into a huddle, pressing against each other with their bills on the bird in front. The exposed surface of each penguin is reduced by 80% and the temperature in the middle of the huddle raised by as much as 20°F (11°C). When the wind blows, the penguins on the exposed side work their way around to the lee, and the whole huddle swirls slowly downwind.

*After the female emperor penguin has laid her egg she leaves it with the male. He balances it on his feet and covers it with a fold of skin (right). The young chick remains in this warm spot after hatching (below).*

While penguins balance eggs on their feet, members of the pelecaniform order – cormorants, gannets, and frigatebirds – wrap their webbed feet around their eggs. For most birds, however, the eggs are warmed by means of incubation patches on the breast. Shortly before egg-laying, feathers drop out under the influence of hormones, or, in waterfowl, are plucked out and used for lining the nest. This leaves an area of bare skin which is covered by the long feathers of the breast and flank. The bare skin is thickened to prevent damage, loose to give good contact with the eggs, and well supplied with blood vessels. When settling on the nest the bird raises its breast and flank feathers and lowers itself over the eggs, wriggling to get them firmly in place against the

*The male yellow warbler (below) supplies much of the female's food while she is incubating, but if food is hard to find, she may have to leave the nest and risk losing the clutch.*

*A European black vulture carrying nest material when it arrives to take over incubation. Like many other birds, black vultures continue to refurbish their nests while they are in use.*

bare skin. The presence of an incubation patch is good evidence that a bird has a nest, or if the feathers are regrowing it can be assumed that it has only recently quitted one. If incubation is shared, both sexes have patches, otherwise they are found only in the sex that incubates, although the bank swallow male and a few others are exceptions, incubating without a patch.

The incubating bird sits very still on the eggs and, in some species, such as chickadees in their nest-holes, eiders and ptarmigan relying on camouflage for concealment, or albatrosses on their mounds of mud, it is possible to approach the bird closely without it taking flight. The only movement is the periodic turning of the eggs, which is performed more frequently among birds with large clutches. The sitting bird rises, examines the eggs closely, arches the neck and draws the bill backwards among the eggs. This

*A red-billed tropicbird defends its single egg. All tropicbirds nest on cliff-ledges, or in cavities, making no more than a scrape for the egg. Both parents incubate and they stay with the egg even if approached closely. This habit was once exploited by Pacific islanders who plucked the long, showy tail plumes of red-tailed tropicbirds while they were incubating.*

rearranges the eggs in the nest so that those on the edge are brought into the middle and the whole clutch is warmed evenly over the course of incubation. The need for egg-turning is illustrated by the 9–11°F (5–6°C) difference in temperature recorded between central and peripheral eggs in a duck's nest.

Another function of egg-turning is to orient the eggs so that they remain the right way up. In the first stages of development, the yolk is free to rotate and because the tiny embryo lies on the lighter part of the yolk, it is always uppermost. Later, the embryo takes up a fixed position within the shell but egg-turning insures that it remains oriented upwards. The movements of the parent's bill separate the eggs and, freed from friction between the shells, they can roll and come to rest with the heavy part of the yolk

environment, and that generated by respiration within the developing embryos. To prevent the eggs getting too warm, it may sit with the layer of breast and flank feathers between eggs and incubation patch so that it transfers very little heat to the eggs.

The environmental temperature markedly affects the time spent incubating. The heating of nestboxes occupied by pied flycatchers caused them to spend less time incubating, and so allowed the birds more time to feed. As the air temperature drops, more warming from the parent is needed until a point is reached when the eggs cannot be kept warm enough to survive. This can have a significant effect on the distribution of a species. Two closely related finches, the chaffinch and brambling, breed in northern Europe but the brambling extends farther north, partly at least because its nest is much better insulated

*A black swan hooks its bill under an egg to move it into the center of the nest. By moving the eggs in a large clutch around, they are warmed evenly, and turning them also aids the development of the embryo.*

downwards and the embryo on top. Rolling in the early part of incubation seems to be necessary for the correct development of the membranes, while the correct orientation later may maintain the chick in the best position for hatching. A few birds manage without egg-turning, for instance the palm swift, which glues its egg to a palm frond, and the mallee fowl and other megapodes which bury their eggs (pp. 175–6).

MAINTAINING THE TEMPERATURE

There is more to incubation than simply sitting on the eggs to keep them warm. The temperature at which the eggs are maintained is several degrees lower than that of the incubation patch: a barn owl's eggs are incubated at 94°F (34°C) while the incubation patch is 9°F (5°C) higher. To keep the temperature of the eggs steady, the adult bird must balance the heat transferred from its body against the heat of the

and the bird can maintain the eggs at the optimum incubation temperature at lower air temperatures. Similarly, the range of the zebra finch in Australia is bounded by the 53.5°F (12°C) isotherm. Where the mean daily temperature drops below this, the birds cannot supply enough heat for incubation.

Incubation behavior explains why the European starling has overrun North America, while a related bird, the crested myna, introduced to Vancouver in 1895, only five years after the starling, has barely spread. Whereas the starling is adapted to a temperate climate and incubates for most of the day, the myna retains the tropical habit of spending little time in its nesthole during the middle of the day and its eggs suffer as a result in the cool climate. The breeding success of the crested myna has been increased, as an experiment, by providing it with heated nestboxes.

In very hot countries, the problem is often one of keeping the eggs cool. Cavity nests or domed nests provide a good insulation that will shield the clutch from extremes of weather but birds nesting in exposed places have to shade their eggs from sun. At very high temperatures the eggs will still be baked and under these conditions the white-winged dove of Arizona and other desert birds sit upon their nest and press their breasts against the eggs. As their body temperature is lower than the air temperature, they act as "heat sinks" that can remove excessive heat from the eggs. The problem is now for the bird to keep itself cool. The yellow-wattled lapwing of India ruffles its feathers so that they act as Venetian blinds, allowing air to circulate but keeping the sun off the skin. Panting, holding the wings out to let heat dissipate from the flanks, and facing directly into or

*An elegant tern rolls its egg back into the nest and arranges it for ease of incubation.*

away from the sun to reduce heat intake are other means of easing the heat burden for desert birds. If there is water nearby, this may be used to keep both birds and eggs cool by wetting the breast feathers or dribbling water from the crop into the nest.

INCUBATOR BIRDS

One way for a bird to avoid the energy cost of keeping its eggs warm with its body heat is to use heat from the environment. The Egyptian plover buries its eggs in sun-warmed sand and the Eurasian partridge keeps some control over egg temperature by covering them with dried grass when it is cool, but earth when it is warm. The earth prevents the eggs getting too hot.

There is one group of birds that has specialized in the use of environmental heat, the megapodes of Australia, New Guinea, Indonesia and Polynesia. These ground-living members of the gamebird order

*A spotted cormorant (above) waits to take its turn at incubation. In cool climates, the eggs are left exposed as little as possible. In hot countries, however, the eggs may need to be kept cool. So, during the day, a wattled plover (left) stands over its eggs to shade them.*

Galliformes are popularly called incubator birds or mound-builders, and none of the twelve species uses body heat to incubate its eggs. Some species lay their eggs in sandy beaches or cracks in rocks where they will be incubated by the sun. Others find sites where the ground is warmed by volcanic heat or hot springs. Somehow the birds are able to choose a site where their eggs will receive the warm, even temperature necessary for incubation. The maleo fowl digs a pit in a sandy beach, like a turtle, and lays its eggs at a depth where the temperature does not fluctuate between day and night.

Another species, the scrubfowl, uses sun-warmed sand, or soil warmed by volcanic steam, but when it lives in dense forest where these sources are unavailable it uses the heat from fermenting

kept busy regulating the temperature to an even 91°F (33°C). He tests the temperature by picking up samples in his bill and alters the nest mound accordingly. At the start, fermentation is rapid and temperatures rise to 122 or 140°F (50–60°C), so the pile is opened to let heat out in the cool of the morning. Later, fermentation dies down, but the summer sun is very hot, so more sand is spread over the top to insulate the pile. In autumn, when sun and fermentation are weaker, the male digs out the sand to let the sun penetrate the nest, spreads it around to warm in the morning sun and then scrapes it back in the evening.

All the time the mallee fowl is testing the temperature and adjusting his activities to compensate for an unusual hot spell in spring, perhaps, or for

*The maleo fowl (left) lays its eggs in sun-warmed sand, at a depth where there is an even temperature. The related mallee fowl (far left) creates a source of heat by building a mound of vegetation that will warm up when it rots. The eggs are laid in the center of the mound and the temperature is controlled by opening it up (below) or piling on sand.*

vegetation. The eggs are laid either in a rotting stump or in dead leaves which the scrubfowl rakes into a pile up to 33 feet (10 meters) across and 16 feet (5 meters) high. Other megapodes, known as brush turkeys, also lay their eggs in large mounds but the most sophisticated nesting arrangement is made by the mallee fowl. It lives in the dry mallee scrubland of Australia where fallen leaves do not easily rot and generate heat.

To get the heat-producing processes of decomposition going, the mallee fowl digs a pit 10 feet (3 meters) across and 3 feet (1 meter) deep and fills it with leaves. When the rains come, the leaves start to rot and the bird covers them with sand to keep the heat of decomposition in. The eggs are laid in a chamber near the surface of the pile over a period of several months, and thereafter the male mallee fowl is

overcast days in autumn. The eggs in one nest are laid over a period of four months and each takes two months to hatch, so with the time spent constructing the nest, the male mallee fowl is occupied with nesting for eleven months each year. That such complicated behavior should have evolved, when most birds simply keep their eggs warm with body heat, is amazing.

The mallee fowl's strenuous work is not even rewarded by a good hatching rate. It seems that the megapodes, as a group, are confined to using environmental heat instead of body heat for incubation. The mallee fowl, in colonizing a drier, cooler environment than the rest of the family, has had to adapt their simple incubation technique, which relies on warm ground, to a more complex procedure that suits its new habitat.

The Cape penduline tit is unique for building a nest with an entrance tunnel that can be closed (far left). The bird uses a foot to open it and then goes into the nest headfirst (left). After it leaves the nest (below left), it turns and closes the entrance by pushing up with its head (below right).

# DEFENDING THE NEST

A nest of eggs or young birds makes an excellent meal, and nest-robbing is a common trait among predators. For the parents this represents a serious waste of investment, and while some can lay a new clutch of eggs to recoup their losses, others must wait until the next season for another chance to breed. Defense of the nest is therefore a priority, but it obviously carries its dangers. It might be the best policy for parents to flee their nests and live to breed another day, and such is often the reaction of small birds faced by a carnivorous mammal, but many species are notably aggressive in the defense of their nests. Hummingbirds, for instance, drive away intruders many times their own size.

The simplest form of defense is to nest in a safe place where predators cannot reach. Trees and cliff ledges are immune from many terrestrial predators but they may be reached by birds, and by climbing mammals and reptiles. Burrows are safer still and studies show that there is a significantly higher breeding success in burrow-nesters than in birds with open nests. Hanging nests, like those of weavers, oropendolas and others, deter some predators but may be robbed by snakes or birds.

Open nests can be sited to avoid the attention of predators and small birds position them where they cannot be easily spotted. Song sparrows raise up to three broods in separate nests each year. The first nest is frequently on the ground, which is not a very safe position but, in early spring, is better than on the bare branches of bushes. Second and third nests are more likely to be built above the ground as by then the leaves have grown to provide effective cover.

Another strategy for protection is to live near a fiercer animal, as when house sparrows and grackles build their nests in the large stick piles of ospreys. Oldsquaws build nests among Arctic terns which can drive foxes away, and African weavers nest in the same trees as kites and buzzards. In tropical countries bees' and wasps' nests provide protection for many kinds of birds including weavers, mannikins, wrens and flycatchers. The birds build their nests near those of the insects but some even nest inside them, like the rufous woodpecker which excavates its nest-hole in the nests of tree ants. That these are not chance happenings but definite associations is shown by the repeated incidences of the same behavior. Thus black-necked (eared) grebes shift their colonies yearly to stay close to those of black-headed gulls, and the southern beardless tyrannulet, a tyrant flycatcher of Central and South America, builds successive nests beside the same wasps' nest.

Ground-nesting birds rely on camouflage for the protection of their nests. The nest scrape is easily overlooked, and the eggs and chicks are usually well camouflaged, so that they tend to go unnoticed. If

*The nest of the Northern "Baltimore" oriole is a flimsy construction of plant fibers and hair, but it is difficult for any predator to reach, when hanging among the slender twigs of a weeping willow.*

*The array of spines on a cholla cactus will defeat all but the most determined attempt to raid a curve-billed thrasher's nest.*

approached by a predator when incubating, the adult often sits tight, flattening itself in an attempt to become more inconspicuous. The importance of camouflage is shown by the Arabian desert lark, of which there are two races, a light form, nesting on pale sand, and a dark race that nests on black volcanic rock. Female pheasants and ducks, which have sole responsibility for incubation, are invariably drab compared with the males, which are brightly colored for display. In the Arctic, ptarmigan hens molt into the dark summer plumage as soon as the snow melts and are very hard to spot, while the cocks retain the white winter plumage longer, for display purposes.

Using a radio telemetry device, it has been shown that when a ptarmigan is approached on the nest, her heartbeat and breathing slow down. Presumably she is harder to hear and smell, and trained hunting dogs certainly have difficulty finding sitting ptarmigan. When an intruder is very close, the "bugged" ptarmigan shows a sudden rise in heartbeat and breathing as she prepares to fly. When these camouflaged, tight-sitting birds eventually seek safety in flight, they "explode" from the nest, startling and confusing the intruder. Eiders frequently defecate over their eggs as they leave, which may put off a potential nest-robber.

Not all ground-nesting birds are camouflaged: terns and gulls are far from inconspicuous and they rely to some extent on nesting in safe places for protection. The eggs and young are well camouflaged, however, and the parents leave them at the first sign of danger and attempt to divert the predator's attention

by attacking it. The form of attack depends on the predator. The birds vigorously attack and peck hedgehogs, which prey on eggs and chicks but are no threat to adult birds, whereas their reactions to foxes and human beings, which are a danger to both adults and brood, are ambivalent. They attack, but not too strongly, with dive-bomb tactics of swooping down, sometimes striking the target with their feet, bill or wing-tip and soaring up again. The predator will not be injured but it may be distracted from its hunt or driven away.

The predator can also be thwarted by distraction displays in which the parent birds seek to lure it from the vicinity of the nest or chicks by making themselves conspicuous. Parasitic jaegers alternate "dive-bombing" with a distraction display in which they land and beat their wings on the ground and call loudly. For many ground-nesting shorebirds, ducks, nightjars and others, the distraction display is the main form of anti-predator behavior.

Distraction displays take several forms. In "injury-feigning" the bird acts frenziedly, tumbling and calling with wings and tail spread, as if mortally wounded and helpless. The "broken-wing display" consists of trailing or beating one or both wings while on the ground and in the "rodent run" of shorebirds the bird scurries along in a crouched posture with wings drooping and tail depressed. In all cases, the bird makes itself conspicuous, and patches of white on the wings and tail are often shown off. The stonechat's distraction display consists of flicking its wings to expose striking white areas and giving the clinking

*A termite nest on a tree is a safe place for a sacred kingfisher to nest (top left). The position of the entrance is very difficult to reach and the termites act as a further deterrent.*

*The willie wagtail, an Australian fantail flycatcher, is renowned for its brave defense of its nest. Here it is landing on the back of a kookaburra, many times its own size (center).*

*Kittlitz's plover hides its eggs at the approach of a predator by kicking sand and pebbles over them (bottom left).*

*Almost impossible to see, a female rock ptarmigan squats motionless on her nest (top right). At the first sign of danger, even her heartbeat and breathing slow down making her less noticeable to predators hunting by sound or scent.*

*A sheep takes no notice as a great skua swoops overhead and gives alarm calls (bottom right). But if it comes nearer the skua's nest it will be attacked violently. The skua will strike with its feet and send the sheep running.*

"chat" calls from which it gets its name. These calls are easy to locate (p. 122) and draw the intruder's attention. There are numerous reports of such displays being effective in luring away dogs, foxes and weasels. A long-billed curlew was once seen running with a "broken wing" in front of a coyote, keeping just ahead of it and leaping away if it came too close. When last seen they were disappearing over a hill, half a mile (a kilometer) away.

BROOD PARASITES

Some of the defenses which birds employ against predators are also effective against brood parasites – birds that lay their eggs in the nests of other species and thus avoid parental duties. The brood parasites known best to Europeans are cuckoos, whereas Americans are familiar with cowbirds, but these

Such a progression can be seen among the different species of cowbirds and cuckoos. The bay-winged cowbird rears its own young but usually takes over the nest of another species in which to lay its eggs, only rarely making its own nest. The shiny cowbird parasitizes a number of small birds and the brown-headed cowbird not only parasitizes many host species but mimics the egg patterns of some. Egg mimicry is a valuable means of ensuring that the parasite's egg is accepted by the host. The brown-headed cowbird is recorded as parasitizing 206 species, some regularly and others occasionally. Finally the screaming cowbird specializes in parasitizing a single host – the bay-winged cowbird.

Among cuckoos, the North American species such as the black-billed and yellow-billed cuckoos

*A European avocet poses no threat to a pair of pratincoles but they still seek to drive it from the nest.*

*A female snowy owl (top left) uses a distraction display to gain the attention of an intruder approaching the nest and so lure it away. The killdeer (above) is achieving the same result by "injury-feigning". It flaps its wings and spreads its tail, so making itself very conspicuous.*

represent only two of the five families in which the habit is known. The other three are the whydahs and honeyguides of Africa and a single species of waterfowl, the black-headed duck of South America.

A few birds occasionally lay their eggs in the nests of others of their own species, and ring-necked pheasants, common moorhens and redhead ducks are examples of such "dump nesters". Many other species have been recorded as sometimes laying eggs in nests of other species. Twenty-one species of ducks are known to do this and casual brood parasitism has also been observed among rails, grebes and pheasants. Occasional parasitism of this nature is presumed to be a stage in the evolution of complete brood parasitism, in which the species never rears its own young.

usually build their own nests and rear their own young. However, they sometimes "dump" their eggs on members of their own species and, more rarely, lay them in nests of other species, although in the latter instance, the eggs do not hatch. From this stage of "accidental parasitism", there has evolved full parasitism in which the egg is incubated, and the nestling cuckoo nurtured by the host, as in the European cuckoo.

Several possible advantages of brood parasitism have been suggested, some fanciful and others possible. One definite advantage must be the saving in energy. A female brood parasite is spared the effort of nest-building, incubation and feeding her offspring. The energy so saved could go into laying more eggs, and in Africa, parasitic cuckoos lay, on average, one

*A blacksmith plover (center) attempts to defend its nest as a zebra walks past, and an oystercatcher (above) confronts a heifer. Both mammals are a serious threat because they could trample the eggs, but the birds' displays are unlikely to deter them.*

egg more than non-parasites. Brood parasitism which involves laying each egg in a different nest could also be a means of reducing the effect of predation (literally not "putting all one's eggs in the same basket") but this cannot be the explanation in some of the cuckoos, the great spotted cuckoo and the koel for instance, which lay several eggs in one nest.

As in other types of parasitism, the relationship is likely to be detrimental to the host. At the least, the host is diverting resources away from its own offspring and jeopardizing their survival, and, at worst, the host loses all its offspring. Indeed, the host invests a great deal of effort in caring for the fosterling forced on it. The host-parasite relationship is, in consequence, one of conflict, although it is fought through natural selection, and individual birds are

Observations show that brood parasites try to avoid detection when approaching a nest and, if detected, they may be successfully driven away. Cowbirds lay in the early morning when the hosts are busy elsewhere. Alternatively, the parasite can mimic its host, and the male koel, a tropical cuckoo, resembles the house crow, its most frequent host. House crows defend their territories vigorously and mistaking the black male koel for an intruding crow, chase after it and so allow the brown, spotted female to get to the nest unmolested.

The European cuckoo overcomes the difficulty of laying in awkward nests by extreme agility and quick laying of the egg. It is impossible for it to sit on the nest of birds which nest in cavities or make domed nests, but it can cling to the side of the nest, straddling

*A red-winged blackbird attacks a mute swan which has come too close to its nest in a reedbed. When hovering around the swan's head has no effect, the blackbird lands on its neck to make its presence felt.*

unaware of the antagonism. While the parasites are evolving stratagems for imposing their offspring on the host, the latter is evolving means of combatting the intrusion.

Potential hosts have several ways in which they can combat the parasites' attentions. Constructing the nest so that it is inaccessible or impenetrable is a common adaptation to prevent predation, and this is also effective against parasitism, as is attacking birds of other species that come too near the nest. The host may recognize an alien egg in its nest, and desertion of the nest, followed by the construction of a new one, is a frequent response. A less drastic measure is to build a false floor over the intruding egg or to eject it from the nest. Brood parasites have developed a variety of strategies to counter these defenses.

the entrance, and "inject" the egg. African weavers and weaver finches build elaborate hanging nests to deter predators but they are parasitized by cuckoos and widowbirds. Cowbirds successfully lay their eggs in the similarly difficult nests of American oropendolas, often gaining access to the nest chamber by tearing a hole in the fabric, which the host later repairs.

Once the egg is installed in the nest, its survival depends on the host's acceptance. The introduction of cowbird eggs results in nest desertion by northern cardinals, and the eggs are ejected from the nest by American robins and gray catbirds among others, but they are accepted by some species. Cuckoos have largely overcome the problem of rejection by mimicking the coloration of their host's eggs, sometimes to make an almost perfect match.

Within most cuckoo species, a range of egg colors is found, but each individual cuckoo lays eggs to match only one host. It is believed that the female cuckoo inherits her egg color exclusively from her mother (so that the egg coloration is not affected by the father's genetic input) and that she chooses the right nests by searching out the host species that reared her. The large hawk-cuckoo of Asia has two different egg colors and the females either lay matching brown eggs in the nests of shortwings and spiderhunters, or matching blue eggs in the nests of laughing thrushes. When these two groups of hosts overlap in range, both types of hawk-cuckoo are found, and each female selects the right nest for her particular egg color.

The situation is much more complicated for the European cuckoo which parasitizes far too many species to be able to match all their eggs. However, in each geographical region it has a few favored hosts which it does match. In central and eastern Europe these are mainly the brambling, great reed warbler and redstart. Eggs matching these species may also be laid in the nests of subsidiary hosts; the blue "redstart" eggs are a good match for the eggs of wheatears and pied flycatchers. In western Europe, matching is less good because some of the main hosts – meadow pipit, reed warbler and pied wagtail – have variable egg patterns themselves and the cuckoos can make only approximate matches. Another main host is the dunnock whose bright blue eggs are not matched by western European cuckoos, even though central European cuckoos lay blue eggs. However, dunnocks are very tolerant of mismatched eggs.

When the eggs hatch, there will be competition between the nestlings of the host and parasite for the parents' attention, except in the black-headed duck, where the ducklings leave the foster nest and fend entirely for themselves. Cuckoos start with the advantage of hatching before the host's own eggs and are then in a good position to outgrow the host's young and dominate them in competing for the food brought by the parents.

The honeyguides of Africa and striped cuckoo of South America go further and destroy any opposition by pecking to death the host's nestlings with the assistance of special hooks on the tips of the mandibles. The European cuckoo and some other species achieve the same end by forcing the host's eggs and young out of the nest. This instinctive behavior operates only for about one day, starting when the cuckoo is a few hours old. It maneuvers each egg or nestling into a hollow between the shoulderblades, then moves backwards until the wings can clasp the rim of the nest, the legs push upwards and the victim topples over the side.

Paradise whydah nestlings are hatched and reared with their waxbill foster siblings. The whydahs, nine parasitic species related to the weavers, have an elaborate method of insuring that their nestlings match their nest-mates and so gain the attention of the foster-parents. Adult waxbills feed their young by

thrusting the bill into their mouths and pumping in the contents of the crop, a method unique among the passerines. They are stimulated to feed their nestlings by the sight of their gaping mouths, but they react only to the specific pattern of their species which consists of colored spots and fleshy outgrowths on the mouth lining. The young whydahs, however, mimic the pattern of the host species with remarkable accuracy and they also imitate the specific begging calls and head movements. The whydah nestling must, therefore, be raised in the nest of the correct waxbill species, not only because it has to match the begging signals but because its digestive system is adapted to the diet of its host, which is different in each waxbill species.

Female whydahs recognize the correct hosts by their songs, and search for nests where a male of the

disadvantages in this association because the bees and wasps sometimes suddenly desert their nests, leaving the birds vulnerable. Crowding around insect nests can also be disastrous, for it causes such a weight of birds' nests to build up that the branches snap. The alternative protection against botfly is for the oropendolas and caciques to allow giant cowbirds to parasitize their nests. The cowbirds pluck the botfly larvae from their nest-mates and reduce their mortality by 90%.

The relationships between the cowbird and its oropendola and cacique hosts are complicated. As with the paradise whydahs, there are several types of giant cowbird. Four mimic the eggs of particular host species and one lays non-mimetic eggs in the nests of any host species. The mimicking cowbirds wait for host females to leave the colony before slipping in to

*By evicting the reed warblers' own offspring, a young common cuckoo secures its fosterparents' whole attention and receives enough food for rapid growth (below). Although the cuckoo is almost bursting out of the nest the warbler still tries to brood it (top center).*

*A cowbird's blue egg contrasts with the eggs of a fostering thrush (center). Although the cowbird may remove some of the host's eggs, those that are left will hatch and be reared alongside the young cowbird.*

species that fostered them is singing. They also mate with a male whydah that incorporates the notes of the same foster species in his courtship song. Among paradise whydahs this careful selection of a mate results in the preservation of seven distinct races, which are very similar in most respects, except that each parasitizes a different species of waxbill.

There is one instance where brood parasitism has become an advantage to the host. Oropendola and cacique colonies in South America are frequently infested with botfly larvae which burrow into the nestlings' bodies and kill them. One defense is to nest near bees and wasps which keep down the botfly numbers. The adult birds are immune to the stings of the bees and wasps and their naked nestlings are protected inside the covered nests. But there are

lay an egg, but the non-mimicking type is aggressive and drives away the host females. Some host birds discriminate against cowbird eggs that do not mimic their own by ejecting them from the nest but others tolerate mismatched eggs.

In any colony, all the oropendolas and caciques are either discriminating or tolerant. It depends whether the colony has the protective umbrella of wasps or bees. If these are absent, cowbirds are tolerated, and save the lives of many host nestlings by ridding them of botflies, but if there are bees or wasps present, cowbirds can lay successfully only if they can deceive their hosts. How the hosts "know" whether to discriminate against or tolerate brood parasites, according to the presence or absence of protective insect nests, is not clear.

*Oropendola nests are positioned at the tips of slender branches for protection against climbing animals, but this does not save the birds from the depredations of either cowbirds or botflies. The relationship between the three is complex and provides a rare example of brood parasitism benefiting the host.*

# HATCHING

A bird starts to behave even before it hatches. In advance of the shell breaking open, the chick inside has begun to become aware of its surroundings and even to communicate with its parents and the chicks in the other eggs. Long before that, its heart began beating, its blood started to circulate around the body and its muscles made their first contractions. But now the chick starts to move with coordination, to breathe air, and to respond to events taking place in the outside world.

In a chicken egg, the embryo starts to flap its wings, in a restricted way, five days before hatching, and ducks at this stage react to their mother's calls with a quickening of the heartbeat. At about this time the embryo changes its position so that the head is no longer resting between the legs but is tucked under the right wing with the bill facing the blunt end of the egg. The next event is the penetration of the airspace at the blunt end by a thrust of the bill and a switch to breathing with the lungs. Until this point, exchange of gases has been taking place through the membrane known as the allantois that lines the shell. A little later, the exchange of air is improved by "pipping" in which the embryo forces a hole in the shell with the tip of its bill. The lungs can now work properly and the allantois dries up.

After "pipping" there is a delay of about fifteen to forty hours before there is any further visible development. Then the chick starts to fight its way out of the shell. The procedure is to knock an arc of holes around the blunt end of the egg, starting in the spot where it first pipped. Bracing itself with its feet against the pointed end, it hammers at the inside of the shell with the bill. The bill tip is strengthened with a chalky 'egg tooth' on the upper mandible, which is seen on newly hatched birds before it drops off, usually at the age of a few days. The thrust for hammering comes from a "hatching muscle" which develops just before hatching as a large bulge on the back of the head and disappears rapidly after the chick has emerged. Between bouts of hammering, the chick relaxes its pressure on the narrow end and, flexing its right leg, it turns counterclockwise, ready to make another hole next to the previous one. Eventually the shell is so weakened that renewed pressing with its feet and heaving with the shoulders forces the top off, and the chick can ease itself free.

The hatching process is the same for all birds with a few exceptions. The woodcock and the willet (both members of the sandpiper family) have a second, smaller egg tooth on the lower mandible. After pipping, they push the bill through the hole and, with a convulsive heave, split the shell longitudinally. The chicks of megapodes lack both egg teeth and hatching muscles and they hatch at such an extremely advanced state of development that they are able to fend for themselves immediately. Megapode eggs are

*A common moorhen chick hatches from its egg by cracking the shell in a ring around the blunt end (top). Then it forces the two halves apart and heaves itself out of the shell. At first the chick is sticky with egg fluids and makes only weak movements. Within a few hours it is dry and fluffy, and begging for food by quivering its wings (bottom).*

laid to stand vertically in the underground chamber (p.176). The head remains tucked between the legs and forceful movements of the wings and feet cause the shell to crack in several places. The feet emerge first and only after the shell has been broken away does the head lift.

Young birds which hatch in an advanced state and leave the nest soon after hatching – known as precocial young – begin to call even before hatching. They start to cheep as soon as the bill penetrates the airspace. One sound is a rapid "clicking" which was once thought to be the chick tapping its bill against the

parents' voices. Experiments with mallard ducklings show that if they hear their mother's calls before hatching, they will follow a model decoy if it is accompanied by a recording of these calls, but not if it is silent.

As precocial birds leave the nest with their parents soon after hatching, an early start to forming a link between adult and young is an advantage. A second advantage of establishing communication while still in the egg is to synchronize hatching. In greater rheas, for instance, the male starts to incubate when the first egg is laid and the female continues

*The chick of the maleo fowl hatches when very well developed and capable of fending for itself. The large feet, which give the megapode family its name, emerge from the egg first, a reversal of the hatching procedure in other birds.*

*A newly hatched silver pheasant already has its full plumage. The flight feathers are protected by horny sheaths which will be shed as the chick dries.*

*The chalky egg tooth shows clearly on the bill of a three-day-old prairie falcon nestling. The tooth is used for cracking the eggshell, and drops off soon after hatching.*

*While only half out of its shell a flamingo chick is already looking alert. Its parent is helping it to dry by nibbling gently at its downy feathers.*

shell, but is, in fact, a vocal sound. These and other calls have a variety of functions. Cooling the egg or turning it upside down causes the chick within to utter distress calls which will stimulate the parent bird to incubate the egg or roll it. Ducklings give a low, quick cheeping to show contentment, or, if distressed, emit the same high-pitched call that they will give after hatching when separated from their mother. Communication between parents and clutch is a two-way process. The exchange of calls with the unhatched chicks stimulates the parents' chick-caring behavior which will soon be needed to replace incubation behavior. At the same time, the chicks learn their

laying for nine or more days, yet all the eggs hatch within the space of two to three hours. The same thing happens with quails, ducks and chickens, and observations show that the chicks are listening to the clicking calls of their siblings and using them to coordinate their hatching times. This process has been studied in experiments using eggs in incubators. Although pipping in a clutch is staggered over one or two days, clicking starts at almost the same time. When the most advanced egg starts to click it stimulates the others to join in and they proceed to the final stages of hatching together so that all emerge within the space of a couple of hours.

Precocial young that leave the nest soon after hatching are a feature of birds that nest on the ground, such as ratites, waterfowl, shorebirds, pheasants and chickens. Such chicks usually feed themselves, although grebes, oystercatchers and rails are exceptions to this. Some birds, such as gulls and penguins, are semi-precocial. Most hatch with a covering of down and their eyes open, but they stay in the nest for some time.

In contrast to precocial young, some birds are almost helpless when newly hatched, and these are known as altricial young. Groups with altricial young include the songbirds, petrels, pigeons, woodpeckers, kingfishers and hummingbirds. With the exception of

*Precocial chicks are active and leave the nest soon after hatching. This turkey chick (top), sleeping on its feet, is only two days old.*

and the down is plastered against the body by egg fluids. The parents have to brood the chicks as closely as they incubated the eggs, because for the first days of life the chicks are poikilothermic (unable to regulate their body temperature) and extremely vulnerable to cold weather. As a general rule, young birds are brooded until they have developed the ability to partially regulate the body temperature, and by this time they are often becoming too large to be covered properly. Fully independent temperature control may not be attained until a later stage of growth, so brooding is resumed in cold, wet or very hot spells. A period of bad weather can be disastrous because, as

*Nidicolous young, like these golden orioles, remain in the nest until their feathers are almost fully grown and they can fly.*

*Pelicans are among the birds whose young may be described as semi-precocial. They are naked at hatching, and their eyes are closed, but open soon afterwards. At about a month old they begin to walk around the colony on legs which are disproportionately well developed.*

the larks and pipits, all these birds nest in trees, burrows or other inaccessible places. Altricial nestlings usually have their eyes closed at first and their bodies are naked or covered with sparse down, although owls have a good downy covering and hawks have their eyes open. These helpless nestlings are fed by their parents until they fly or even later. They stay in the nest, and are often termed nidicolous, whereas fully precocial young are described as nidifugous – "nest-fleeing". Not all nidicolous young are altricial, however – as noted above, the semi-precocial young of penguins and gulls also stay in the nest.

When they are first hatched all young birds are weak and wet. The head flops on the floor of the nest

well as making food difficult to find, the extra brooding reduces the time available for foraging.

For nidicolous birds, care of the young includes sanitation, and unless the chicks are going to leave the nest very soon after hatching, the empty eggshells are removed. This may be to prevent the sharp edges injuring the small birds, but for ground-nesting birds the white inner surface of eggshell fragments can also destroy the camouflage of the nest. To remove the shells, the adults generally pick them up in their bills and fly away with them, but some birds eat them for the calcium they contain (p.71). In colonial species, carrying the eggshell away can render the newly hatched chick vulnerable to attack by neighboring birds, and the black-headed gull compromises by delaying removal for several hours. It leaves the eggshell until the chick is dry and fluffy, since it is then more difficult for another gull to swallow.

For many nidicolous birds, nest sanitation also involves removing their nestlings' droppings. Among woodpeckers and passerines, for example, the nestlings produce dropping in gelatinous sacs which are removed or eaten by the parent. The sac is usually produced immediately after the nestling has been fed and the parent seizes it as it is expelled. The removal of the droppings probably helps to prevent disease, but there is also a link with temperature regulation and the stage of development of the young. In tits and starlings, at least, the parents become less zealous in removing droppings when their nestlings grow their feathers and develop the ability to regulate their body

and the nests of hoopoes, trogons and many pigeons become filthy. Kingfisher nestlings eject droppings down the burrow with the result that the adults become fouled and need to bathe after visiting the nest. The nestlings' own feathers are protected by growing within waxy sheaths until well developed.

## FEEDING THE YOUNG

Among nidifugous birds the chicks can usually forage independently soon after hatching, but, for nidicolous species, feeding the young in the nest is a major task that makes great demands on the parents. Pied flycatcher nests receive thirty visits an hour and over 6,000 provisioning journeys are needed to rear the brood. This work has to be crammed into the daytime and one advantage of breeding at high latitudes is that daylight is almost unlimited in the summer. In the Arctic, snow buntings and bluethroats spend most of

*A ruddy turnstone examines a chick as it emerges from the egg (top left). Once the chick is free, the adult carries away the eggshell whose white interior would make the nest conspicuous (top corner).*

*Although active soon after hatching, the ruddy turnstone chick returns to the nest to be brooded (top right).*

*One of the parental duties of many altricial birds is to remove the droppings of their nestlings. They become less conscientious about this once the brood grows, as shown by the stained nest of this American robin (bottom left).*

temperatures. Before this, fouling wets their bodies and the nest material, spoiling the insulating properties of both, and making the nestlings more susceptible to chilling.

Another reason for removing droppings is to maintain the camouflage of the nest and it is very noticeable that birds nesting on inaccessible cliff ledges, like kittiwakes or peregrines, or those found in dense colonies, like albatrosses, penguins and gannets, make no such provision. The area around the nests becomes fouled, although droppings are usually cast over the side of the nest, or out of the burrow, so that the nest itself remains clean, but becomes extremely conspicuous. Others are less scrupulous

the twenty-four hours feeding their young and rest only around midnight when the temperature drops and insects are harder to find. At the other extreme, penguin, albatross and shearwater nestlings may receive meals at intervals greater than twenty-four hours. Their parents travel long distances to forage but can deliver a large amount of food at one visit.

The transfer of food from parents to nestling is efficient and little time is wasted. Birds of prey need to dismember each kill and feed fragments to small nestlings, but they leave larger nestlings to engulf entire animals, or tear the prey up for themselves. Where the meal is made up of smaller items, transfer is achieved by the parent placing food into the gaping

*Nestling swifts deposit their droppings over the side of the nest. The parents remove some but the nest area gets very dirty (bottom center). Nests become a breeding ground for parasites, such as poultry mites, which could threaten the health of these swallow nestlings (bottom right).*

mouth of the nestling, as in passerines and hummingbirds, or the young bird thrusting its head into the parent's mouth, as in penguins, pelicans and cormorants. The nestlings of albatrosses and petrels place their bills between the parent's mandibles and, with adroit use of their tongues, a slippery meal of fish, crustaceans or squid, mixed with oil which is produced by partial digestion of the food, is transferred without spillage.

Although mostly helpless, nestlings of altricial birds have one well developed response which is instinctive. When hungry, they beg for food as the parent arrives at the nest. Young thrushes respond to the vibrations set up by the adult as it lands and they immediately rear up vertically with their mouths gaping wide. As the nestlings grow and their eyes open, they react to the visual stimulus of the parent's head moving above them and later still, the gaping is directed towards the parent. The stimulus which triggers begging varies between species: for woodpeckers and rollers it is the darkening of the nest cavity as the adult blocks the entrance; for chimney swifts it is the draft of the parents' wingbeats, while bank swallows, coal tits and crows call to the young on approaching the nest. The edge of the mouth is very sensitive in some birds and if the nestling does not react to other stimuli, the parent taps it on the mouth to get a response.

The sight of the gaping mouths of their brood and the sound of their begging calls are the signals that stimulate and guide the behavior of the parent birds. Many nestlings, especially those that live in cavities and burrows, have a brightly colored lining to the mouth to act as a beacon directing the adult's attention. They are usually orange, yellow or white and may be patterned. The Gouldian finch has glistening "beads" in the mouth that glow in the dark.

Begging and feeding are adjusted so that the nestlings are kept well fed. As soon as one is replete, it ceases to beg and its less fortunate nest-mates receive the attention of the parents. When food is plentiful, all will be fed in turn and grow accordingly, but a shortage will lead to some going hungry and possibly

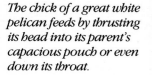

dying. If a limited food supply is shared out equally between the chicks this can result in the death of the whole brood, which is a serious loss for the parents.

Some species make use of what food is available in a more efficient manner by staggering the hatching of the eggs and giving priority to the oldest chicks when feeding them. In most bird species, the clutch hatches at about the same time because, although the eggs are laid at intervals, incubation does not start until laying is almost complete. But in the birds of prey, owls, cranes, swifts, bee-eaters and herons, incubation starts with the first egg, so that they hatch at intervals. All these birds have widely fluctuating food supplies and are likely to face a sudden shortage of food while rearing chicks. When an owl has a large clutch there can be two weeks between the laying of the first and last eggs and a similar spread in their hatching. If food supplies dwindle, the oldest owlets get the major share because, being larger and stronger, their begging attracts the parents and they push their younger siblings aside. The latter gradually weaken and become less able to compete, and they may then be killed, and sometimes eaten, by the older nestlings. Thus the older nestlings survive at the expense of the younger ones, and the result is that the adults will stand a chance of rearing at least a few young rather than losing the whole brood.

Within limits, the adults adjust the amount of food they bring to the demands of the brood. As an experiment, a nestbox containing pied flycatchers was divided so that the parents could see only one nestling. The single nestling received many more feeds when the parents could hear the hidden nestlings' begging calls. Removing some nestlings from the nest altogether reduced the number of feeding visits because the stimulation to bring food was reduced by fewer begging cries.

With an increasing number of birds in the nest, growth rate drops because the parents cannot deliver enough food to sustain maximum growth. For pied flycatchers, although the maximum rate of growth cannot be achieved in a brood of more than two, five to seven is the usual number in a nest.

*A western reef heron (left) and a blue-footed booby (below) shade their young from the heat of the sun. The booby is also feeling the heat. It is panting, and has raised the feathers of the back to allow air to circulate.*

*An osprey tears up a fish and gives the pieces to its nearly fledged youngster.*

*In nestlings that gape when begging for food, the lining of the mouth is brightly colored, as a signal to the parents. These young reedlings show an elaborate pattern of white, fleshy projections on a black and red background.*

*A tawny owl nestling swallows a mouse. The rodent's body will be broken up and digested in the owl's stomach and the indigestible fur and bones will be regurgitated as pellets. The pellets gather around the nest and can be used to determine the nestlings' diet.*

## COOPERATIVE BREEDING

In at least 300 species of birds, the parents are assisted in raising their young by adults other than their mates. These helpers bring food to the nestlings and join in defense against predators, but some also share nest-building, incubation and territorial behavior. Biologists have been interested to discover why the helpers should assist with other birds' families rather than rearing their own.

Most cooperative breeders are tropical or subtropical species that nest colonially or have permanent pair bonds and year-round territories. There are only a few cooperative breeders in temperate countries, where permanent partnerships and pair bonds are rarer. In common moorhens, fledglings from the first brood of the season help to feed the young of the second brood, and the first brood of eastern kingbirds sometimes help to feed younger siblings and remove their droppings. In these examples the helpers are related to their charges and it is easy to see the advantages in caring for them. On average, siblings will share half their genetic make-up, which is the same as a parent and its offspring have in common. So helping to rear a brood of brothers and sisters has roughly the same genetic reward as rearing a brood of one's own offspring. In other cases there is no relationship and cooperative breeding is more difficult to explain, as in bushtits where the helpers may be adults who have lost their nest. From studies of species with regular nest helpers, it has become clear that the social organization can be very complex and the advantage of cooperative breeding to the helpers is not always clear.

On the American continent there is a range of communal behavior in jays. The scrub jay shows the simplest form of social organization, with pairs living in territories and rearing their young without helpers. From this "basic" situation two lines of social behavior have developed. One is towards a colonial life, as exemplified by the pinyon jay in which several hundred pairs nest in one colony and forage together. A few adults may serve as helpers to nesting pairs but this behavior has become more important in the second line of development. An early stage of this is shown by the Florida scrub jay, an isolated population restricted to the Florida peninsula. Like other cooperative breeders, it lives in permanent territories. The pairs are assisted by helpers who feed the young, give warning of danger and join in attacks on predators, such as snakes, which menace the nest. Their presence significantly increases the number of offspring reared. The helpers are nearly always siblings or offspring of the breeding pair. The Mexican jay of oak and pine forests lives in flocks of up to twenty birds in a group territory. Each flock is composed of two or more breeding pairs with several non-breeding juveniles and adults. These non-breeders help to feed the nestlings and may bring more food than the parents themselves. The close family relationship in these jay flocks means that the helpers are assisting to rear offspring which will be

*A parent blue tit has six hungry mouths to feed. When the nestlings are young, they gape vertically (top left) when a parent arrives.*

carrying some of their genes. Cooperative breeding is favored where there is competition for space, and most helpers are males who have not been able to set up a territory. Helping their parents is worthwhile until there is a vacant territory for them to fill.

Among African bee-eaters, some species employ helpers and others do not. The white-fronted bee-eater nests in colonies, and of ninety-six nests examined in one study, sixty-nine were occupied by a pair, twenty-three had three adult birds, three had four adults and one rather crowded nest had five. The

arrangement is that, if they are young, the experience will improve their breeding success later when they rear their own families, and they will, in turn, be assisted by the nestlings they helped to rear.

Another form of cooperation is called communal breeding. Rather than helpers joining a breeding pair, several breeding birds join forces. The best known example of this occurs in the anis, members of the cuckoo family ranging from the southern United States to Argentina. These birds live in flocks, feeding on insects and making use of cattle to flush prey.

*The hungriest nestlings gape most but sometimes one cannot swallow a caterpillar and the parent has to remove it and give it to another (top center).*

*There is a dilemma when the adult tit's attention is caught by the production of a fecal sac (top right) while it has a caterpillar in its bill. It quickly pushes the caterpillar into a waiting gape and grabs the pellet (bottom left).*

helpers may be older offspring of the pair or of a neighboring pair, widowed birds or failed breeders. The breeding success of bee-eaters can be seriously affected by a shortage of flying insects in bad weather and the assistance of helpers is a great advantage. Hatching is asynchronous and, of the four chicks, the two youngest, and sometimes even the second oldest, may die of starvation. In a colony of red-throated bee-eaters it was found that a brood of two nestlings grew faster if there was a helper and that, with such assistance, a third nestling could grow almost as fast as its elder siblings. One benefit for helpers in this

Groups of one to four pairs live in communal territory, all the females laying in one communal nest and sharing incubation duties. In the groove-billed and smooth-billed anis communal life has gone one stage further and pair bonds have broken down so that males and females mate freely within the group. The problem with the anis' communal nest is that there are too many eggs to be incubated properly. The females roll eggs out of the nest before laying their own and the dominant female "wins" by laying last, after the others have stopped evicting eggs and have settled down to incubation.

*Older nestlings are still gaping at random when the parent arrives (bottom center), but when nearly fledged, they direct the gape towards the nest entrance (bottom right).*

# GROWING UP

The concentrated hard work needed to rear the family to fledging in the space of a few weeks is rewarded in the long run. Feeding the nestlings at such a frenetic pace reduces the time when they are vulnerable to nest predators and allows the parent birds to end their responsibilities soon and begin to regain condition, or start a second brood. Even if the fledglings still require feeding, the effort of flying to the nest with each meal can be saved by the fledglings following the parents to the food source. However, in birds that nest in places secure from predators, the urgency of fledging is decreased. Atlantic puffins fledge at the advanced age of seven weeks, having been safe from marauding gulls in the nest burrow, and fly out to sea alone. By contrast young common murres and razorbills leave the nest even before they can fly properly. On the cliff ledges they are vulnerable to gulls, since they tend to nest on wider ledges than the kittiwake (p. 8), so they flutter down to the water on part-grown wings, then swim out to sea with their parents. Xantus' murrelet of California takes this development to the extreme and the young leave the cliff ledge when only two days old.

Young passerines will leave the nest early if disturbed. This is an embarrassment for bird banders who try to handle nestlings of advanced age. The brood may "explode" out of the nest and scatter although they cannot fly properly. This could prove fatal for many of the brood, but to stay in a nest that has been discovered by a predator means certain death. Escapees may survive if their parents find and continue to feed them.

Small passerines reared in vulnerable nests fledge before their wings and tails are fully grown. They are reluctant to leave the nest initially and a certain amount of "persuasion" may be needed from the parents who wait and call nearby. For a while they spend their time perched near the old nest while food is brought to them. As flying becomes easier, they follow their parents and start to search for food, while continuing to receive meals. Woodpeckers, swallows and wrens return to the nest at night but gradually the

*The wood duck lays its eggs in a hollow tree up to 50 feet (15 meters) above the ground. When less than a day old the ducklings jump to the ground in response to their mother's calls and follow her to water.*

*Leaving the nest prematurely is disastrous. Although out of reach of an alligator, this egret's plumage has not grown enough for it to fly properly.*

ties with both nest and territory are lost as the young birds wander farther away, either in family parties or alone. The process may be hastened, as in birds of prey with permanent territories, by the parents switching from feeding their offsprings to harassing them.

## MOBILE FAMILIES

With the few exceptions mentioned earlier, precocial birds are spared the labor of feeding their chicks, and their parental duties are concerned with leading them to suitable feeding places, and protecting them from predators and adverse weather. Precocial chicks are hatched in an advanced state of development compared with altricial nestlings. Their legs are strong, the eyes open and a coat of down helps to keep them warm. The chicks are altogether more alert, being able to walk, preen and peck at things within a few hours of hatching. While the newly-hatched nestling does little more than gape to receive food when hungry, a precocial chick of the same age must be capable of following its parent even over rough terrain. The agility, strength and persistence of these chicks is amazing, as when a brood of eider ducklings is attempting to join the duck as she leads them into the sea. Despite repeatedly being thrown back by the breaking waves, the ducklings eventually get into the calmer water beyond, through a combination of buoyancy and hard paddling.

If the family is to keep together it is vital that parent and offspring identify one another and respond to each other's behavior. The imprinting of young chicks, a form of rapid learning which enables them to recognize their parents, is described on pp. 53–4, and the communication between parent and unhatched chick on p. 125.

Among mallards, the soft quacks of the duck and the shrill piping of the ducklings serve to keep the family together. The duck cannot tell by sight if one duckling is missing but she will respond by calling louder and searching when distress calls from a duckling tell her that it has strayed, lagged behind or is simply cold and hungry. Even at an early age, ducklings give a whistling call of alarm when a hawk or airplane passes overhead, and they can recognize and react to the duck's calls of alarm. In the pheasant family, which includes the domestic chicken, the chicks react to one type of alarm call by "freezing" – crouching motionless, head lowered and eyes closed. Another call – abrupt and low-pitched – sends the chicks diving for cover (p. 124), and a "flocking call" brings them back when danger has passed.

Precocial young can walk, run, and often swim, at an early age but there are occasions when the parents carry them, particularly when danger threatens. Apart from the regular rides given to young grebes and swans that nestle on their parents' back while they swim, carrying of young appears to be relatively rare. There are reliable reports of spotted sandpipers, common moorhens, water rails, clapper rails and whistling ducks flying with young clasped between the feet, and many records of this behavior among European and American woodcocks. The African jaçana stoops to gather its chick under its wing before escaping from danger and barnacle geese have been seen carrying newly hatched goslings in the bill, from a nest high on a cliff ledge, but no one has been able to investigate whether this is regular behavior.

CRECHES

Broods of shelduck often combine to form flotillas of a hundred or more ducklings with a few adults, and the same sort of crèches are also found among eiders. In shelduck, the adults are guarding a crèche that includes their own young, but with eiders, some of the adults, known as "aunties", are unrelated to the ducklings. Despite this, they help to drive off predators and the ducklings gather round them when danger threatens.

It seems that crèches such as these form because there is safety in numbers, large groups of young birds helping to reduce the effects of predation, as in a flock of adult birds (p. 136). In ostriches, up to half-a-dozen broods may band together. When two broods meet, the chicks run unhesitatingly together while the guardian adults display aggressively until one is left in control. The victorious male is believed to stay in charge of the crèche thereafter, but it is possible that the adult ostriches take turns in caring for the crèche.

The advantage to a male ostrich of looking after someone else's family as well as his own may be that it reduces the chances of his offspring being taken by predators, as in the case of several female ostriches laying in one nest.

Crèches are also a feature of a number of semi-precocial species where the young leave the nest some time after hatching but continue to be fed. Such gatherings are found among terns, flamingos, pelicans and penguins. In these colonial birds, the crèches form once the chicks are largely able to regulate their body temperatures and have become too big to be covered by the parents. The young birds leave their nests and begin to gather in small groups which eventually form into large, close-packed crowds. With the exception of emperor penguin chicks, which

*Young artic loons frequently rest or sleep on their parent's back. They can also be carried about in this position when the parent is swimming.*

*A young jaçana chick runs from danger across the waterlily leaves (left). Its parents may come to its aid and carry it away tucked under a wing (far left).*

huddle for warmth as their parents did during incubation, the crèche is a protection against predators. At penguin colonies, skuas can harass single chicks and drag them away from adults that might come to their defense, but they cannot deal with a group of chicks, which bunch together and huddle around adults when the skuas appear. Crèching starts at an age when the chicks would be vulnerable if left alone on the nest, yet their increasing dietary requirements cannot be satisfied unless both parents go foraging. Later, as the penguin chicks increase in size and become too large for the skuas, the crèches begin to break up and the chicks may return to their nests.

Despite the masses of chicks gathered into the crèche, adult birds feed only their own offspring. The

*A male ostrich guards more chicks than could have hatched from its nest. The extra chicks have come from another brood. Gathering of broods also occurs in Canada geese (below) and these crèches of young birds are probably a defense against predators.*

*Most penguin chicks go into a huddle as a defense against skuas, but for emperor penguins, which are not threatened by these aerial predators, huddling gives protection against the bitter cold.*

chicks recognize their parents'' calls and advance to meet them. Young flamingos who have lost their parents will search for them and prod sleeping adults to make them call.

PLAY

Play is common among young birds, as it is among young mammals, yet this is the most difficult type of animal behavior to define. It is not always easy to decide when an animal is playing, or whether play has a function because, unlike other types of animal behavior it is not elicited by a certain set of circumstances. Characteristically, playing involves incomplete, exaggerated or repeated patterns of normal behavior, and there is a general impression that the animal is "not in earnest" in its actions. While it could be said that young birds might be playing because they have nothing to do between receiving meals from their parents, the form of play suggests that it is training for the serious activities of adult life. Young birds of prey pounce on sticks, sometimes tossing them in the air first, fledgling frigatebirds steal feathers or seaweed from each other while in flight, and young hornbills toss and catch sticks, and then crush them with their bills in the way that they will later treat snakes and scorpions.

The greatest difficulty in explaining this type of behavior comes with the seemingly pointless play of adult birds. Eiders have been seen, sliding down a cascade of water rushing over a rock, then hauling themselves out, walking back up to the starting point, and repeating the game. Ravens, crows and rooks hang upside down by their feet from branches or overhead cables, or suspend themselves by their bills. In such situations, it is very difficult not to believe that the bird is gaining some sort of pleasure from its odd behavior.

*An immature great white pelican playing with the head of a dead nestling. Play is difficult to explain but in many cases it seems that the bird is practicing skills that will be needed in its adult life.*

*Some populations of sandhill cranes are sedentary and do not migrate. Others nest on the tundra, mountain meadows and prairies of North America and migrate to the southern states and Mexico. In winter, flocks roost in damp places often with other waterbirds, such as the ducks seen here. At daybreak, the cranes fly out to feed in fields.*

The problem of where birds went for the winter puzzled naturalists for centuries, and even when the pattern of an annual journey to and from the breeding grounds was finally accepted, there still remained "the mystery of migration". In the last three decades there have been enormous advances in our knowledge of all aspects of migration. Destinations and routes are being discovered; the impulses that trigger the journey and the energetics of the flight are better understood, and the value of undertaking a potentially hazardous journey twice a year is becoming clearer. Yet the mystery remains: how does a bird find its way to its destination, perhaps halfway around the world? Birds are known to use the sun, stars or the Earth's magnetic field to set a compass course, but their capacity for true navigation has still to be explained.

The term migration is usually used to describe regular movements of animals between two areas, typically at different seasons of the year and usually covering a considerable distance. The local movements of the capercaillie are rarely considered as migrations, neither are the daily journeys made by sandgrouse to waterholes in the desert, nor the morning flights of gulls into cities to feed, although these are as regular as the popular idea of an annual migration and serve the same purpose of exploiting two different environments. Migrations are usually journeys across the face of the Earth but they can also be vertical movements like those of the mangrove kingfisher, which moves from the coastal mangrove swamps of Africa to mountain streams, or the North American blue grouse, which spends the winter in the mountain pine forests and descends some 1,000 feet (300 meters) to nest in deciduous woodland where there is an early crop of fresh leaves and seeds.

Bird species are often described as either "migratory" or "resident" but this is a simplification. In temperate Europe and America, typical songbird migrants "fly south for the winter", but bird banding has revealed extensive seasonal movements in other directions, even among species that are considered as resident. The picture is one of extreme complexity and in almost all species there are a few individuals which will travel at least a short distance. The migration is not always immediately apparent. Lesser black-backed gulls nesting in Britain move to Spain and Portugal for the winter, but their place is taken by birds coming in from Scandinavia that are barely distinguishable from them.

There is every degree of movement between a species being migratory or sedentary, and, when only a portion of the population is involved, migration is said to be partial. Even such strongly migratory species as swallows and warblers leave a few individuals behind, but the swallows, at least, are very unlikely to survive the winter.

In some species one sex, or one age group, is more likely to migrate than another. When Linnaeus embarked on his monumental classification of living things, he gave the name of *Fringilla coelebs* – the bachelor finch – to the chaffinch. In his native Sweden, female chaffinches migrate south, leaving flocks of males to survive the winter. Farther south, chaffinches are sedentary and they are joined in winter by immigrants from the north. Juvenile chaffinches are more likely to migrate than adults, and females more than males. This seems to be due to the more dominant chaffinches being best able to compete for the limited food supplies on the home ground. So it pays the less dominant juveniles and females to migrate, whereas it is an advantage for the males to remain on the breeding grounds in order to establish territories as early as possible and improve their chances of breeding. This pattern of movement by age and sex is not invariable. In North America female dark-eyed juncos migrate farther south from their breeding grounds in the boreal forests than the males, but juveniles of both sexes remain farther north than the adults.

## WHY MIGRATE?

There must be some advantage in leaving a familiar place, where the details of the environment – the whereabouts of food, water, safe roosts and so on – are well known, to embark on an exhausting and hazardous journey across the world. Birds may migrate to avoid the energy stress of the winter or a dry season when food and water are hard to find, or they may move to avoid competition with other birds for food and nesting places. Both factors may be operating, as when birds leave crowded winter quarters to exploit a temporary season of plenty elsewhere; but whichever is the primary reason, food supply is always the main force behind bird migration.

The competitors that a bird escapes from by its spring migration may be members of its own species or other species with similar habits. This can be illustrated by two North American seed eaters. Field sparrows living in North Carolina spend the winter in fields of blue-stem grasses, where there is a plentiful supply of grass seeds. Some stay to breed there, but about two-thirds of the sparrows move into other habitats to breed. The benefit of the move is an increased success in breeding, which is at a low level in the crowded fields. The dickcissel, another member of the finch family, winters in the grasslands of northern South America. Here it meets intense competition from other seed eaters, but wintering flocks can always move on in search of food. Breeding birds suffer a double handicap since they are tied to one place at the very time when they need extra food

to raise their families, so dickcissels "escape" into the North American prairies, thus avoiding the high level of competition with other seed eaters.

When it comes to moving south for the winter, food supply is again the primary driving force, as shown by birds that have abandoned their migratory habits and now survive the winter on bird-table offerings. These include the blackcap in Europe and the mourning dove in America. The problems of getting enough to eat during the lean winter months is made worse for birds that rely on sight to find their food by the shorter days in which to forage or hunt. In addition to this, extra energy is needed to keep warm, and extreme weather conditions can cut off food supplies. The freezing of fresh waters and soil, or a persistent layer of snow, form a barrier between a bird and its food, so that geese and shorebirds must leave the Arctic regions where they breed. However, low temperatures and snow do not make the tundra impossible for all birds. Ptarmigan survive by digging to uncover Arctic willow and other plants which remain fresh under the blanket of snow; they can keep warm by sheltering in their excavations.

In temperate regions flying insects disappear in winter so that the airspace can no longer support swallows, martins, swifts, nightjars and flycatchers. In general, therefore, it is the insect eaters which leave temperate latitudes, but there are exceptions. Much depends on the precise feeding habits of the birds, so that the warblers that pluck insects from foliage are migratory, while the titmice and creepers that pick hibernating insects from crevices are sedentary.

Emphasis is usually given to adverse conditions as the impetus for migration, but this may be a bias on our part, since we see the disappearance of the birds as an omen of the approaching hardships of winter and their return as a welcome portent of warmer weather. The place where the birds nest and rear their families is seen as "home", yet the birds may have a different perspective. Many species spend more months of the year in their non-breeding areas, and the summer movement is a comparatively brief foray to take advantage of the summer abundance of food. So, are swallows, warblers and flycatchers refugees from the winter, or are they tropical opportunists taking advantage of the northern summer? There are about 400 species of Old World warblers and most are African residents, with only one-eighth making long-distance migrations. Of eleven species of swallows living in Africa, only one comes to Europe. In the New World, less than half the 114 species of warblers and only thirty out of 375 tyrant flycatchers migrate up to North America; and of 319 hummingbirds, twenty-one reach the United States and four reach Canada. It is also significant that the American warblers spend only about three or four months on the breeding grounds but six to seven months on the wintering grounds (the remainder of the year being spent in traveling). These figures suggest that the nesting area is not the true home of such migrants and that these birds should be thought of as tropical species.

One way in which a migratory lifestyle can develop is illustrated by the history of the serin. A century or more ago this was a Mediterranean species, but it then began to spread northwards and has now reached southern Sweden. In its original home the serin is sedentary, but at the far north of its new range it is migratory, since the scant winter food supplies do not allow it to survive the year round.

In temperate climates the advantages of migrating or staying for the winter are often finely balanced, as shown by the British populations of stonechats and

*Flocks of red-winged blackbirds gather in the southern United States before migrating northwards. They are one of the first birds to return, in February and March, the males appearing a few days before the females.*

whinchats. Both species inhabit open grasslands, heaths and areas of recently planted conifers, eating a similar diet of insects, but the stonechat either remains in Britain the year round or migrates only as far as south-western Europe, while the whinchat is a regular long-distance migrant and spends the winter south of the Sahara. A cold winter in Europe results in a serious reduction in numbers of stonechats, but the whinchats are unaffected and the long journey to Africa usually proves in the long run to be no more hazardous than remaining in Europe. Nevertheless, the stonechats do derive some advantage from their lifestyle. By remaining on or near the breeding grounds, they can start nesting early and, not only do they lay three clutches a year to the whinchats' two, they are more successful in rearing their broods. Thus, the stonechats produce twice as many young and can rapidly compensate for the losses from a cold winter. Both species thrive, since the vagaries of the British climate benefit first one and then the other.

MOVING WITH THE WEATHER

The regular pattern of movements by migrants is often obscured by irregular "weather movements". A cold snap can lock up a bird's food and force it to wander far afield. Ducks that need open water, thrushes and

shorebirds requiring soft ground to probe for invertebrates, and finches that find feeding impossible when bushes are imprisoned in snow make long-distance movements. Once again, Britain is the target of Continental birds and, if the weather is still too bad, they fly on to areas of even milder climate. Should the bad weather be coming from the east, they continue towards Ireland, whereas, if the storms are blowing in from the west, they move south to Spain and Portugal.

Once in a while there is a particularly spectacular arrival of birds, prompted by a genuine shortage of food rather than a change in the weather making food unavailable. These movements are called eruptions and are most common in birds which feed on fruits or

seeds during the winter. Many trees do not produce an equal crop each year, and sometimes the crop fails entirely so that the population of birds must move in search of alternative food. The situation is compounded if there was a good crop in the previous year: winter survival would then have been high so that a much increased population is faced by the subsequent crop failure.

Crossbills that feed on conifer seeds, redpolls feeding on birch, siskins feeding on birch and alder, and waxwings feeding on berries, are among the birds

*Fork-tailed flycatchers nest in South America and migrate northwards to Central America for the winter. They are rare vagrants to North America, probably because of mistakes in their navigation.*

*The stonechat and whinchat are closely related birds but the British populations have different life-styles. The stonechat (center top) is resident the year round, or migrates only as far as south-western Europe, but the whinchat (below) regularly migrates south of the Sahara.*

which frequently erupt out of Scandinavia and northern North America. Birds of prey breeding in the Arctic are also subject to regular eruptions, caused by the cyclical rises and crashes of their lemming prey, and snowy owls sometimes reach California and Bermuda. Northern European jays also erupt fairly regularly, and in the fall of 1983 Britain had an unusual invasion of jays from Europe. Normally solitary, retiring woodland birds, the jays were seen arriving along the English coastline in flocks of a hundred or more. They were only stragglers compared with the flocks moving westwards across Europe, apparently because of a failure of the acorn crop which is a major food at this time of year.

One of the marvels of bird migration is that such small creatures can travel so far as a matter of routine. Records of migration are full of superlatives. The Arctic tern nests in high latitudes of the northern hemisphere and migrates into the Antarctic pack-ice, a distance on the order of 11,000 miles (18,000 kilometers). Although this bird is interesting because it must enjoy more daylight than any other animal, its migration is not so remarkable a feat as it might seem, since a seabird can feed on the way. The most prodigious feats of endurance are made by birds

*Migration takes its toll of many birds. This brambling was so exhausted by its flight across the sea to England that it succumbed before it could find any food.*

which make non-stop migratory flights over a hostile environment. The bristle-thighed curlew has to fly 6,000 miles (10,000 kilometers) or more across the Pacific Ocean to reach its winter home on the Polynesian islands, and for long stretches of this journey it cannot rest or feed. The longest non-stop stretch is over 1,800 miles (3,000 kilometers). The same sort of endurance is shown by the tiny ruby-throated hummingbird when it makes a 600-mile (1,000-kilometer), twenty-hour hop across the Gulf of Mexico.

To make a non-stop migration, a bird must be well prepared for the journey. Fuel, in the form of fat, must be laid down before migration starts, and in some species the flight muscles are built up. Regular migrants are not driven to migrate by immediate hunger. They must migrate to avoid a future food shortage, and the migration is timed to follow a period of abundance, perhaps lasting several weeks, during which the birds can prepare for the journey.

It seems incredible that a bird can carry enough fuel to cross an ocean. However, its flight range is not dependent on the absolute amount of fuel carried, but on the proportion of fuel to the body weight. Warblers burn up 0.5% of their body weight per hour during flight and, since they double their weight before migrating, they will have the capacity to make their longest flights, in the order of 1,200 miles (2,000 kilometers), with sufficient reserves to cope with adverse winds. Blackpoll warblers gather on the east coast of North America in the fall, weighing ⅓ ounce (10–13 grams). They feed there for ten to twenty days, until they weigh ¾ ounce (20–23 grams), and then set out for South America. They have fuel for over ninety-five hours' flying time, which gives them a safety margin for a flight which lasts eighty-five hours in fair conditions. Larger birds cannot carry such large reserves of fat because of the problem of generating sufficient power to get the extra weight airborne: a goose or swan could not possibly carry 50% extra weight. The advantage that large birds have over small ones is that their optimum flight speed is greater and they are less influenced by wind. A hummingbird would be stopped in its tracks by a headwind of 20 mph (35 kph), but geese and swans can press on. The most efficient migrators, in terms of flight endurance, are the medium-sized birds – those weighing up to 1¾ pounds (800 grams) without fat – such as the large, fast-flying shorebirds. Until slaughter rendered it virtually extinct, the Eskimo curlew bred in large numbers on the tundra of Alaska and Canada and migrated to the pampas of Argentina. In the fall, it flew south-east to Newfoundland and Nova Scotia, where it fed on ripe crowberries before heading down the New England seaboard. It put on so much weight before the start of the journey south that it was nicknamed "the doughbird" because, when skinned its breast revealed a thick layer of fat looking like dough.

## FUEL ECONOMY

Whether a bird doubles its weight for a long flight or proceeds in stages with stops to feed, it must use its reserves economically in case of delay by bad weather or a temporary famine at the destination. There are several ways in which birds strive for economical flight. First, a species may evolve structurally. Among both New and Old World warblers, the shape of the wing is longer and narrower in migratory species than

*Left: common cranes breed over a wide area of northern Eurasia. Those from the eastern part of this range fly to China for the winter, those from central Asia travel to northern India, and the Scandinavian cranes migrate to Africa, the Middle East or Spain. Cranes tend to soar less frequently than storks and regularly make long sea passages.*

*Below: brants make prodigious journeys. Breeding birds from the Arctic islands of Canada may fly as far south as Florida or northern Mexico, and some even come to the British Isles for winter, where they are joined by darker-breasted birds from the northern coasts of Siberia.*

*Although they are not often seen in the air and prefer to run when disturbed, many rails are long-distance migrants. The sora migrates from North America to the West Indies in a journey that entails a long sea crossing. On rare occasions it is swept across the Atlantic to Europe.*

*Black kites circle over a ship at port in Queensland, Australia. These birds are found over much of the Old World and many populations migrate long distances, in flocks that travel together and gather in communal roosts or bathing places en route.*

in their sedentary relatives. Comparison of wing lengths of American wood warblers shows that the migratory species, such as Blackburnian and Nashville warblers, have longer, more pointed wings than the tropical residents, such as the russet-crowned warbler and yellow-crowned redstart. In Europe, the migratory willow warbler and reed warbler have longer wings than the largely sedentary Cetti's and Dartford warblers. Short, broad wings are suited to the hovering sallies used in picking up insects, while sustained flight is more efficient with long, narrow wings, and the wings of migratory species reflect the importance of sustained flight.

The bird can also adapt its flight to give the greatest economy. With a tail-wind, it can fly less strenuously and save fuel by being blown along. If caught by winds blowing it off course over the sea, it can fly slowly, saving energy and increasing its endurance, until the wind drops or it is blown to land. It can also save energy and maintain its optimum cruising speed by gliding between bouts of wing flapping. Small birds typically migrate with a "bounding" flight in which they rise and fall in the air through brief bouts of flapping and gliding. The smaller passerines close their wings instead of gliding, to reduce drag (p.22).

The largest birds – broad-winged raptors, storks, cranes and herons – dispense with flapping where possible and gain lift by soaring, making extensive use of thermals for migration. A stork's journey from central Europe to equatorial Africa covers 4,000 miles (7,000 kilometers). With six to eight hours' thermal soaring per day, the journey would take twenty-three days. A stork carries fuel for forty-eight days, so it has plenty of reserves. If it had to rely on flapping flight, it has been calculated that its energy consumption would be so great that four refueling stops would be needed. As thermals do not develop over the sea, soaring birds use the shortest possible sea crossings. Those leaving Europe for Africa and Asia are channelled across the Strait of Gibraltar and the Bosphorus, and to a lesser extent via Italy. By soaring high over the land, the birds can glide over the thermal-free sea. During the migration season, the Strait of Gibraltar and the Bosphorus witness the marvelous sight of thousands of large birds passing in flocks overhead, and there are occasional news reports of "battles" between eagles and storks as they swirl around together in a thermal!

The stress of flight can be further reduced by selecting the appropriate time of day, altitude and wind direction. Land birds crossing the ocean have no

*White storks nesting in northern Europe (right) fly to Africa (far right) for the winter. They take the shortest possible sea routes into Africa, some populations using the Straits of Gibraltar, others crossing the Bosphorus at Istanbul. Here they can be seen soaring in thermals above Istanbul (below) in preparation for the sea journey. Once they have soared to a certain height they can glide across the open water and reach the other side without the need for flapping flight.*

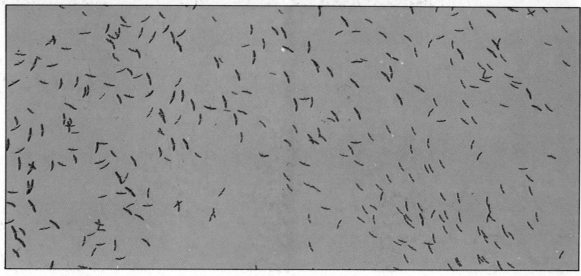

option but to keep going throughout the twenty-four hours, while the thermal-soaring raptors and storks fly by day, as do buntings, orioles, starlings, finches, swifts and swallows. Warblers, thrushes, flamingos, rails and, not surprisingly, owls and nightjars, travel by night. The reason for these preferences is not always clear. Night travel has several advantages: the danger of predation is lessened and insect eaters, in particular, can make use of the day for feeding if they fly at night. It is possible that the heat of the day could distress small birds which normally do not fly at great heights or travel very far. Combined with the exertions of flying, the sun's rays could cause overheating; it is known that budgerigars overheat and stop flying when the air temperature rises to 97°F (36°C).

In general, birds prefer to start their migration when the weather is fair and the wind will help them on their way. Geese will land or turn back over the sea if contrary winds spring up. Departure depends to some extent on the birds' urge to move. At the beginning of the season, they wait for favorable winds. Later, they will take off even in foul weather and battle against strong winds. Spring migration is often more rapid, as the birds are in a hurry to reach the breeding grounds and start nesting. For example, European wood warblers take thirty days to reach northern Germany in spring and sixty days to return to Africa in the fall.

Unexpected strong and contrary winds may lead to loss of life, though they bring delight to birders who have the chance to identify stray birds well outside their normal range. Every year American species are blown off the normal course down the Atlantic seaboard and carried across the Atlantic along the normal westerly storm tracks. Occasionally there are conditions which carry birds in the opposite direction. In 1927, and again in 1966, hundreds of lapwings from Europe arrived on the Atlantic coast of America, from Baffin Island to Barbados. In both instances, cold weather had spread westwards across Europe, pushing the lapwings through Britain and into Ireland as part of a "weather movement". Winds then carried them in a westerly arc, around the north side of a huge depression lying across the Atlantic.

The weather conditions which are sufficiently good to cause birds to depart, but which are then likely to sweep them off course, are known well enough to predict movements of birds. Thus, birders use weather forecasts to alert themselves to a good influx of birds. Most of the birds they find in the fall are juveniles which suggests that adult birds can make better judgements about the weather.

*Flocks of lapwings from Europe move around in winter to avoid severe weather. Freak conditions occasionally sweep them out to sea and across the Atlantic to America.*

In the temperate countries of Europe and America there are, at first sight, two great waves of migration: summer visitors from warmer climes and winter visitors from the Arctic. Viewed globally, there is no real distinction, and both are part of a general movement southwards in the fall and northwards in spring. The reasons behind the waves of migration are the same: escape from a crowded environment to take advantage of the summer season of abundance farther north, then a retreat as the climate becomes unfavorable in winter. The Arctic migrants stand out because their breeding grounds are so markedly seasonal. From continuous sunshine and a flush of insect and plant food, the environment changes to the permanent darkness of the winter, with snow and ice locking up the remaining supplies of food to all but a few species.

*The whimbrel (center) and the greater golden plover (below) are two of the birds that fly long distances to take advantage of the short but productive Arctic summer. The season is just long enough to nest and put on weight for the journey south.*

Arctic birds are champion migrants, particularly shorebirds such as the golden plovers. Greater golden plovers from Europe spend the winter in Britain and around the Mediterranean, while the Siberian and western Alaskan populations of the lesser golden plover (also known as the American golden plover) converge on southern Asia, the Pacific islands, Australia and New Zealand. The north Alaskan and Arctic Canadian populations fly to the southern end of South America, including Tierra del Fuego. Several Old World species have crossed into the New World, especially to Greenland and neighboring Canadian islands: barnacle and white-fronted geese, banded plover, sanderling and ruddy turnstone, for instance.

For some birds it is clear that the present-day migration route retraces the track of their original dispersal. The wheatear, for example, spread from

However, the superabundance of food in the Arctic is often more apparent than real. The birds are well spaced out across the tundra and, while there is often sufficient food to rear a family and fatten up before migration, their success can be easily overturned. A late spring delays the thaw and keeps food supplies hidden under the snow. The arriving birds may be so short of food that breeding is not attempted, and they may even starve to death. Ducks and loons are sometimes prevented from breeding by the failure of lakes to thaw. At the end of summer, a cold snap will cover tundra pools and the seashore with a brittle skin of ice that locks up the insect larvae and intertidal crustaceans which are important foods for shorebirds before they migrate south. Such occasional lean years, when the Arctic summer fails, are apparently a small penalty to pay for the advantage of escaping the heavier predation and competition farther south.

Europe into Greenland and eastern Canada, and from Asia into Alaska, yet both American populations still return to Africa for the winter, one flying eastwards and the other westwards, rather than heading down the American continent. The yellow wagtail and Arctic warbler also have Alaskan populations, which winter in Asia. But the gray-cheeked thrush, an American species, has spread the other way; it has a Siberian population which flies to Central America for the winter, where it mixes with related thrushes. These transcontinental routes have apparently been formed since the last glaciation as birds re-established themselves in the wake of the retreating ice cap, but for some species there are now separate wintering grounds on the two continents. Bewick's swan stays in the Old World, and the whistling swan (which is so similar that the two are now classed as one species – the tundra swan) stays in the New World. The same holds true for New and Old World populations of

*A family of two adult and three juvenile trumpeter swans. This North American race of the whooper swan almost became extinct through hunting. Once strongly migratory, the remaining populations mainly winter on ice-free freshwaters and move south only in severe weather.*

pintail ducks. Presumably, the two populations became separated by Ice Age glaciation at an earlier date and new migration routes had to be formed.

### DUCKS, GEESE AND SWANS

The Arctic is the breeding ground for many of the world's waterfowl. Most Arctic ducks feed on aquatic animals, and they retire to ice-free seas or inland waters after breeding, but the swans and geese are vegetarians that migrate long distances to find plant food well south of the Arctic.

Swans and geese can exploit the Arctic because the growing parts of Arctic plants contain more protein than those in lower latitudes, so they form a rich food for the growing young. The spring migration takes the birds into the Arctic before the grass has started to grow, or is even uncovered by the thaw, and they have to rely on their stored fat not only to fuel the flight but to sustain them during the early stages of nesting. Indeed, the amount of fat and protein stored in the body largely determines how many eggs the female lays.

The male goose needs fat reserves so that he can devote his time to guarding first the territory and then the nest and brood, while the female needs her reserves to carry her through incubation. She alone incubates the eggs, and female snow geese may, on rare occasions, starve to death on the nest, since their food is still hidden under the snow. Even later on in the summer, breeding can suffer because in poor years both parents spend a great deal of time searching for food and predators take advantage of the relaxed guard on the brood.

Goose migration is well known because each year hunters wait for the flocks to arrive at traditional feeding grounds. In North America, geese are funnelled along regular flyways with staging posts, where the flocks alight to rest and feed. Their existence is a result of the geography of North America, where the land mass is traversed by features that run roughly north to south and are used as guides by the migrating birds. Mountain ranges, large rivers, seashores and forest edges constitute these "leading

*Wetland refuges such as Tule Lake in California are important wintering grounds for waterfowl, many of which have flown there from the Arctic. Preservation of these places is essential for the survival of the birds.*

*Ruddy turnstones rest on their spring journey northwards. These birds nest on the tundras of the New- and Old-World Arctic and migrate to coastal areas, reaching central Chile and Argentina, South Africa and New Zealand. Ruddy turnstones from Greenland and north-east Canada cross the Atlantic to winter in Europe.*

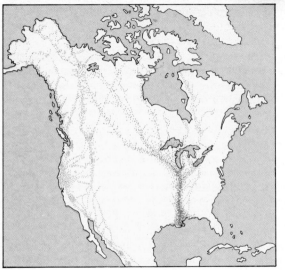

*The geographical features of North America channel migrant birds into routes that run north-south. Birds from breeding grounds all over the northern part of the continent collect into four main flyways leading to their wintering grounds. The Pacific and Mississippi flyways are shown on the right-hand map, the Central and Atlantic flyways on the left-hand map.*

*The snow goose nests in the Arctic, from Wrangel Island in Siberia across Canada to Baffin Island.*

*Snow geese gather in flocks on the tundra before leaving to fly south along the major flyways. By traveling in flocks, it is possible that young geese migrating for the first time can learn details of the route, but they are also capable of making the journey by themselves.*

*Snow geese often fly in a V-formation, like other geese, but their undulating flight makes the pattern rather irregular. These V-formations do not have a particular leader, neither is there any evidence that keeping in formation makes flying easier. Here the typical lesser snow geese are mixed with the darker forms of the species, known as blue geese.*

lines", and they create a network of paths that make up four main trunk routes. Flyways are less obvious in Europe because the major geographical features are oriented mainly east–west.

The wintering grounds of Arctic geese and swans are concentrated in areas which remain ice- and snow-free during most of the winter. In Europe these are mostly in the British Isles and a coastal strip on the other side of the North Sea. Populations from different parts of the Arctic separate into discrete wintering areas. The barnacle goose was the one-time mystery bird which was thought to spring from goose barnacles growing on ships' timbers. Its three widely separate breeding grounds were not discovered until this century. The Russian population on the islands of Novaya Zemlya and Vaigach once spent the winter confined to the coast of north-west Germany, but drainage has pushed them around to the coast of the Netherlands. Barnacle geese from Svalbard still have a restricted distribution; they gather on the Solway Firth, which forms the west-coast boundary of Scotland and England. The third population nests on the ice-free ground of east Greenland, and winters in western Scotland and Ireland. Their departure from Greenland depends on the timing of the first winter frosts, and initially they gather in Iceland to feed on seeds and rhizomes for a month or more. Just before the Iceland winter begins, and when there are favorable winds, they make the final crossing to the British Isles.

SHOREBIRDS

The end of the Arctic summer also sees the departure of the shorebirds. As with the geese, the time between nesting and migration is occupied by feeding in preparation for the journey. Unlike geese, shorebirds do not migrate in family parties, and in some species the juveniles and adults travel separately. Although they are champion long-distance fliers, with the ability

*Migrating snow geese stop at traditional staging posts such as Hudson Bay and the Sand Lake National Wildlife Refuge, South Dakota (left).*

to fly several thousand miles non-stop, shorebirds make use of staging posts.

Each spring and fall, shallow bays with large areas of sand and mud exposed at low tide are filled with flocks of shorebirds that are either stopping temporarily or remaining for the winter. There is a great confusion of birds, but over the years they have been caught in huge numbers and, by ringing and taking measurements that show racial differences, the complex patterns of movements of the different species have become clearer.

The red knot is a common and widely distributed shorebird, a high-Arctic breeder with populations in both the New and Old Worlds. Those from eastern Siberia winter in South-east Asia, Australia and New Zealand; from central Siberia westwards to Greenland and eastern Canada, they go down to western Europe and Africa; but west of Baffin Island red knots migrate through America.

The Greenland and eastern Canadian red knots winter mainly in western Europe. In spring, along with other shorebirds, they fly to Iceland and spend three weeks feeding before continuing the journey over the Greenland ice-cap. It would be possible for them to fly from Europe to the Arctic without a break, but the stopover allows them to reach the nesting grounds in much better condition and with good reserves of fat. In the fall they are heading for rich feeding grounds in Europe, and Iceland is visited only briefly or missed altogether.

"American" red knots fly to Argentina, although a few remain in the southern United States for the winter. On both outward and return journeys, they stop off at rich coastal feeding grounds in Suriname, but, whereas in the fall they reach Suriname by the direct ocean route, in spring they fly up the coast of the United States and tens of thousands gather in Delaware Bay to feed on the eggs of spawning horseshoe crabs.

*Wintering grounds include areas of Texas (left) at the end of the Central and Mississippi flyways, and California, at the end of the Pacific flyway. Here a large flock of snow geese has gathered near Mount Shasta, in California (right). A small number of snow geese migrate down the Atlantic flyway to Chesapeake Bay.*

*Siberian white cranes mingle with sarus cranes in India. The former, now rare, breeds across Siberia. The western population migrates to the Caspian region as well as India, while the eastern poulation flies to China.*

The annual migration of landbirds from the great landmasses of North America and Eurasia into the tropics and beyond is not evenly distributed. Africa receives the most migrant birds, South and Central America fewer, while India and Australia are the destination of only a minority of species. The reasons seem to lie in geographical history. The link between Africa and Eurasia is ancient, but South America was separated from the North until comparatively recently (about two million years ago), and relatively few tropical American species have spread northwards. The Indian subcontinent is walled off by the Himalayas and the Tibetan plateau, and has only limited habitats suitable for visiting migrants. Although some birds fly over these mountains, fifteen species, including corn crake, swift and red-footed falcon, travel from eastern Siberia across the vast breadth of Asia, skirting north around the mountain ranges and into Africa. Far-eastern migrants heading south mostly stop in South-east Asia, from Burma to the Philippines, although a number of shorebirds continue to Australasia. Only a few landbirds, such as the white-throated needletail, a swift, regularly make the long flight from eastern Asia into Australia. The reasons could be the lack of suitable habitat for immigrants and a failure of Australian species to take up a northern breeding ground, as the tropical African and American birds have done.

Of 589 species of birds living in Europe and northern Asia, 238 are long-distance migrants and 185 of these travel to Africa in winter. About half settle in the huge crescent of grassland and dry woodland that stretches from Senegal across to Somalia and south to Zimbabwe. A large number of birds settle in the Sahel region bordering the Sahara desert, which is surprising because they arrive at the time of the dry season when the Sahel is particularly inhospitable. People and their livestock must rely on shrinking lakes and deep wells for water, but even at this season some plants will be in leaf, and bearing flowers and fruit for birds to eat. The whitethroat, for instance, is mainly an insect eater in Europe, but relies heavily on berries while in Africa. The warm weather and freedom from nesting duties reduces its energy requirements to about two-thirds of its needs during the northern summer. Nevertheless, the recent series of droughts in the Sahel has had a devastating effect on this and some other species. Surprisingly few birds occupy the bush forests of the Congo basin, only the hobby, nightingale, barn swallow, several Old World warblers and wagtails. By contrast, North American migrants are more abundant in the forests of Central and South America, than in open country. This has important implications for the conservation of migratory birds. Deforestation in Africa provides more open country of the type preferred by the migrants,

*The ruff is a shorebird which, unusually, lives inland in both summer and winter. This flock from eastern Europe is migrating along the Blue Nile, past Khartoum, on its way to eastern and southern Africa.*

*A flock of black-tailed godwits, in winter plumage, feed in a stream in New Guinea, while on passage between Siberia and Australia.*

*A lesser golden plover in a paddy field in the Philippines. It will have migrated from eastern Siberia and may be on its way to New Guinea or Australia.*

*Massed waterfowl on an East African lake. These migrants have come from Europe or Asia, and some may have nested as far away as Siberia the previous summer.*

whereas the destruction of tropical forests in America is seriously affecting some migrant species so that populations are dwindling on the breeding grounds.

AFRICAN MIGRANTS

The main routes into Africa from Europe and Asia are channelled to avoid the worst of the Sahara desert, either westwards through the Iberian peninsula and down the western border of North Africa, or eastwards through the Middle East and down the Nile Valley, although many birds enter Africa below Italy and fly across the middle of the Sahara. The desert, and to a lesser extent the Mediterranean Sea, form a very considerable barrier to migrants entering and leaving Africa. The desert crossing is 900 miles (1,500 kilometers) and, for a small bird, will take thirty-five to forty hours. Its fat reserves will be quite adequate, providing that it fed well before the journey and does not meet difficult conditions, such as contrary winds, on the crossing. Occasionally there are mass mortalities of small birds around the Sahara when a catastrophe has struck. During the migration seasons, there is always a scattering of birds sheltering among piles of rocks or among the bushes growing in dry river beds. These are presumably birds which failed to make the crossing in one flight. They probably have a slender chance of finding sufficient food to complete the journey unless, like the barn swallows and yellow wagtails, they can feed on flies swarming around oases.

Within sub-Saharan Africa, the migrants disperse, often to traditional areas. Three very similar European warblers, which are famous for being virtually indistinguishable except by their songs, have quite different winter ranges. Willow warblers spread over most of the African continent south of the Sahara and the bordering arid lands; the wood warbler is confined to a narrow band of Africa just north of the equator; but the chiffchaff is hardly found south of the desert zone and winters mainly in North Africa, the Middle East and even in parts of Europe. Most migrants remain north of the equator, but the barn swallow reaches South Africa, and banding gives good evidence that different European populations remain largely separate in Africa: German swallows turn up in the Congo basin and British swallows in South Africa.

Banding also shows that individual birds of many species regularly return to the same winter home: one yellow wagtail was caught at the same spot in Nigeria in seven consecutive years. There are also, however, regular and large-scale movements of European migrants within Africa. They went unrecognized until recently because they take place at night. Presumably they are related to changing food supplies, such as the flush of insects which follows the onset of the rainy season.

The movements of marsh warblers are known in some detail. From all over Europe, they travel around the eastern end of the Mediterranean and probably stop for some time in Sudan and Ethiopia. Then they move on, passing through Kenya and Zambia to arrive in South Africa in December. There they remain until March, spreading back through Zambia, Tanzania and Kenya from April to May and then rapidly covering the remaining distance to Europe.

AMERICAN MIGRANTS

Of the 650 or more species that breed north of Mexico, 332 fly south in the fall. Their destinations are principally the scrubs and forests of Central America, from southern Mexico to Panama. More infrequently they fly into northern South America, and only a small number reach the grasslands of the pampas and beyond. Of the thirty tyrant flycatchers that breed in North America, only the eastern phoebe and a few others remain in North America, while the greatest proportion fly to southern Mexico and Guatemala; only four species reach Peru. Birds which migrate beyond the tropics include the barn swallow, Swainson's hawk, the bobolink and several vireos and nighthawks.

The Gulf of Mexico and the Caribbean Sea act as a barrier similar to the Mediterranean Sea on the other side of the Atlantic. Many passerines and shorebirds take a direct sea route to South America passing over the general area of Bermuda. Others, including the birds of prey which are ill-suited for long sea voyages, travel overland through Central America, or hop along the West Indies island chain, like the blackpoll warbler and Connecticut warbler. A few, including some Connecticut warblers and the scarlet tanager, fly directly across the Gulf of Mexico to Yucatan.

Radar tracking has been used in a telling way to show what happens to the hordes of birds which fly out from the American coast between Nova Scotia and Virginia and apparently disappear into the empty expanse of the Atlantic. Over ten million birds, mostly shorebirds and songbirds, may leave Cape Cod alone in a single fall night. Observations at a chain of radar stations were needed to reveal the rationale behind this seemingly strange behavior. The birds head out to sea on a south-easterly course until they are in the region of Bermuda and the Sargasso Sea, when their flight path swings to the south-west, and they eventually make a landfall in South America. The flight takes them over 2,000 miles (3,000 kilometers) of sea and is among the longest non-stop flights recorded for small birds. Yet it is a more direct route to eastern South America than the apparently safer routes through Central America or along the chain of Caribbean islands. The birds are turning the weather system to advantage and making considerable energy savings. They gather at the coast and wait for a cold front to pass over, so getting the benefit of the strong winds from the north-west behind it. A wave of birds takes to the air and is carried south-east in the direction of Bermuda, a journey taking about eighteen hours. They fly at altitudes of around 6,500 feet (2,000 meters), dropping slightly over Bermuda as they pass through an area of light and variable winds until they

reach the Sargasso Sea, where they meet the north-east trades. They climb again to over 13,000 feet (4,000 meters), and sometimes as high as 21,000 feet (6,500 meters), to find the trade winds that will push them south-westwards towards South America, to make a landfall after about eighty hours in the air.

Another advantage of this route is that navigation is simple. Analysis of radar-tracking data suggests that the birds set off on a steady south-easterly heading with the wind behind them. They do not have to change course at any stage. On the second leg of the journey, the south-easterly heading combined with the north-east trade wind gives an actual track in the direction of South America.

A feature of many species is that birds nesting in the north and west swing across North America and pass through the eastern United States. This seems to be the ancestral route, which has been retained as the birds have spread north-west, either as the climate improved or, as in the case of the bobolink, settlement of the prairies has extended the habitat.

*Barn swallows line up on papyrus stems in Kenya, as they had on telegraph wires in Europe a few months earlier. Swallows from particular parts of Europe have been found to gather in specific wintering grounds in Africa.*

*Shovelers from Europe spend the winter alongside flamingos on Lake Nakuru. The teeming aquatic life of the Rift Valley lakes of Kenya attracts many waterfowl and shorebirds during the European winter.*

The migration routes in both Africa and America are complicated by some species carrying out loop migrations in which they enter winter quarters by one route and leave by another. In Africa, the bank and barn swallows fly in across the Straits of Gibraltar and return on a broad front farther east. In America, the lesser golden plover flies between the Arctic tundra and the Argentine pampas using the sea route on the way south, but returning overland through Central America. This loop can be explained by the rich crop of berries along the Atlantic coast of North America which the birds gorge on in the fall before they set off for the flight to South America.

Recent researches, especially in America, have aimed at determining how migrants fit into the ecology of the tropics, and the results have revealed a complicated picture. One reason why there may be so few migrants in the African forests is that, in a lush habitat with little seasonal variation, all the ecological niches are filled by the residents. In the surrounding savannahs, however, there are distinct rainy seasons which produce sudden flushes of plant and insect food. The resident breeding birds are tied to their nests and need a steady supply of food, whereas the migrants are free to move around the countryside and take advantage of local abundance.

In South America there are relatively few migrants from the north among the residents in the even climate of the lowland forests. More appear in the grasslands, where there are alternating wet and dry seasons, and in the seasonal forests farther from the equator. Here they make use of sporadic gluts of food such as fruit, swarming termites or the panicking crowds of insects disturbed by army ants, or they occupy niches which are not used by residents. In the region of Central America and the Caribbean, most immigrant birds are "gleaners" such as warblers that pick insects off leaves, or flycatchers "sallying" from perches. There are few residents of this type in Central America, but many more are found in the incomparably rich bird fauna of South America, where immigrants become less common.

*The tanagers belong to a tropical family and only five out of 233 species breed in North America. The scarlet tanager is one of the northernmost, nesting in broadleaved woods throughout eastern North America. It winters from Panama to Peru.*

*The ruby-throated hummingbird (left) is the most strongly migratory of the hummingbirds. It flies north each spring to breed in the eastern areas of North America and Canada, making a non-stop crossing of the Gulf of Mexico. The black-chinned hummingbird (below left) is its counterpart in the western states, breeding as far north as south-west British Columbia. Like the ruby-throated hummingbird it winters in Mexico.*

*A satellite picture shows the band of cloud that signifies a cold front moving into the Atlantic from the coast of North America. Migrating birds use the north-westerly winds that these fronts produce to carry them out to sea. By changing altitude over the Sargasso Sea they can find north-easterly winds that will push them towards South America.*

# MIGRATION IN THE TROPICS

*Periodic flooding of rivers is a feature of many countries in the warmer parts of the world. Fish flourish in the newly created aquatic habitat but perish in large numbers as the waters subside. They attract birds which arrive to feed and breed. Here, maguari storks are catching stranded fish, in northern Argentina. The carrion-feeding caracaras have also been attracted by the fish, but the coypu is feeding on floating plant stems.*

Over a huge area of the tropics there are forests and savannahs which are subjected to alternating seasons of rain and drought. In the dry season, the vegetation becomes dry and brown, standing water disappears and conditions become unfavourable for birds. Once or twice a year, there is a regular and sudden break in the weather, and the rain pours down. The ground is soaked; pools and streams fill, plants revive, produce flowers and set seed, insects swarm, and birds nest and raise their young.

There is a migration of birds within the tropics to capitalize on the shifting rains and the season of plenty that they bring. Its scale has only been realized in recent years, mainly in Africa, because many visiting ornithologists have been attracted there. Migrations within the tropics are stimulated by the start and finish of the rainy seasons, but the ultimate cause of migration is the same as in higher latitudes: variable food supply.

The rainy season produces swarms of termites, grasshoppers and other insects which attract the insectivorous birds, while the seed crop attracts the grain eaters. Swollen streams and lakes provide fish for herons, storks, kingfishers and others, but their easiest pickings come when the waters drop again and fish are left floundering in shrinking pools. On the other hand, flooding can cut off food supplies for some birds, and the American wood stork migrates between the Amazon and Orinoco rivers, which run low at different times of the year. As one river fills up, the stork transfers to the other so that it can always wade in shallow water by the river bank.

These seasons of plenty are usually regular in their appearance, and the cycle of migration and breeding therefore follows an annual pattern. There are generally some individuals of a species breeding in every month of the year, but the peak number of clutches is laid around the rainy season.

Most African migrants travel north–south, and migration is commonest on the strongly seasonal savannahs whereas birds of the evergreen forests rarely move. In West Africa, many bird species spend the dry season (September to June) in the damp savannah woodland belt, lying north of the rainforest, where the raptors, nightjars and waders breed. Just before the rains, the migrant population moves into the dry savannahs and Sahel region, and here species such as the kingfishers, sunbirds and herons breed beside the temporary lakes and rivers.

The pattern of migration in Africa is usually regular, as birds follow the annual cycle of rains. Abdim's stork makes a long transequatorial journey, breeding in a broad belt from Senegal to the Red Sea during the northern rainy season (June to September) and then flying to southern Africa for the remainder of

the year. Thus, it spends its whole life among fresh grasslands with teeming insects to eat. The pennant-winged nightjar, named after the long streamers trailing from its wings, does the reverse. It breeds in the southern rainy season between September and October and then flies northwards, following the shifts in rainy season and feeding on the resultant insect swarms until it reaches the savannah countries between Nigeria and Uganda.

A more complicated timetable of movements is shown by the red-billed quelea. More often known simply as the quelea, this relative of the weaver birds is a serious agricultural pest that often lives in enormous flocks numbering millions of birds. It generally moves north–south in tropical Africa, but this varies over the continent in line with the pattern of shifting rain belts. The quelea's main food is grass seeds lying on the ground, but at the start of the rains these germinate, so the quelea turns to the burgeoning insect population, especially swarming termites and grasshoppers. It puts on fat and migrates back in the direction that the rains had come from until it reaches an area where the plants have had time to set a new crop of seeds since the rain belt swept past. There it settles to breed and feed itself and its young on insects and seeds. In East Africa, this results in a migration north from Tanzania as the rains begin in November, through Kenya to Somalia. There the rains stop and the queleas move south, stopping to breed somewhere on the way between December and February. In April the rain belt moves northwards again and there is another cycle of breeding. The result is colonies of nesting birds forming at different times and places, as food supplies become available, and then moving on.

AUSTRALIAN MIGRANTS

Cycles of rainfall and the resulting crops of seeds, fruit and insects are predictable throughout most of the tropics and subtropics, but the climate of Australia is capricious. Over the interior of the continent rainfall is low and unreliable. There are long droughts interrupted by downpours at extremely irregular intervals. As a result, a large number of Australian birds are nomads that traverse wide areas in search of food and water and then gather in large numbers in 'sumps' – depressions into which rainwater drains and where vegetation flourishes. Emus scan the horizon for storm clouds and set off in their direction. The journey on foot is slow and, by the time the emus have reached the spot, fresh vegetation has sprouted.

In times of drought there can be huge mortality of birds as waterholes dry up, but the survivors have the capacity for rapid breeding. The grey teal is a duck which has adapted to desert life through its ability to arrive at a newly formed lake and quickly nest. The best-known Australian opportunists are the budgerigar and zebra finch, so familiar as cage birds; the latter starts courting within a few minutes of rain falling and starts nest building a day later. The black-faced wood swallow has an even more rapid response. It has been seen picking up sticks as soon as a cloud passes over!

*Long-tailed cormorants rest by a temporary pool in Nigeria. These birds are seen on permanent lakes but they quickly move into newly flooded areas to breed.*

*Abdim's storks make a regular migration around Africa to take advantage of the shifting rains that bring out swarms of insects for them to eat. This flock is preening by a waterhole in Namibia.*

*Queleas (far left and left) are members of the sparrow family which live in flocks that can number millions. They are nomadic, moving around Africa in search of crops of grass seeds and stopping to breed when food is plentiful. A flock that settles on a grain field can do enormous damage.*

The pattern of seabird migration is broadly the same as that of landbirds in that the birds leave the breeding grounds and head for alternative feeding grounds. Those from temperate waters head for warmer places, which may take them across the equator. Patterns of tropical migrations are less clear because breeding can generally take place throughout the year and the birds may never move far. The main contrast with landbirds is that seabirds on a long journey have more opportunity to feed or rest, although observations at sea suggest that migrating seabirds are traveling fast.

petrel as long ago as 1940. The species is very numerous on the fringes of the Antarctic, and the race which breeds in the sector below South America later migrates into the North Atlantic. At the end of the Antarctic summer, in March and April, the petrels quickly spread north in flocks of several hundred. The majority fly round the "bulge" of Brazil and into the western Atlantic, and head for the rich fishing waters off North America (at one time they were caught and used as bait by fishermen). Another, slower stream crosses to Africa, but by July all are "wintering" in the

*The Wilson's storm-petrels (top center) which are to be seen all over the Atlantic Ocean are birds which have bred in the Antarctic.*

*After leaving their cliff-top nests in the Antarctic, young giant petrels set off around the world. They are carried from west to east by the prevailing winds and birds raised on islands near South America may reach Australia within a matter of weeks.*

*Noddies are known as "navigation birds" in Polynesia because they always return to roost on an island at night, and were once relied on by local sailors seeking the nearest landfall. After the breeding season these birds leave their nesting colonies and disperse into the Pacific. As with most tropical seabirds, their migration patterns have been little studied and no one knows exactly how far they go.*

This is especially true for shearwaters and petrels, but these birds may well be feeding at night. Even the short-tailed shearwater which was banded in southern Australia and then traveled 10,000 miles (16,000 kilometers) to the Bering Sea in six weeks averaged only 10 mph (16 kph) over the period. Its actual flying speed would have been much faster, so leaving it plenty of time for feeding and resting en route.

Seabirds' movements are particularly difficult to study because they take place out of sight of observers, except where the birds are channelled into a narrow stream around a headland. Nevertheless, the behavior of many species has been worked out, at least in outline. Shipborne observers get only a fleeting glimpse of passing birds, but the collection of logs over the years allows the pattern of movement to be reconstructed. This was done for Wilson's storm-

temperate zone of the North Atlantic, especially around the waters of the Gulf Stream. The return in October starts with a gathering in the eastern North Atlantic and a journey down the African coast.

The drawback to using ships' records is that the plots record the shipping lanes as much as the paths of the birds. Movements in rarely visited parts of the ocean go unrecorded. The same difficulty occurs with banding studies, the details of movements being hard to gather. A very wide-ranging movement of giant petrels, an Antarctic species, was discovered because birds are frequently blown ashore in storms. Young birds have been banded on the nest at Signy Island, lying south-east of Tierra del Fuego, for many years. Within a few months of fledging, juveniles are picked up on coastlines and islands around the Southern Ocean. The juvenile giant petrels leave the nest in late

*Some waterfowl perform special "molt migrations", leaving the breeding ground to carry out the post-breeding molt in another habitat which provides safety and a plentiful supply of food. These king eiders (center bottom) are among the 100,000 males and immatures that molt in the Davis Strait between Greenland and Baffin Island.*

April or early May, and it seems that they first fly northwards into the South Atlantic because, between five and ten weeks later, they are turning up off the east coast of South America. Then they are carried eastwards under the influence of the prevailing westerlies and are found on the west coast of South Africa. After about three months they have reached Australia and then New Zealand. Ten months after leaving the nest the giant petrels reach the west coast of South America, having almost circled the world.

Because of the difficulty of following the movements of seabirds, it is not always easy to classify these movements. Some are doing no more than dispersing, leaving their nesting colonies on cliffs and shores and spending the winter at sea, not far from

and spend three months in the vicinity of the Bering Sea. At each stage the shearwaters make use of prevailing winds to assist their passage. Thus, they set off from Australia in an easterly direction towards New Zealand, then turn north and north-west to Japan. On the way home, they come down the west coast of North America before turning south-west across the open Pacific. Crossing the out-going track around Fiji, they arrive back off eastern Australia about five months after setting off.

Migration is sometimes more extensive among young birds than among adults. Juvenile great skuas from Scotland spend their first winter mostly off the Iberian peninsula, where banded birds are caught in fishing lines and nets. Some fly up to Arctic waters for

land. Others are nomads which keep moving and cover vast tracts of sea looking for good feeding grounds. Nomads tend to drift over a regular course because seabirds are strongly influenced by prevailing winds. So nomadic wandering may not appear very different from a regular migration in which the birds keep moving for most of the time. Young giant petrels are best described as nomads because they do not appear to have winter quarters but merely drift with the westerlies, following the clipper route of the Roaring Forties.

Short-tailed shearwaters (known as mutton-birds because the nestlings were once taken for oil, feathers and meat) fly with the wind in a huge circle around the Pacific Ocean, but they are true migrants rather than nomads. They leave southern Australia and Tasmania in April or May, take a month to reach Japan,

the summer. As they grow older, the skuas stay nearer home in winter and eventually remain in British waters. The difference between adults and juveniles is even more marked in gannets. Almost all juveniles head for West Africa, swimming for the first week after gliding from the nest. They spend two winters in tropical waters, some making a long detour into the Mediterranean. The adults remain farther north and young gannets start to winter in European waters in their fourth year. On the other side of the Atlantic, most young Canadian gannets migrate to the Gulf of Mexico. When they become adult, at four years, nearly all gannets abandon the migratory habit completely. It seems that it may pay the young, inexperienced gannets to make a long journey for an easy life in the tropics, but competent adults can cope with the North Atlantic winter weather.

*In the North Atlantic, nearly all newly fledged gannets migrate southwards for their first winter. As they grow older they stay nearer the breeding ground, and, as adults, most do not move as far.*

# NAVIGATION

A migrant bird needs to know which direction to go. But does it have to learn which way to fly or is it born with the knowledge? A young bird might learn its migration route and destination from its elders. Geese migrate in family parties, with the youngsters accompanying their parents to the wintering grounds, so inexperienced birds could be learning as they go. However, young Canada geese sometimes migrate alone from the breeding ground by Lake Manitoba to the winter quarters in Minnesota, so they must be born with the necessary skills to make their first migratory voyage. The classic examples of migration guided by instinct are the parasitic cuckoos of the Old World, such as the European cuckoo, which never sees its parents and has to find its way to Africa alone.

emerged. The experiments have been carried out on rather few species, so generalizations are dangerous because of the possibility of there being more than one system. A common experimental bird has been the homing pigeon, which is not a migrant but which is a very convenient subject for the study of navigation. Yet it would be rash to extrapolate from pigeons to hummingbirds, gannets or penguins without further data.

## PILOTING

When a young bird leaves its nest, it spends some time wandering at random, presumably learning details of its environment and finding feeding places and roost sites. Sedentary birds do not move far, but strong-flying migrants can survey large areas. Eventually, the bird sets off on migration, having a clear idea of local landmarks to guide it on its return. It will also be noting details of its route as it goes, particularly if flying by day, though even at night the general lines of

*Adverse winds can be disastrous for small migrants. This wheatear found refuge on a ship 200 miles (320 kilometers) out to sea. Providing that it has enough energy reserves to survive, its navigation system will get it back on course when the wind changes.*

*Although its ancestor, the rock dove, is not migratory, the racing pigeon has been bred for its homing abilities and it is used extensively in the study of bird navigation.*

To understand the problems of bird navigation, an analogy may be made with a ship sailing, say, from Southampton to New York. The first stretch can be guided by *piloting*, using landmarks, buoys and beacons to guide the ship down Southampton Water. The final stage is accomplished in the same way. Once clear of land the ship is oriented on a *compass course*, which should take it to its destination, but in practice allowance must be made for winds and currents. At intervals the ship's position is checked by sextant, or other navigational aid, and, by comparison with the position of New York on the ship's chart, a new course is set. This is *"map" navigation* or *true navigation*: the ability to calculate a position and compare it with a known destination. Experiments with birds have aimed at determining whether they have a similar system. Displacement experiments show that some birds taken to an unfamiliar place, perhaps thousands of miles from their nests, can return quickly, and it seems likely that they achieve this by true navigation. They have been carried in covered boxes so, when released, they must have been able to work out where they were and what course to set for home. As yet, no satisfactory explanation of how they do this has

rivers and coasts remain visible. Flying high and with a "bird's-eye view", it will become familiar with a wide span of ground laid out like a map. The fact that birds removed from their homes return more quickly if they are released along their normal migration route than in strange territory shows a memory of previous journeys to be helpful, though not essential.

To date, birds have been shown to use landmarks over a short distance, in the final guidance to their destination, but landmarks need not be restricted to visual features on the ground below. It is theoretically possible for infra-sounds generated by wind tumbling over mountains or waves pounding on the shore to be heard for thousands of miles. Over shorter distances, choruses of frogs in their spawning ponds might be heard as migrants pass overhead. The sense of smell could also play a part in piloting, according to results from experiments with homing pigeons (p.48).

## ORIENTATION

Classic experiments on the ability of birds to orientate, or set a fixed compass course, were performed by Gustav Kramer at Wilmshaven in the 1950s. He had noted that, in October, captive starlings regularly took up position in the south-west of their cages and showed all the characteristic restlessness of migratory birds (usually known by the German term, *Zugunruhe*). They maintained this orientation when they could see nothing but the sky. In the following spring, the starlings faced north-east. The starlings were, it seemed, getting their bearings from the sky. To check this, individual starlings were housed in a pavilion (now called a 'Kramer cage"), which had six large glass windows around the circumference. The windows were fitted with movable mirrors, and, by adjusting the angle of the mirrors, the apparent position of the sun could be altered. The starlings inside were completely fooled. When the apparent position of the sun was changed by 90° to the east, they changed the direction of their fluttering accordingly. When the sun became overcast, the starlings fluttered at random. Here was proof that the starlings were using the sun as a compass. The position of the rising or setting sun seems to be

bird must be able to allow for the movement of the sun through the day and maintain a course by continually altering the angle between its path and the sun, otherwise it will fly in a circle. It is known that birds, like other living organisms, have an internal clock which regulates their daily cycles of activity and rest. That this internal clock also enables them to make the necessary calculations for orientation by the sun is shown by experiments in which birds are kept in artificial regimes of light and darkness out of step with the sun's rising and setting. Their internal clocks become reset and, when they are allowed to see the sun again, they orientate incorrectly. For example, starlings were given an artificial day in which the sun rose and set six hours early. When they were returned to natural daylight, they oriented at right angles to their proper heading, as was to be expected if their clocks were six hours slow.

Following the precise track taken by a bird when

*Many birds, like these geese, migrate at night. They can use the setting sun or the position of the stars to set a course, and some species also have a magnetic sense. The moon is probably only useful for illuminating landmarks.*

*The actual track of a migrating bird can be traced by following Adélie penguins as they walk over the snow.*

important, but the bird need not see the actual disk of the sun. Birds are sensitive to polarized light which means they can locate the sun's position when it is covered by cloud or just below the horizon, as long as part of the sky is clear.

Further experiments, using a planetarium, showed that night migrants such as blackcaps and indigo buntings were aware of the rotation of the stars and were able to identify the one stationary star around which the others moved – the Pole Star. Having identified the Pole Star, they oriented their flight away from it, which took them south. In one experiment, the planetarium was programed so that the stars rotated around Betelgeuse, a star in the constellation of Orion. The birds duly treated it as the Pole Star and oriented by it. These experiments also showed that young birds learn the position of the stars before their first migration.

It is clear that for a sun compass to work, an accurate knowledge of the time of day is needed. In the northern hemisphere the sun is due south at noon, whatever the season of the year, but a migrating

it flies home is not easy, even after equipping them with tiny radio transmitters so that they can be followed in a car or airplane. This problem was overcome by studying penguins in the Antarctic. Some Adélie penguins were released on a flat, featureless expanse of snow, many miles from their nesting colony. As each penguin was released, it peered about and then plodded off. The researchers could easily plot its track by watching its black back moving slowly across the white background and then following the trail of footprints. When the sun was shining, the penguins held a steady course but, if the day clouded over, they became lost immediately and wandered erratically. When the sun reappeared, the penguins resumed their original course.

The sun cannot be the only compass available to birds because radar plots show that migrating birds keep a course at night, in heavy weather or when flying between two cloud layers so that both sky and landmarks are obscured. An alternative compass used in these conditions is now known to be magnetic. European robins kept in a windowless room continue their *Zugunruhe* fluttering in the correct direction but, when the magnetic field is changed by an electromagnet, their orientation alters accordingly. They can orient only when they are moving through the magnetic field, and they detect it by means of tiny crystals of magnetite in the head. Similar crystals have been found in species ranging from bacteria to human beings, but how they work is not known. The birds do not detect the polarity of the magnetic field, like a compass needle pointing to magnetic north, but perceive the angle of dip, the acute angle between the lines of the Earth's magnetic field and the horizontal plane.

Several species have been proved to possess a magnetic compass. Among nocturnal migrants these include the indigo bunting and savannah sparrow of North America, and the blackcap and garden warbler of Europe. Some evidence suggests that the magnetic compass is the master mechanism and is used to calibrate the sun or star compasses over a period of time. The latter may be more useful in practice because they can be used for instantaneous "readings", whereas a magnetic compass takes some time to set.

## TRUE NAVIGATION

There is little mystery then about how birds perform the two basic navigational processes: piloting and orientation. For piloting they can use visual landmarks, smells or sounds. To orientate, they can set a course by the sun, the stars or by a magnetic sense. But this does not explain how a homing pigeon can find its way home after being released in an unfamiliar place many hundreds of miles away, nor how a shearwater, taken from its nest in Wales and transported to Massachusetts, flew directly back to its nest site in just twelve and a half days. These skills in natural circumstances, allow migrants to reach their destinations after being blown off course. Such feats require true navigation: calculating the current position, comparing it with the destination and laying a course to link them.

In theory, many species could manage without this ability. As long as they were not diverted by strong winds, simple orientation combined with an instinctive knowledge of the direction to take and when to stop would be sufficient. From experiments with European warblers it transpires that this is how juveniles on their first journey navigate: the direction of flight and distance covered on migration are under genetic control, so that they reach their goal by instinctive "dead reckoning". Captive warblers show an amount of *Zugunruhe* proportionate to the time, and consequently the distance, they would have traveled if free to do so. Thus, spectacled warblers which migrate about 60 miles (100 kilometers) show very little restlessness when kept in a cage, while garden warblers that travel 3,000 miles (5,000 kilometers) flutter very much more frequently. Captive blackcaps show an amount of *Zugunruhe* which depends on the latitude where they were bred and hence the time they would need to travel to winter quarters. The direction of migration is

indicated by the birds' orientation. Garden warblers leave their breeding grounds in Germany on a south-westerly course through Europe and cross the Straits of Gibraltar, where their heading changes to due south as they fly down through Africa. Captive garden warblers mimic these headings with their fluttering in the cage, and even swing from south-west to south at the time that free-living warblers would be leaving Europe and entering Africa.

In the case of starlings, a similar form of instinctive navigation has been shown to operate in juvenile birds. In a classic experiment 11,000 starlings were captured in the autumn as they flew through the Netherlands. They were banded, then flown to Switzerland and released. Of the 354 that were recaptured later, most adults had found their way to the normal winter quarters on each side of the English Channel, or were heading in the right direction, but most of the young birds were in quite the wrong place. They had flown south-west from the starting point, which would in normal circumstances have led them from the Netherlands into southern England and north-west France, but instead it landed them in southern France, Spain and Portugal. In other words, these juveniles were traveling on a fixed compass course and stopped when they had gone "far enough"

The most interesting aspect of this experiment was the discovery the following year that the displaced juvenile starlings went back to their birthplace for the summer but returned to south-west Europe for their second winter, rather than to England or northern France, showing that they had now learned the position of their first winter home and were not relying on the inborn compass course and flight time. With the experience of their first migration behind them, they were using true navigation.

How this is achieved is still a mystery. The birds must have a "mental map" or "grid" so they can establish coordinates, like the human navigator's latitude and longitude, to tell them their position and that of their destination. Armed with this knowledge, they can calculate the correct course to steer. One theory that was popular for some years is that birds plot the movement of the sun with extreme accuracy to calculate its position. Comparison with the known movement of the sun at the bird's destination gives the information needed to set the course. This was an attractive theory because the birds could be envisaged as having a mental sextant and chart which they used rather like a human navigator. Unfortunately, there is little evidence to support the notion, and there are theoretical problems in deciding how it might work.

Other ideas are that birds use a magnetic map based on the changes in angle and strength of the Earth's field, or a map based on scents in the environment. Again, there are theoretical problems as well as lack of evidence, and the conclusion has to be that, despite all the research which shows that birds have the potential to navigate by sun, stars, magnetic field and other clues, the nature of their map is one of the most elusive mysteries in animal behavior.

*Emperor penguins returning to a rookery at the start of their nesting season. The ice cliff is continually moving, so the landmarks change from one year to the next, but these penguins always return to exactly the same spot, as determined by a sextant. This suggests that they are migrating with the help of a very precise navigation system, but exactly how such a system works remains a mystery.*

Page references in italics refer to illustrations. Bird names are shown in capitals (eg ALBATROSS, LARK) where there are two or more species listed under that group name, or where there are general entries for the group. These general entries are listed separately (under Albatrosses, Larks) to avoid confusion.

The scientific name of each species is given in brackets beneath the common name. Where a name is used in a general way for several species, the generic name (eg *Cacicus*) or family name (eg Falconidae) is given. This does not imply that all members of the family or genus are identified by the common name shown.